Falcons Forever—
Rob Dollar

FATHER
Of THE FALCONS

Coach P's Military Brats & 'The Game of Life'

By ROB DOLLAR

FLYING FALCON PRESS
HOPKINSVILLE, KENTUCKY

i

FLYING FALCON PRESS
105 Sherwood Drive
Hopkinsville, Kentucky, 42240

ISBN978-0-692-70953-5

First Edition, 2016

Good faith efforts have been made to trace copyrights on materials included in this publication. If any copyrighted material has been included without permission and due acknowledgement, proper credit will be inserted in future printings after notice has been received.

The photographs in this book—including those on the front and back covers of the dust jacket—are from Fort Campbell High School yearbooks and publications as well as the personal collections of the author and friends of the Falcon Nation.

Printed in the United States of America on acid free paper.

DEDICATION

This book is dedicated—on behalf of the Falcon Nation—with love and gratitude to the family of Marshall H. Patterson and also to the wonderful faculty of FortCampbellHigh School who, through the years, forever made a difference in the lives of thousands of proud Military Brats, including the author.

TABLE OF CONTENTS

Foreword.. vii

Highway of Memories...1

A Job for Life 31

The Early Falcons 47

Two Old Quarterbacks...65

Voices for CoachP...103

Making Headlines 129

The First Time...163

Portrait of a Military Brat 177

Young and Stupid 197

'Broadway Joe' 219

Forgive and Forget..249

The Final Whistle..261

Coach's Funeral 271

The Movie 285

The Hall Comes Calling 293

For The Record 305

Afterword 306

Acknowledgments 308

References..311

FOREWORD

This is the story about the legend of Marshall H. Patterson, one of the finest high school coaches ever to walk the sidelines of a football field in America. It's also the story of thousands of appreciative Military Brats, including this author, who were lucky enough to have this great man as a teacher, coach, mentor, and sometimes surrogate father. For many, if not most of us, he made the difference for lives lived well and to the fullest— when it comes to success and happiness.

An employee of Fort Campbell Dependent Schools for 35 years, Coach Marshall Patterson—or "Coach P" as he was known to just about everyone —was the father of the Fort Campbell High School football program, launching it in 1962 and serving as the head coach of the Falcons through the 1993 season.

The very first Falcon football team took the practice field for the first time more than a half-century ago at the old junior high school (now known as Wassom Middle School), close to the Army post's hospital of the era and the Gate 5 entrance into Fort Campbell. Facilities and equipment were primitive back then, compared to today's standards. It was an era of the traditional family and stimulating conversation around the dinner table. There were few, if any, "super-sized" high school athletes, perhaps because the fast-food industry had yet to explode in America. There were trophies that actually meant something, not those handed out in political correctness to everyone on a team for simply trying to play a sport. And, in those days, there were true champions left standing on the football field, unlike nowadays when just about every team in the district—even those with losing records—is given an invitation to the playoffs every season and the opportunity to compete for a state championship.

From absolutely nothing, Coach P built a football program, worked to keep it respectable during some early lean years and then put it into a position to become a perennial power in Kentucky.

It is a little known fact that FortCampbell and FortKnox, both located in the Commonwealth of Kentucky, are the only stateside Army posts with high schools to exclusively educate dependents of active-duty soldiers. Both schools in the BluegrassState fall under the umbrella of the U.S. Department of Defense Education Activity (DoDEA).

Because the military is a transient profession by nature, Coach P and his coaching staff faced the difficult task of rebuilding the Falcon football team just about every year. This was especially true in the 1960s, 1970s, and 1980s when soldiers—with their families—were stationed at their military installation for a few years, at best. Unlike opponents who grew their teams from the junior varsity ranks, FortCampbell coaches could never count on the return of experienced players to lead them to glory. Those blue-chippers were gone with the wind whenever the Army called and transferred their fathers to another post somewhere else in the world. Returning starters and multiple-year players in those early years, in fact, often were as rare as pink parachutes at the sprawling Army post on the Kentucky-Tennessee border.

When this huge disadvantage is given the consideration it deserves, Coach P's overwhelming success as a high school football coach over the years was nothing short of amazing, to say the least.

Capitalizing on his circumstances, he posted 227 victories on the gridiron during his tenure at FCHS, including state championships in 1976, 1978, and 1979. His 1980 team was only nine points shy of a fourth state crown, finishing runner-up to Corbin in the Falcons' first year of Class AA competition after moving up from the small high school division.

Make no mistake about it, Coach P's miracles on the football field with his ever-changing Band of Military Brats were recognized across the commonwealth as well as the nation. Three times he was named Kentucky Coach of the Year and his 1982 team was ranked No. 17 in the country by *USA Today*.

In his spare time—a thought probably amusing to those who knew him well—Marshall Patterson learned a few wrestling moves from some books and then coached the Falcons for 17 years in that difficult sport. Just seven year after starting the FCHS wrestling program, he brought home the sweetest of rewards—the 1971 state championship. His 1970 and 1978 wrestling squads were runner-up to the eventual team champions.

The icing on his cake was serving 33 years as FCHS athletic director. With Coach P at the helm, Falcon athletes claimed 27 combined team sports championships.

When Coach P ended his football coaching career at FCHS after the 1993 season, he was in the Top 10 on the state's all-time wins list with a record of 227-120.

In 1995, family, friends and FCHS colleagues gathered at a retirement dinner to honor the man they celebrated in a wonderful video presentation as "The Captain of The Game of Life." What no one knew at the time was "The Captain" still wasn't finished with his work of changing the lives of young people…There was much more work to do.

After just months of retirement, Coach P un-retired and returned to the world of high school football, accepting the head coach's job at Northwest High School in Clarksville, Tennessee. In only six seasons, he rebuilt the lackluster program and turned the Vikings into a playoff team before he left the game for good after the 2000 football season. The Tennessee coaching stint added an additional 18 victories to his career wins total.

Yes. Marshall Patterson loved the game of football. He loved it because he said it was just like life. There always are ups and downs in life. Nevertheless, according to Coach P, success is within reach of anyone willing to work hard and leave *everything* on the field of battle.

To this day, I can still hear his booming voice: *Don't ever give up. Never quit. When someone knocks you down, get up no matter what, and with even more determination to come out on top.*

Marshall Patterson's inspiring lessons for winning "The Game of Life," taught on a football field and in a classroom, made life-changing impressions on many Military Brats who later achieved great success in their chosen professions.

For many, Coach P was that all-important primary authority figure who filled the void left by a parent at war in Vietnam, Grenada, Panama, the Persian Gulf or Somalia.

And, you can bet your bottom dollar he was there and rose to the occasion for those who needed him on that darkest day ever at Fort Campbell, Thursday, December 12, 1985, when a jetliner with 248 soldiers from the Army post—returning home for Christmas after a six-month peacekeeping mission in the Middle East—crashed and burned after a refueling stop in Gander, Newfoundland, killing everyone aboard the plane, including the eight-member crew.

On the football field, Marshall Patterson definitely set the highest of standards and expectations for Falcon head coaches who would follow in his giant footsteps. Not surprisingly, every one of Coach P's successors—Rocky Cobb, Ronnie Bell, Shawn Berner, Tony Butler, and Josh McKillip—discovered almost immediately they had some mighty big shoes to fill, for sure, after taking the hand-off from the "Father of The Falcons."

No doubt there will be many more exceptional head football coaches at FCHS in the future. But there will *never* be another Marshall Patterson.

Teacher, coach, administrator, longtime sponsor of the Fort Campbell High School Chapter of the Fellowship of Christian Athletes (FCA)…

Coach P died on January 19, 2014, at Gateway Medical Center in Clarksville, Tennessee, at the age of 79, most certainly called home by "The Almighty" to coach and mentor the best of the best in Heaven.

Tennessee's General Assembly, just three weeks later, passed a resolution—signed by Governor Bill Haslam—recognizing Marshall Patterson for his life's accomplishments. The special honor from the Tennessee Legislature is afforded to very few Tennesseans. But Coach P was special, and everyone knew it.

He was, and forever will be, Mr. Fort Campbell High School Football. Falcons Forever!

Rob Dollar, Spring 2016

CHAPTER 1: HIGHWAY OF MEMORIES

It was near the noon hour on a sunny but crisp autumn day in Hopkinsville, Kentucky. The smell of football wafted through the air, but for this old Military Brat and Fort Campbell High School alumnus—Rob Dollar—there would be time today for just one game: "The Game of Life."

Climbing into my Mustang convertible, I slipped on my shades and backed out of the driveway of my Sherwood Drive home. I eased the powerful mechanical pony up the short, dead-end street and turned left onto Country Club Lane, headed in the direction of Fort Campbell Boulevard. As I drove along the tree-lined road, I marveled at the vibrant hues of the autumn leaves.

Always the rebel with too many causes, I was on a mission of mercy to nearby Clarksville, Tennessee, on this beautiful Friday. Someone who counts on me as a friend was feeling mighty low. Yes, just like everyone else in this crazy world, I have friends in low places. A few of them even pretend to be in high places.

Anyway, the poor guy was feeling sorry for himself because LIFE ISN'T ALWAYS FAIR.

My friend already saw himself as an old man—and now, all of a sudden, he was an old man without a job. The powers-that-be in his life decided to replace him with a much younger man or maybe a woman who had far less experience on the job than him, and apparently fewer aches and pains. His replacement was willing to work for less money, too. Now, if that life crisis wasn't bad enough, my old buddy had also just lost the love of his life. Once again, he was replaced by a man or maybe a woman with more get-up-and-go and much more money. My pal was a nervous wreck, and I was really worried about him. He had even deluded himself into believing he could right the wrongs done against him by seeing a doctor for one of those unnecessary medical procedures for people who want to look and act young again. Maybe the old guy was thinking of restoring the hair on his near-bald head, having plastic surgery to get rid of the wrinkles on his face, or finally getting rid of that beer belly with a tummy tuck. It really didn't matter, I suppose, because it probably wasn't going to do him much good anyway. Like P.T. Barnum once told anyone who would listen, *"There's a sucker born every minute."* And, the guy I was going to try and rescue—for anyone watching the clock—was right on the dot with his foolishness. Still, there was a bottom line to the madness of this unfolding drama: I had a friend out there in the wilderness—unfortunately not a Military Brat, so unlike me, not nearly as tough as nails—who needed a helping hand in his life. The guy was drowning and looking for a life preserver. Someone—and that someone would be me—had to step forward to read the old fool the riot act, and as another old fool, I knew I was the perfect person to talk some sense into him and get him through his life crisis. For long ago, I learned that bad things happen to good people all the time, jobs come and go like the wind, the good guy doesn't always get the girl, and every story doesn't have a happy ending. In life, there's a bottom line, and I knew where to find it. As my old and wise college classmate—Don "Gringo" McNay, aka "The Incredible Shrinking Man"—was known to opine: *Only the lucky few live a long life—always LARGE.* It's just not in the cards for everyone.

LIFE ISN'T ALWAYS FAIR.

DRIVING AND THINKING….As a seasoned and tested Baby Boomer anxious for retirement and a life of leisure, I considered myself somewhat of an authority on losing jobs and aging with grace. Early in life, I got fired from my job as a crime reporter at the Clarksville newspaper for simply applying to become the city's new police chief. Years later, in another crime against humanity, I was canned from a high-profile position in the Hopkinsville Mayor's Office. A new mayor, who once had been a neighbor, kicked me to the curb. Of course there were no hard feelings. It was what it was—nothing but politics. The "beautiful people"—you know, the ones who can't take the word "*No*" for an answer—wanted my scalp, and they got it (or what was left of it…). As for the curse of growing old, I'd discovered years ago and reaffirmed only lately that there's really no way of ever getting around it until, or unless, someone actually discovers The Fountain of Youth. Body parts break down with a vengeance the closer a person gets to those golden years of retirement. There's simply nothing that can be done except to duck the issue and roll with the punches.

The same advice—ducking and rolling with the punches—holds true for dealing with the fairer sex. You just do it more often. For those who believe it's possible to tame the ladies, listen closely to someone who's been down that rocky road far too many times: DON'T EVEN GO THERE.

No doubt about it. I was quite confident I could speak to my troubled friend with authority, and from a position of strength. The lessons I had learned, and learned so well over the years, convinced me that my rescue mission that day would end in success, and that the good deed I was doing definitely needed to get done. Friends help friends. It's as simple as that…It's what they're supposed to do—because LIFE ISN'T ALWAYS FAIR.

Now, before continuing with my story, there's something everyone should know about me. Like many of my time-ravaged friends—life survivors who these days make far too many visits to hospitals and funeral homes— yours truly starts every morning the same way. It's a routine honed to near perfection, given my more than four decades as a "man of many words" while scratching out a living as a newspaperman and independent journalist.

For the record, I suppose it's only right that I should confess to having an odd habit that was much more important years and years ago—when newspapers mattered, and most people actually read them. Because I'm such a dinosaur (maybe a more descriptive word is *"NEWSOSAUR"*), the first thing I had done after hobbling out of bed on this fine morning in Kentucky was to hunt down the newspaper and check the obituaries for my name. Not seeing it, I let out a sigh of relief and immediately gave thanks to the Creator for what I hoped would be another meaningful day on this Earth. It was with this frame of mind—a recharged enthusiasm for life—that I began my mission of mercy to Clarksville and the Volunteer State.

The distance between downtown Hopkinsville, Kentucky, and Fort Campbell is about 13 miles along heavily-traveled U.S. 41A. In the early 1970s, there was little retail and commercial development in this area of Christian County, which made for a relaxing drive between the two communities. (Photo by Rob Dollar)

After a few minutes on Country Club Lane, my Mustang pulled into the southbound lanes of Fort Campbell Boulevard, where I then eased into my comfort zone for a straight shot to Clarksville down old and familiar U.S. 41A. But, just before I crossed into Tennessee and arrived in Clarksville—"The Queen City on The Cumberland"—I'd first have to pass the front gates of Fort Campbell, Kentucky. One of the largest Army posts in the country, the fort—located on the Kentucky-Tennessee border—was about 13 miles down the road from my tidy Ranch-style house in Hopkinsville.

As I navigated through the Fort Campbell Boulevard traffic, still in the Hopkinsville city limits, my mind slowly drifted into mental playback mode, back to a time in life that was so much simpler—happier, too, in so many ways—than the new America.

There's a popular phrase that describes this most special place in everyone's lifetime: People refer to it as "The Best Years of Our Lives," those glorious days when—because you're young (usually ages 17-24) and believe you'll live forever—life is so promising, and no one wants to wait another minute to set the world on fire.

For me, and I'm sure for many of my oldest and dearest friends, "The Best Years of Our Lives" took place at Fort Campbell High School during the period of time that came to represent the bittersweet ending of our lives as active Military Brats.

Flashbacks of those fond and carefree days from more than 40 years ago flooded my mind as I glided down this highway of memories...Family vacations...Friendly neighbors...Summer barbecues...Campouts in the back yard...Opryland USA...Hanging out with friends at the Officers' Club pool... Drive-in movies...High school athletics...Falcon Chocolate Cakes...First dance....First kiss...First car...Cruising the backroads with Pink Floyd's *The Dark Side of the Moon* blasting out of the 8-Track Player...The Teen Club...Midnight visits to Ghost Bridge in Oak Grove, Kentucky, or "The Bell Witch" cemetery in Adams, Tennessee....Parties (sometimes wild, especially when parents were out of town)....Playing golf (at night)...Visiting "Heaven Lee" and Printer's Alley in Nashville, Tennessee ...Graduation Day...Going off to college...

DRIVING AND THINKING….These 13 miles between Hopkinsville and Fort Campbell…The drive, both ways, was as familiar as an old friend…I had been up and down this stretch of road thousands of times since moving to the area as a teenager during the height of the Vietnam War. The Dollar family—piled into an early 1960s Rambler station wagon—arrived in Kentucky in November 1969 after the Army assigned my father to Fort Campbell, where he would continue to serve his country for almost another decade.

Dad—Floyd Amos Dollar, who, at the time, was a 37-year-old chief warrant officer—had just completed what would be the first of two tours in Vietnam with the Screaming Eagles of the 101st Airborne Division. A Georgia native, he had already served 20 years in the Army at this point in his career, including combat as an infantryman during the Korean War. While Dad was overseas, our family—which included my mother, Rose (Savant) Dollar, and three younger sisters, Adele, Linda and Dede—lived with my maternal grandmother, Adele Rosa (Frola) Savant, at her home in Hurley, Wisconsin. Not far from the shores of Lake Superior in Northern Wisconsin, Hurley was our home for the last five months of 1968 and nearly all of 1969, while Dad first attended a military school and then left to fight the war in the jungles of Vietnam.

Grandma Savant and the love of her life—my grandfather, Bert Savant, who was 76 when he died in early October 1961—had immigrated from Italy to America, through Ellis Island, in the early part of the 20th Century, searching for a better way of life. My mother was the youngest of their seven children born in the new country.

Over the years, and up until my grandmother's death at the age of 89 on Christmas Eve 1982, the old Savant house on Second Avenue in Hurley had always been our place of refuge whenever the Army sent my father overseas to places that were too dangerous for family members.

Hurley, where U.S. 51 ends and the ground remains covered with snow seven months out of the year, sits on the Wisconsin-Michigan border. Within walking distance from the small town is Ironwood, Michigan, a community that has a most unusual tourist attraction—a giant Indian statue. Billed as "The World's Largest Indian," the legendary Hiawatha statue is 52 feet tall and weighs two tons.

During one of those many visits to grandma's house, my father—a warrior for his country and a man who certainly had a funny bone—tagged the Indian chief with a memorable nickname that still draws uncontrollable laughter in our family decades later: "BIG CHIEF STINKING BUTT."

Dad's orders to Fort Campbell in the late fall of 1969 presented the Dollar clan with a rare gift that few military families ever enjoy—a period of stability. Finally, after many years of traveling the world, The Dollars were putting down some firm roots at an Army post that our family would call home for nearly five years.

DRIVING AND THINKING…Those new to the Fort Campbell area probably don't know it, but there once was a time when motorists saw nothing but beautiful rolling farmland while traveling U.S. 41A, between Hopkinsville and the Army post. In those early days, when my family was new to the area, it was a relaxing and breathtaking drive between the two communities. The view for the entire trip was like a painting that could be hung on a wall with pride. No commercial or residential development. No traffic lights. No stress of too many vehicles on the road. No Interstate 24 flying past the local communities at breakneck speed. Time almost stood still on every drive.

It's different now, of course. Everything has changed, thanks to greed and Korporate Amerika's obsession to break everything that isn't already broken. Some people like to call it progress. Development along this beautiful stretch of highway began at a creep in the 1980s. And now, with new construction exploding, many people fear the days are fast approaching when the drive between Hopkinsville and Fort Campbell will come to resemble the chaos and mess of U.S. 41A, from Clarksville to Fort Campbell. Curiously enough, motorists navigating the north and south lanes of U.S. 41A are likely every now and then to stumble upon a contradiction to this ever-growing hectic pace of life: The occasional horse-drawn Amish buggy.

Nevertheless, there's no stopping progress—or greed. In the end, as is always the case, the common folks—those who do most of the working, paying, living and dying in this great country—won't have a choice except to sell their land and give up an honorable way of life, so that others can get filthy rich off the real estate and development deals. It may happen in our lifetime, only because money is, and always will be, KING.

LIFE ISN'T ALWAYS FAIR.

DRIVING AND THINKING…Nothing stays the same. Back in the day, I got to know every nook and cranny of U.S. 41A that ran through Christian County, between Hopkinsville and Oak Grove. There had been an entire year—when I was a senior at Fort Campbell High School (1974-1975), just after my family moved from on-post quarters in Werner Park, off post and into our own house on the southwest side of Hopkinsville—when my sister, Adele, and I commuted, Monday through Friday, between home and school on the Army post. While the two high school seniors had to hit the road daily to get to classes, the remaining Dollar siblings—Linda, a sophomore, and Dede, who was in the eighth grade—were enrolled in the Christian County school system in Hopkinsville.

The Dollar family lived on post at Fort Campbell from late 1969 through the summer of 1974. Their home was located at 1335-B Werner Park, a housing area on the Tennessee side of the military installation. Above is a photo of the four Military Brats, taken sometime around 1972. From left are Robert, Adele, Linda, and Dede. (Courtesy of Rose Dollar)

Fort Campbell authorities—at my family's request—granted special permission for the two oldest Dollar kids to complete their senior year at FCHS and graduate with their friends. The same courtesy was extended to one of our classmates, Preston Owens, after his family also moved out of their post quarters around the same time and into a house in North Clarksville.

The first class of 22 graduating seniors from Fort Campbell High School ventured out into the world in the late spring of 1963. The Class of 1975—my class, with 122 seniors—was the 13th in the history of the post high school to don caps and gowns on Graduation Day.

In hindsight, there certainly was nothing unlucky about the Class of 1975. In fact, the future—as the years to come most certainly would prove—was so bright that practically everyone in the high school gymnasium should have been wearing shades during our commencement exercises.

There was no better place to learn about life than Fort Campbell High School. With only our senior year to finish up, Preston Owens and yours truly—basically "Straight-A" students—had positioned ourselves to graduate at the top of our class. Those were the days before many high schools in this country began naming multiple students to share valedictorian and salutatorian honors instead of only the top two graduates. Thanks to political correctness, there's no choice nowadays other than to appease proud parents at all costs in the high school honors process. Heaven forbid that their super-sensitive teens ever feel the sting of disappointment.

At FCHS, schoolwork was a walk in the park for Mr. Owens. My good friend never took a book home and always aced his tests. It was quite amazing. As for me, I had to hire someone to help me carry my books. I also had to study like a fool—every night. Nevertheless, our battle for top of the class was a friendly competition. With two semesters to go before graduation, Preston's GPA was just a few hundredths of a point higher than mine—only because I left my comfort zone and enrolled in two very risky elective classes (Typing and Bookkeeping). They were taught by one of my favorite teachers, Sherrie Pennington, and I earned "B's" in both of the challenging courses.

In the end, those two "B's" and the unfortunate (for me) transfer to FCHS of a beautiful and brilliant student—Mary Saunders—cost me that coveted yellow honor stole. On Graduation Day, after the dust had settled, sweet and smart Mary Saunders—with her perfect GPA—was named valedictorian of the Class of 1975. Preston Owens earned the honor of salutatorian, and the author of this book—as the No. 3 graduate—was just a sad face in the sea of graduates. But, there still was a silver lining for my academic honors letdown: As the Senior Class president, the school administration put me on the program to deliver what would be a most forgettable, five-second "Welcome Speech" at the graduation ceremony.

LIFE ISN'T ALWAYS FAIR.

No, it certainly isn't…But, sometimes there's some humor in it if you think about it long enough….The funny thing about my fall from perfection in high school, as it turned out, is that learning the ABC's of typing proved to be one of the best decisions a future journalist could make—even though I didn't know at the time that newspapers were in my future, and it might help if I knew how to type my stories. But, I suppose I should have had a clue, since I already had ink on my hands from delivering newspapers on the Army post for nearly four years while going to school. Heck, I even was named *The Clarksville Leaf-Chronicle's* "Newspaper Carrier of the Year" as the co-winner of The Meyer Brick Award back in the fall of 1973.

Fittingly, it may have even been the longtime librarian at Fort Campbell High School, Irene Proctor, who kept me on track for that future newspaper career. The sweet lady actually rescued me from the humiliation of being recognized as a top-notch "paperboy." She shamed classmates unmercifully for even daring to tease me about the honor. Decades later, I still smile about those experiences that marked my humble beginning in the world of newspapers. Looking back with a critical eye, I honestly believe Mrs. Pennington's typing class was the most valuable learning experience I had in high school since it actually proved useful to me in later life…So, I guess the "B" in typing was well worth the loss of that honor stole. I'll forever be grateful to Mrs. Pennington, the outstanding and caring teacher who taught me how to type and gave me the grade I had earned, not the one that would have made life

10

easier for me at the time. As for Irene Proctor, who passed away in May 2007 at the age of 84, she believed in me, and newspapers—and, throughout my later life, I never forgot it.

DRIVING AND THINKING....That coveted, blue-cased high school diploma, of course, represented what my Falcon classmates and I hoped at the time would be the start of many good things to come. Leaving the hallowed halls of Fort Campbell High School to find our places in the cold, cruel world, our life's journey and chase after those mighty big dreams had only just begun.....

But, as the great John Lennon pointed out in a song just a few years later, *"Life is what happens to you while you're busy making other plans."*

Things happen in life (I've heard some people actually replace the word *"things"* with a four-letter synonym for crap)....Plans change or veer off in another direction...Preston Owens is a perfect example. A serious knee injury on the football field in high school cost him an appointment to West Point, thereby ending his dream of following in the footsteps of an older brother who went to the U.S. Military Academy and became an Officer and Gentleman in the U.S. Army.

Preston, in character, responded to the setback by joining the Navy and serving on active duty for six years. After he got out of the service, he returned to school for his bachelor's degree and then began a career as a successful industrial engineer.

Disappointment, hard luck and even tragedy are not strangers to anyone on this Earth. Like other graduates before us and those who have, and will, come after us, there is no one who escapes from the mother of all life's lessons.

LIFE ISN'T ALWAYS FAIR.

DRIVING AND THINKING....Many days during my senior year in high school, there were multiple road trips in my blue 1968 Ford Mustang Sports Coupe between Hopkinsville and Fort Campbell, just so I could hang out with my own kind—fellow Army Brats who understood me and our way of life.

As sons and daughters of soldiers, my classmates had always been patriotic when patriotism wasn't cool. We grew to love the daily bugle calls at sunrise for Reveille and at sunset for Retreat when everything on post would halt as soldiers saluted and civilians stood at attention during the lowering of the American flag. We learned to accept the dangers and sacrifices of our fathers' chosen profession. Still, we couldn't help but worry whenever a dark sedan, with uniformed officers and a chaplain, showed up in the neighborhood, knowing all too well what was about to happen—a knock at someone's door, an unearthly cry and precious lives changed forever.

The first time I saw Fort Campbell in 1969, it was about half the size it is today. Many of its buildings and facilities dated back to World War II. Soldiers and their families who made the Army post their home did not live in the best of conditions. They were paid less than their counterparts in the private sector and many qualified for food stamps. Off post, the civilian communities were not always friendly to military families, and soldiers and their dependents seldom, if ever, got a military discount at the movies or when shopping at any business. Believe it or not, there were even parents out in the civilian communities who wouldn't allow their daughters to date a soldier.

Unlike The Post-9/11 Era—when anyone who puts on a uniform becomes an instant hero—the general public, back then, was not very supportive of the military. No "Welcome Home" ceremonies or parades. No American flag lapel pins. Patriotism was anything but popular, and it sure wasn't in abundant supply.

As I kept pace with the moving traffic on the Boulevard, the memories kept coming at me, reminding me in stark detail that the old America and the new America were as different as night and day.

Well, with that one glaring exception, of course….

LIFE ISN'T ALWAYS FAIR

DRIVING AND THINKING…Four decades is a long time and things change, I suppose, often not for the best. Contrary to the joke of jokes, I'm someone who lived during the tempestuous Sixties and Seventies, and I actually recall most, if not all, of what happened during those crazy days. My good memory makes many of my closest friends very nervous, particularly during reunions when forgetfulness sometimes is seen as a virtue.

The late 1960s and early 1970s were days that definitely were wild, sometimes scary, and always unpredictable. Looking back, they were exciting times, too. People actually were interesting….The "Hippies" more so than the "Squares"…Man, you know, when the Hippies talked, the slang was really far out.

They used cool words like *dig, brother, dude, chick, heat, hassle, bread, crash, trip, dibs, fuzz, jam, rap, shades, threads, downer, bummer…*

Remember the "Don't-Trust-Anyone-Over-30" crowd and those heavy slogans that marked the times? Catchphrases that were spot-on: *Do Your Own Thing…It's Been Real…Keep the Faith…Lay it on Me…Make Love Not War… Don't Have a Cow…GimmeSome Skin…*Even Richard "Tricky Dick" Nixon—who, at the time, was only months away from his election as America's "I-Am-Not-A-Crook'' president—got into the act when he appeared on TV's *Rowan & Martin's Laugh-In* in 1968: *"Sock it to me?"*

In the Swinging Sixties and Seventies, the guys (dudes) wore their locks long, sometimes to their shoulders, and the ladies (chicks) had flowers in their hair. Everyone dressed in groovy or psychedelic outfits. Remember those worn-out, patched blue jeans, Tie-Dyed T-shirts, bell bottoms, field jackets, unbelievably short skirts, baby doll dresses and even those ugly leisure suits during the Disco craze? The times….They, for sure, were a-changin'…There was Vietnam, the Civil Rights Movement, political assassinations and riots, protests, women burning their bras, free love, muscle cars, cheap gasoline, space missions and man walking on the moon, Nixon and Watergate, and Jimi Hendrix, Bob Dylan, The Beatles and the hippest music of all time. Everyone, everywhere, was flashing the Peace Sign or maybe flipping someone—usually *"The Man"*—The Bird.

DRIVING AND THINKING…..I know…I know…I'm not forgetting THE DRUGS. "Weed," for sure, was here, there and everywhere in those heady days of the Sixties and Seventies. You know what I'm talking about…Grass…Mary Jane…Marijuana. There was plenty of it out there. Most everyone I know probably tried it, but just like Bill Clinton, they certainly never inhaled…

Lots of other drugs were around, too. Remember the "Head Shops" in every neighborhood in America?

But, seriously, an argument easily could be made that the drug problem is much worse in the new America. Today's "War on Drugs"—and other substances that make people feel better than they should—is much harder to fight. You've now got new epidemics like crack, crystal meth and synthetic drugs. Don't forget about the legal painkillers. The money-making healthcare industry has far too many Americans hooked on prescription drugs and medicines they don't need and sure can't afford. In the meantime, Americans are drinking alcohol like there's no tomorrow and replacing cigarette smoking with "Vaping"—a new fad that might prove even more dangerous than tobacco. Completing what might be The Perfect Storm is the acceptance of medicinal marijuana in some parts of the country and the legalization of small amounts of weed for consumption in states like Washington and Colorado.

Let's get back to The Days of Cool…Folks who made the scene in those days will tell you they never felt so alive. There were people walking around who actually had a soul that wasn't for sale, and they were FOR something—anything, it didn't really matter what—and not AGAINST everything.

The new America, in many ways, pales in comparison to the old America. Today, it's hard to find passion for anything except making money, and lots of it. Too many Americans can't wait to climb aboard The Gravy Train, and once on it, they'll do anything to keep from giving up their seat.

It's all about "ME." People spend too much time these days buying stuff they don't need and probably won't ever use in a Global Economy where the stock market crashes every time someone breaks wind in China. There's too much drama everywhere and absolutely no shame. There's a lack of civility and respect for authority out in public. There's an epidemic of fragmented families, and it's crippling the country. There's no loyalty to anyone or anything. There's no desire to do the right thing—especially if no one is watching.

Those looking at the world through rose-colored glasses might argue that our lives are so much better, thanks to the advanced technology now at our fingertips. But, maybe, just maybe, our society finally has reached the point where there's just too much information out there for a world so much smaller. Think about it. Back in the old America, things were simple and slow, and everyone got their 15 minutes of fame. In the new America, with our fancy gadgets and instant communication, the pursuit of fame never stops. ALL THE WORLD'S A STAGE—24 hours a day, seven days a week. With the Internet, social media, and picture- and video-taking smart phones, everyone's suddenly got an opinion to share—even the village idiots and evil-doers. Instant communication—which can, and often does, take place without the communicator actually taking the time to THINK—might have its place in this fast-paced world. But, it's not always a positive thing—especially when people fail to act in a responsible manner.

Thanks, in part, to Al Gore—the inventor of the Internet (A claim the former vice president sometimes makes, but never during this ex-reporter's past interviews with him because he knows I would have called him a liar)—there are too many distracted people running amok in today's world. They're living their lives on Facebook and going back and forth with sociopaths on Twitter, responding to Tweets of Hate or Silliness. As for those smart phones, so absolutely necessary in this day and age of instant gratification, I guess the 1960s and 1970s were the days when no one was smart enough to need them or important enough to have them. Take it from me: Most of the smart phone users I know have the attention span of a gnat. They walk around distracted—day and night. Most of the young people of the Sixties and Seventies never had a problem finding something worthwhile to do with their free time. Now, with these toys of new technology running our lives, there's little opportunity to think about the really important things. It's become a world of "Mind Control by

Consent." Don't even get me started on drones, and issues like privacy. The government and private sector—in the new America—have the ability to track movements and monitor the communications of anyone walking down the street, and they use it, legally and sometimes maybe even illegally. In this Age of Political Correctness and Dysfunctional Leadership, people walk around every day OFFENDED about anything and everything. Incredibly, there are few complaints from the masses about Big Brother. It's what happens, I suppose, when most people choose to bury their noses in their smart phones.

TMI....Too much information is not a good thing in a Twitter world. *(Hashtag) PleaseKeepItSimpleStupid.* Go ahead and Tweet or Text that plea for a saner and slower world. It's a desperate statement from an old newspaperman suffering from a bad case of information overload, thank you very much.

Now, while I'm on my soap box here, let me make something perfectly clear. I don't hate new and advanced technology. I like, and welcome, anything that improves the quality of life and makes the world a better place. What I hate is the abuse and misuse of knowledge. Korporate Amerika is really good at selling anything, and everything, to the public— whether it's useful or not. I think often these new thingamajigs and technological wonders become crutches for some people and prevent them from living meaningful and productive lives. Technology, anyway, isn't the answer to all the problems in the world. In many ways, it's made things worse. We still don't have peace in the Middle East. And now, bloodthirsty terrorists are using the Internet and social media to target disenfranchised youth, spread their distorted ideology, and encourage death and destruction in the world. Because of things that many people don't, or can't, understand, there also are many new challenges and headaches to face now like identify theft, cyber-attacks, and the dumbing down of our way of life.

Back in the old America, no one would have thought twice about even borrowing my identity. Heck, sometimes I didn't want it. Now, I'm getting daily e-mails and telephone calls from foreigners—barely able to speak English—pretending to help me rescue my identity while they're actually trying to steal it. And, it looks to me like there's really no way to stop the hackers—domestic and foreign—who are breaking into government and business computers just about every day and gaining access to the most sensitive information. A can of worms has been opened, my friends, and it isn't a pretty picture.

DRIVING AND THINKING….Dumb and dumber? Look at the kids of today if there's any doubt there hasn't been a Dumbing Down of America in the past few decades. Teenagers are busier than birds and bees, spending most of their time sexting each other with their camera phones. One of America's most respected journalists, Tim Ghianni, who teaches writing at a Nashville, Tennessee, university, blames the world of Texting and Twitter and their abbreviated form of language and communicating for the relative inability of many young people to write coherent sentences. Too many of our kids nowadays are overweight and intellectually lazy because they're spending too much time on video games instead of getting some fresh air and exercise outdoors while playing with friends—growing their imaginations.

This failure to nurture imagination is evident in our everyday lives. Look at television as an example. Now an inescapable part of modern culture, television was hailed in the 1950s as the invention that would transform the world. There was a time when most everyone in this country had television—and no bill to pay at the end of the month. All it took was an inexpensive antenna that was mounted on the roof of the family home to capture the free airwaves. At Fort Campbell, in the early 1970s, our family had three channels to watch day and night, and it didn't cost a dime. And, back in those days, there actually were programs on TV worth watching—like *The Tonight Show Starring Johnny Carson* and *The Lone Ranger*. It was a different time, for sure. Believe it or not, families actually spent time together in front of the television or at the dinner table. There was never any fighting over the remote control because it hadn't been invented yet. If memory serves me correct, yours truly—young Robert Dollar—was the remote control in his house. As a teenager, I'd jump out of my easy chair and manually change the channel on the television set whenever a family member pitched a fit to watch something else. Then, I'd sit back down again until someone else started whining for a channel change. There was a beneficial side to this unpaid internship in television. As a human remote control, I never needed a gym membership to stay in shape, and I sure didn't have to do any of those crazy aerobics. Imagine that! OK, I know exactly what the fine folks paying those outrageous cable and satellite TV bills every month are thinking right about now. Back in the day, paying nothing got you nothing, right? The critics will claim that nothing worth watching was ever on those three Nashville television stations, and they went off the air sometime after midnight. Well, here's my argument: I'm still seeing nothing, and paying an arm and leg for it. In my humble opinion, it's a sad state of affairs when the most entertaining thing on the Boob Tube in the new America is a commercial for Viagra that features beautiful and scantily-clad women. The lovely ladies promise viewers, while whispering sweet nothings, that the wonder drug will help every man GET and KEEP an erection—maybe for up to four hours or more before the need arises to call a doctor. Try and picture that…

In the new America, imagination and good storylines on television are missing in action. The public is tormented by around-the-clock "Reality" television shows. I don't know about you, but as for me, I've always watched television or gone to the movies to escape from reality. I don't really care about the size of Kim Kardashian's butt. And, speaking of butts, I've also grown sick and tired of those buttheads on TV—you know, the annoying "Talking Heads" on entertainment programs masquerading as the news. They never stop with their holier-than-thou opinions, they're always shouting like everyone is deaf, and there's no getting away from them because they're on every channel on the dial.

The Kardashians…..Jerry Springer…..Honey Boo Boo. Are you kidding me? Stick a fork in it…The Golden Age of Television is done and long gone—just another victim of the Dumbing Down of America. Never mind the sophisticated technology and those hundreds and hundreds of cable and satellite channels. The sad recognition of what's happened to the world of entertainment reverberates with me whenever I watch that old classic war movie on TV—*Sands of Iwo Jima*. John Wayne's character, Marine Sergeant John M. Stryker, hit the nail on the head: *"Life is tough, but it's tougher if you're stupid."*

Forgive me friends. I guess I just miss the old America, and I'm disappointed that the new America seems STUCK ON STUPID. With apologies (and credit, of course) to The Beach Boys, maybe I just wasn't made for these times.

DRIVING AND THINKING....The old America and the new America, I muttered to myself as I continued my rant and drive down the Boulevard, past Bradford Square Mall and the overpass for the Pennyrile Parkway (also known as the Edward T. "Ned" Breathitt Parkway) that, in the early 1980s, had been the ending point for developed property on the south side of Hopkinsville. Of course, in the decades to follow, this invisible barrier would crumble and big chunks of land along both sides of the highway, toward Fort Campbell, would be purchased and developed—thanks, in part, to the construction of Interstate 24 through Kentucky, with the Christian County segment, just miles north of Fort Campbell, opening to traffic in the fall of 1975.

As my car passed the parkway overpass, I looked over to my immediate left to admire the beauty of Fort Campbell Memorial Park— Hopkinsville's gift of friendship to their military neighbors to the south, built in the aftermath of the December 12, 1985, plane crash that killed those 248 fort soldiers returning to post for Christmas after a six-month peacekeeping mission in the Middle East. The soldiers on that plane— along with its eight-member crew—gave their lives in the name of peace.....

LIFE ISN'T ALWAYS FAIR.

The southward development—The Good, The Bad & The Ugly, and I use those descriptions very loosely—that had come to fruition in the past three decades was now before me to see in full living color during my drive toward Fort Campbell: Completion of the Hopkinsville Bypass, the seven-mile parkway extension to a second intersection with Interstate 24, Trover Clinic (Baptist Health), Walmart Supercenter, James E. Bruce Convention Center, Murray State University-Hopkinsville Campus, Kentucky Veterans Cemetery-West, The Links At Novadell (golf course and upscale housing), Southpark (industrial complex) & Walmart Distribution Center, Cumberland Hall psychiatric hospital, three major car dealerships, scores of new retail businesses and restaurants, and a handful of new residential developments.

SEEING IS BELIEVING …Maybe, but, it still was difficult for me to digest what had already happened, and what was continuing to happen, to my dream highway. It wasn't a nightmare, at least not yet. But it was getting there.

Not far into my drive along U.S. 41A, about half-way to Fort Campbell at a curve just before getting to the beautiful Novadell Golf Course, I spotted the old abandoned railroad overpass in front of me. This particular location, decades ago, had been the scene of one of Christian County's most notorious and deadly traffic accidents.

Six Fort Campbell soldiers, riding in one car, were killed at the Masonville Underpass in a fiery wreck that stunned the community on December 30, 1958.

At the time of the tragic crash, the commanding general of the 101st Airborne Division at Fort Campbell was a 44-year-old Army officer named William C. Westmorland. Destined by history to one day become known as the architect of the Vietnam War, Westmoreland already had been tested by heartbreak in early April of the same year, just days after assuming command at the fort.

A parachute maneuver at a drop zone on post—part of Exercise "Eagle Wing," involving 1,400 troops—went awry, killing five soldiers and leaving another 137 with injuries. Because of gusty winds, paratroopers were blown across the drop zone, against rocks and trees. Unable to collapse their chutes, those killed were strangled to death.

Over the years, I had heard many accounts of both incidents. The tragedies never lost their impact on me as a newsman, and I often thought about that deadly year of 1958 whenever I was traveling U.S. 41A and passed the familiar highway landmark.

LIFE ISN'T ALWAYS FAIR.

Still lost in the nostalgia of my youth, I soon was brought back to reality by a speeding car that roared by me in the passing lane like a rocket. The music coming from it was so loud that the car was shaking like a leaf. It was full of teenagers and every one of them, including the driver, was holding a smart phone or speaking into one of the gadgets. The young fools were taking "SELFIES." They were TWEETING and TEXTING up a storm, maybe about the awesome bargains they had just gotten at Wally World. I can't swear to it, but I'm pretty sure most of the teens had ugly tattoos and piercings and were probably allergic to work.

Of course, I had to let off some steam. "Good God!" I yelled out my window, shaking my fist as the speeding car disappeared into the distance. "What's the world coming to? Why don't you kids get a job or join the Army?"

Feeling better after my outburst, I glanced into my rear-view mirror and looked closely at the face staring back at me. "Damn. I think I'm becoming MY PARENTS," I blurted out, with a chuckle.

It wasn't long before I was at the Interstate 24 and U.S. 41A interchange, approaching the city limits of Oak Grove. Off in the distance, I observed a huge C-5 Galaxy aircraft about to make a landing at Campbell Army Airfield—probably bringing home fort soldiers from a deployment to some hostile spot in the world.

DRIVING AND THINKING….There was a time when the City of Oak Grove consisted of several trailer parks and a few dozen businesses— some of them seedy—that either catered to the sometimes lusty needs of soldiers or targeted them for their money. That was THEN.

NOW, Oak Grove is recognized as one of Kentucky's fastest growing cities with a population of around 7,500. It has neighborhoods of modern houses and apartment buildings, brand-named retail stores, a recreation complex with an amphitheater and convention center, and its very own Walmart Supercenter. Years ago, a new entrance to Fort Campbell—Gate 7, which provides direct access to the airfield—also was constructed by local, state and military authorities.

Passing the Interstate 24 turn-offs to Paducah, Kentucky, and Nashville, and now officially in Oak Grove, I looked to my right and left and saw that the chain hotels, gas stations and restaurants were doing a thriving business—as usual. I remembered, when as a young newspaper reporter decades earlier, I was at a meeting where folks actually burst out laughing when then-Mayor Jack Elliott and Oak Grove City Council passed a hotel and restaurant tax to fund recreational projects in the community. At the time, there were NO HOTELS and very few restaurants. Life is always full of surprises. No one is laughing now.

Further up the highway, I couldn't help but start chuckling when my car passed some signs in a huge empty field that advertised the future development of a multimillion-dollar village mall project and a movie theater complex, directly across from Fort Campbell.

I smiled, with the knowledge that I knew one of Oak Grove's dirty little secrets. Quite a few people—including curious Fort Campbell teenagers anxious to learn about "The Birds & The Bees"—had been entertained in that same field many, many years ago when the infamous Family Drive-In was showing movies and selling popcorn. Now, for those unfamiliar with the history, this was a drive-in that wasn't in business to entertain families. No Disney movies there. Adult or Triple-X movies played nightly at the Family Drive-In. It was one of the local locations for pornography before the Internet came along.

For far too long, there was no fence around the adult business to block the view of the large movie screen—and what was on it—from non-patrons. Therefore, Peeping Toms in the immediate area—including those in the not-so-distant Lee Village housing area on Fort Campbell, where a good pair of binoculars was all that was needed to make out the naked action on the screen—always got a free show. Of course, there was no sound. But who was listening, anyway?

Over the years, there were many traffic accidents on U.S. 41A, in the vicinity of the drive-in, caused when motorists were distracted by the sex on the screen. Public safety and complaints from mothers worried about the moral welfare of their teenage sons eventually got a fence put up, but it still wasn't enough to keep the determined from sneaking a peek now and then.

Young, sex-starved soldiers weren't the only ones watching the flicks at the Family Drive-In. Not that I have any first-hand knowledge—I choose to invoke my Fifth Amendment on this subject—but it wasn't hard to get into the drive-in as long as money changed hands. The business had a history of run-ins with the law, and I seem to recall a former Christian County lawman getting into some trouble while working there after his law enforcement career was over.

The Family Drive-In is now just a bad memory for the town fathers of Oak Grove. It's the same story for the numerous "Head Shops" that, at one time, dotted the community, selling music, posters and drug paraphernalia to the counter-culture.

Nevertheless, sex still sells at a few adult businesses that continue to this day to bring crowds to Oak Grove. One of the most notorious, The Cat West, a private club that features nude dancing, opened in 1984 amid controversy and has withstood numerous court challenges to close it over the past three decades. As a newspaper reporter, I was there for much of that journey—including the time when Bill Dillard, then the sheriff of Christian County, threatened to shut down the club if the girls didn't wear their "pastries." Yes... he said "pastries"... like he expected the girls to wear donuts on their breasts. Cops just have a thing for donuts, I guess.

As The Cat West came into my view, just before the intersection with Fort Campbell's Gate 6, my heart began to ache a bit. The large lot, across from the strip club, remained empty. Still nothing there—yet. But maybe one day....

One of the area's most iconic businesses had once occupied this prime location at the corner of U.S. 41A and Kentucky 911—Charlie's Steak House. Known internationally for its fine steaks and salads, the business—opened in the early 1950s by Max Read and family—was almost as old as the Fort Campbell Army post when it burned to the ground in mid-April 2011.

Many great memories were made over the years at Charlie's Steak House by soldiers and their families. Return visits to the area almost always included a stop at the steakhouse. It was really popular for making new memories during reunions.

The list of the famous who dined at Charlie's Steak House was long and distinguished, to say the least. Because the restaurant was world-famous, regular folks often found themselves sitting near tables occupied by the likes of celebrities such as The Tommy Dorsey Band, Minnie Pearl, Barbie Benton, Floyd Cramer, Chet Atkins, Ray Stevens, Boots Randolph, Tom T. Hall, Jeff Gordon, Adolph Rupp, Kentucky governors Edward T. "Ned" Breathitt and John Y. Brown Jr., and Army generals William C. Westmoreland, H. Norman Schwarzkopf Jr., and Colin L. Powell.

General Powell—who, in his later years, served as President George W. Bush's secretary of state from 2001 through 2004—ended his military career as the Chairman of the Joint Chiefs of Staff. In April 1990, while serving as the nation's highest-ranking military officer, he returned to the area to make a speech at Austin Peay State University in Clarksville. The general made sure everyone knew he still had fond memories of his days at Fort Campbell, joking that he was glad businesses like Grandpa's— a discount box store ahead of its era that was located in North Clarksville along U.S. 41A—were still going strong.

Powell served at Fort Campbell in the mid-1970s, residing at 1560 Cole Park, just down the hill from the log cabin that was occupied by the post's commanding general at that time and future Army chief of staff—Major General John A. Wickham, Jr. As a colonel, Powell assumed command of the 2nd Brigade of the 101st Airborne Division (Air Assault) in July 1976. He succeeded then-Colonel Fred K. Mahaffey, the father of four lovely daughters, two of whom attended high school with me. The 2nd Brigade commander, back in those days, was assigned the additional duty of serving as the president of the Fort Campbell School Board. As a result, Fred Mahaffey and Colin Powell are remembered, and revered, to this day for playing important roles in the success of the Army post's nationally-recognized school system.

Throughout his career, timing and good fortune always seemed to smile on Colin Powell. Therefore, it really should come as no surprise that he had only been at Fort Campbell for a few months when FCHS won its first state football championship, and as part of the command staff, he helped them celebrate the milestone.

Fred Mahaffey missed the celebration. But his Army career was on the rise. A native of New Mexico, he was promoted to four-star rank in 1985 at the age of 51, making him one of the youngest four-star generals ever at the time. A shining star among America's top generals, Fred Mahaffey died of cancer the following year, the result of exposure to Agent Orange during his heroic service in the Vietnam War.

The old Fort Campbell High School on South Carolina Avenue, now known as Mahaffey Middle School, is named in his honor.

Looking into the distance, down Kentucky 911, my mind conjured up another painful memory from the past. The intersection was very near the site where a car driven by one of my Fort Campbell High School classmates, Charles Cunningham—19 years old at the time, with his entire life ahead of him—collided with another vehicle. Charles was killed in the crash, and the other driver—Jack Elliott's son, Richard—was injured. The fatal wreck occurred less than two years after our June 1975 graduation.

The tragedy left friends agonizing about what could only be described as a cruel twist of fate…Sometime after graduation, Charles Cunningham and another of our classmates, Mike Hellums, surprised everyone by enlisting together in the Navy. But, before he shipped out for Boot Camp, Charles had a change of heart, and instead of becoming a sailor, took a job in the area as a skilled trade professional.

An iconic business destroyed by fire, a rising military star darkened forever by cancer, and a young man who died way before his time…..

LIFE ISN'T ALWAYS FAIR.

Passing the fort's Gate 6, and cruising toward the Tennessee state line, I flipped on my car's radio to catch the news headlines for the day: Terrorists Seize Hostages…..South Braces for Tornado Outbreak….Jobless Rate Rises…..President Raps Do-Nothing Congress….Poor Get Poorer Rich Get Richer….Military Reducing Troop

Levels….Police Shooting Spurs Riots…Government Cuts
Coming….Stock Market Crashes…

The headlines sounded just like the ones from the days of my youth.

No news is good news—THEN and NOW, I muttered to myself. It was
knowledge gained from worldly experience. If there was one thing I had
learned during a lifetime as a journalist, it was that news, unfortunately, is
rarely good or positive…It usually involves something bad happening to
someone good.

LIFE ISN'T ALWAYS FAIR.

As I got to Gate 4, the main entrance to Fort Campbell, the traffic light
turned red, and I braked my car to a stop. There was a time when the fort
was an open post, with quick easy access to the public. But those days
ended with the Age of Terrorism. In addition to high-security gates, a
"Force Protection Wall"—an 8-foot, 4-inch barrier of brick and block
design—now paralleled U.S. 41A for about three miles, from Gate 1 to
Gate 6.

Waiting for the light to change, I reflected on my long, strange trip
through life—from the old America to the new America.

"HOW IN GOD'S NAME IS IT THAT I'VE BEEN ABLE TO MAKE
MY WAY THROUGH THIS CRAZY, DYSFUNCTIONAL WORLD
WITHOUT LOSING MY SANITY AND SELF-RESPECT?" I asked
myself, not really expecting a response. But, out of nowhere and in the
blink of an eye, came an answer.

Before I even had the opportunity to think another thought, I glanced off
into the distance, over the fort wall and through some trees, and spotted in
all its glory the old high school, now Mahaffey Middle School. At the
very moment my eyes focused on it, just like magic, an old Trini Lopez
song started playing on the car radio. I had heard it before—many times.

I grinned, and out of my mouth, without even thinking, came the answer
to my prayer of frustration: "COACH P."

Like a reflex, I started singing along with the familiar tune: *"If I had a hammer I'd hammer in the morning... I'd hammer in the evening all over this land... I'd hammer out danger... I'd hammer out warning... I'd hammer out love between my brothers and my sisters... All over this land..."*

When the song ended, I smiled, remembering that it had been Coach Marshall Patterson who had hammered an important lesson into my head long ago at Fort Campbell High School, a lesson that put me on the right path in life: *"When the going gets tough, the tough get going."*

Still waiting for the light to change, I looked back at the old high school and thought I saw a 1968 light blue Volkswagen Beetle parked in front of the gym. I wanted to see it...It probably wasn't really there, but it sure should have been because, in my mind, that's where it belongs for all of eternity.

It was the man who drove that car for nearly two decades—I've heard it finally quit and died on U.S. 41A sometime in the 1980s, and then was sold to a Falcon football player—who prepared me and thousands of other Military Brats for "The Game of Life." And, knowing now the things I didn't know way back then, Marshall Patterson—coach, teacher, and mentor—sure got the job done, and done right. He taught the sons and daughters of soldiers the art of adapting to a changing and difficult world. He inspired them—and me—to deal with adversity and to never give up. He made winners out of his students and athletes.

I don't know if Coach P liked listening to Trini Lopez, but the singer's lively tunes were on a synchronized tape-recording of popular music he put together for the June and July conditioning workouts that always preceded the start of football season at Fort Campbell High School. That tape was probably played until it was finally worn out.

I spent three summers with Trini Lopez's music spinning through my head, so whenever I heard it, I was instantly returned to the days of those summer workouts at the old high school gym. Despite the years that had passed, I could still smell the sweat and hear Coach P's whistle to move to the next workout station…Peg Board…Rope...Bench Press…Military Press…Sit-Ups….Pull-Ups….

When I was at FCHS, trying to play football in the early 1970s, Coach P and his three assistant football coaches—Houston Mills, Rocky Cobb, and Ronnie Bell—were just years away from reaching the highest peak of their coaching careers. By the end of the decade, they would have three state football championships under their belts.

Coach P taught the student population at Fort Campbell High School many life lessons, and one of the most important was that life isn't always fair, because it was never supposed to be fair. Life is full of ups and downs—mountains and valleys. And, we all have our crosses to bear.

He told us that everyone, at some point in their lives, gets handed a few lemons. The thing to do, whenever that happened, was to learn from your mistakes, work even harder and find a way to turn those lemons into lemonade. It was God, family and then football and everything else—in that order—that were the real priorities in this life, according to Marshall Patterson.

Coach P represented everything good and decent about this country. He personified the traits of old America in all its glory—character, discipline, loyalty, work ethic, and respect for authority. He made everyone he met, in this life, a better person and forever shaped the lives of thousands of Military Brats.

I don't ever remember Coach P quoting Ralph Waldo Emerson, but I'm pretty sure he agreed with him: *"Life is a journey, not a destination."* Marshall Patterson, for sure, knew the world—and everything in it— would always be changing, for the better or for the worse…There was no getting around it. But the one thing that would never change—it was forever—was the impact that a mentor could have on the lives of teenagers coming of age. Coach P saw his opportunity to make a difference as a young teacher and coach, and he seized it and never let go.

The thoughts in my head about my old football coach changed my mood. Now feeling much better, with a huge smile on my face, I thanked Trini

Lopez for the timely reminder of those valuable lessons taught to me by Coach P, especially the ones that sometimes are so easy to forget when life gets crazy.

As the traffic light changed to green, I pushed on the gas and sped off toward Clarksville to pay forward some of Coach P's Pearls of Wisdom. With excitement and enthusiasm, I couldn't wait to mentor my troubled friend and tell him that the time had come for him to stand up and spit in the eye of adversity. Life isn't always fair, and never will be....But—in the end—everything is good because every new day is a new beginning.

It was just the kind of speech that someone who felt sorry for himself needed to hear from a student of Coach P well acquainted with "The Game of Life."

Not everyone, after all, was lucky enough to have been a Military Brat and had a Marshall Patterson in their life to show them the way.

Above is an early photograph of Fort Campbell's very first, brand-new high school, which opened for the 1968-1969 school year. It was built just inside Gate 4 on South Carolina Avenue, near Stryker Village. Today, the facility is known as Mahaffey Middle School. (Courtesy of Fort Campbell High School)

Marshall Patterson turned his first job as a teacher and coach into a career at Fort Campbell High School. Above, Coach P gets a kiss from cafeteria manager and booster Lucy Shaw. Smiling her approval is PE teacher Shirley Bell. (Courtesy of Fort Campbell High School)

CHAPTER 2: A JOB FOR LIFE

In what may be the irony of ironies, one of the greatest warriors and heroes ever to serve at Fort Campbell, Kentucky, spent nearly his entire career at the Army post without ever wearing a uniform and returning a salute.

Marshall Patterson was not a soldier, but instead a top-notch educator and coach who gained legendary status in the Commonwealth of Kentucky for mentoring the sons and daughters of servicemen at Fort Campbell for more than three decades.

His name, for many years, was synonymous with Fort Campbell. The son of the late Marshall Gray Patterson and Grace Holman Patterson Liggett, "Coach P"—as he would become known for most of his life—was born in Lewisburg, Tennessee, on October 13, 1934.

Lewisburg, a city of about 10,500 residents, sits in central Marshall County in the rolling hills of Middle Tennessee, about an hour south of Nashville, Tennessee, and only 115 miles from the Fort Campbell Army Post.

Marshall County is known worldwide for its connection to the Tennessee Walking Horse Breeders' and Exhibitors' Association (TWHBEA), which has its headquarters in Lewisburg. Founded in the mid-1930s, TWHBEA is the oldest and most prestigious organization devoted to the promotion of the breed.

The future high school football coach's father was a die-hard Democrat who worked for the Tennessee Highway Department. As a child growing up, young Marshall Patterson was known to his family and friends by a nickname that stuck with him for life—"Buddy." Like other youngsters in rural Tennessee, he enjoyed the outdoors and playing sports. Apparently, he also was known on occasion to tease his older sister, Aldene, who was responsible for putting a permanent scar on his forehead. According to the family story, young Marshall tore the head off of Aldene's doll, and she retaliated by hitting him in the head with a Coke bottle.

Marshall H. Patterson was born and raised in Lewisburg, Tennessee—the county seat of Marshall County. His father worked for the state highway department. In high school, he starred in three sports for the Marshall County Tigers. (Courtesy of Marshall Patterson family)

A star athlete for Marshall County High School, Marshall Patterson played football, basketball and baseball for the Tigers. His ambition, according to his high school yearbook, was to one day become a coach. After graduating from high school, he enrolled at Castle Heights Military Academy in Lebanon, Tennessee, where he spent six months before heading off to Tennessee Tech on a football scholarship. At the Cookeville, Tennessee, college, Patterson earned praise and honors for being a hard-nosed lineman for the Golden Eagles football team for four years. While at Tennessee Tech, he met the woman who later would become his wife for 56 years, Rebecca (Roach) Patterson.

A hard-nosed lineman, Marshall Patterson played football for the Tennessee Tech Golden Eagles for four years in the 1950s. He also served as president of the Wesley Foundation. (Courtesy of Marshall Patterson Family)

Known to everyone as "Cissie"—her childhood nickname—she was raised in Savannah, Tennessee, which is about 115 miles east of Memphis, Tennessee.

According to Rebecca Patterson, Tennessee Tech was a small college back in the mid-1950s, so she and her future husband knew each other for years, running with the same crowd. "At one time, he was even dating one of my friends," she said, with a laugh.

When he wasn't studying or playing football at Tennessee Tech, Marshall Patterson served as president of the Wesley Foundation, a United Methodist campus ministry. He also was in the school's ROTC program.

"In high school and college, during the summers, Buddy earned money by measuring tobacco out in the fields, and he also sold fireworks during the Fourth of July and Christmas holidays," Rebecca Patterson recalled.

During their senior year in college—when Rebecca "Cissie" Roach was crowned "Miss Tech" and Marshall "Buddy" Patterson received campus recognition as the "Bachelor of Ugliness"—the friendship bloomed into a full-scale romance.

Commissioned a second lieutenant in the U.S. Army upon his graduation from Tennessee Tech in 1957, Patterson reported to Fort Monmouth, New Jersey, for basic training. His future wife moved to Memphis, where she began her career as a schoolteacher.

Within a year, the couple was married, but the blessed event got off to a shaky start. Rebecca Patterson, with a big giggle, pointed the finger at her father, Lucian Roach. She said it was her father who introduced Coach P to the other great love of his life—FISHING. "He took Buddy fishing on the day we got married, and they didn't get back until almost noon. I started to wonder if he was going to show up."

The Army assigned Lieutenant Marshall Patterson to Fort Gordon in Augusta, Georgia, to fulfill his two years of military service. Initially, he was a commander of a signal training company and later served as the athletics and recreation officer. While at Fort Gordon, the new Mrs.

Patterson taught school in Augusta. After leaving active duty, Marshall Patterson served in the Army Reserve and eventually obtained the rank of captain. He also returned to school at the prestigious George Peabody College in Nashville, where he prepared himself for a career in education by earning his master's degree. Peabody now is a part of Vanderbilt University for those trying to find it on Google or maybe an old-fashioned map.

Rebecca Patterson said it was a chance encounter with a stranger on the Peabody campus a few months before graduation that brought her husband to Fort Campbell. "He struck up a conversation with this man and mentioned he was graduating and looking for a job," she said. As fate would have it, the stranger—most certainly impressed by the attitude and enthusiasm of Marshall Patterson—had just left his position as superintendent of Fort Campbell schools, and he sent the teaching prospect up to the Army post and told him who to see about a job.

And so it was, with the Sixties now under way, that Marshall Patterson got his first teaching job, initially for the summer at an elementary school on the Army post on the Kentucky-Tennessee border. Not long after starting the job, he switched schools and went to work at Fort Campbell Junior High School, where he taught physical education and coached junior high football for a few years. The new coach, as one of his first tasks, also launched intramural programs in boys' and girls' basketball and volleyball for eighth- and ninth-grade students.

It was Bill Perry—the future longtime principal at Fort Campbell High School, but at the time, serving as junior high school principal—who hired Coach P and shared his dream of building a top-notch football program. That first meeting between these two great visionaries evolved into a close friendship that would last more than 40 years.

Making his home in nearby Clarksville, Tennessee—less than 10 miles away from his new job at Fort Campbell—Marshall Patterson's first career stop would also turn out to be his last. He and his wife never left Clarksville, and over the years, attended New Providence United Methodist Church and raised three wonderful children—a son and two daughters. In the years after his retirement, Marshall Patterson coached his church's softball team and taught an exercise class for senior citizens three times a week.

Today, the three Patterson children are grown adults and happily married, with children. They also are successes in their chosen professions.

Stephen Patterson, who was Coach P's lifelong fishing partner, is a teacher and coach who eerily looks and sounds just like his legendary father. He has many of the same mannerisms. A graduate of Middle Tennessee State University, Stephen Patterson attended the school in Murfreesboro, Tennessee, on a wrestling scholarship and later earned a master's degree at Auburn University in Alabama. For more than 30 years, he taught and coached in Georgia before retiring and moving his family to Paducah, Kentucky, in 2014 to take a teaching and coaching job at Paducah Tilghman High School.

Dr. Jeanann (Patterson) Pardue, lives in Knoxville, Tennessee, where she's a respected pediatrician, while Marsha (Patterson) Anderson, works as a lawyer in Nashville.

As a doting father, there wasn't anything Marshall Patterson wouldn't do for his two daughters, regardless of the sacrifice. When it was time to leave home for college, Jeanann, and later Marsha, had their hearts set on obtaining their undergraduate degrees from prestigious, and expensive, Vanderbilt University in Nashville. Coach P—who had a tendency to be softhearted—made those dreams a reality for his two girls despite the severe financial hardships on the family.

Rebecca Patterson, before retiring, taught school for 34 years in the Clarksville-Montgomery County School System. Although Coach P had many other job opportunities over the years, Mrs. Patterson said she was not surprised that her husband retired at the same place where he started his career.

"Early on, I knew he would never leave Fort Campbell," she said. "He was always so excited to go to work....The people at Fort Campbell were good to him and our family."

When Marshall Patterson first passed through the gates at Fort Campbell, the Army post had not yet celebrated its 20th birthday, and its handful of schools had only been in the education business for less than a decade.

Driven by his optimism and the opportunity to live and make history at the fort, Coach P probably saw a challenge and some promising opportunities in his future.

The roots of Fort Campbell stretch back to the beginning of World War II in Europe, when the calls for preparedness and mobilization became more urgent throughout the United States. Many Americans were of the opinion that the military should be grown—just in case the United States entered the war.

Ironically, as early as the summer of 1940, the Chamber of Commerce in Hopkinsville, Kentucky, already had mounted one of the first major efforts to woo the Army to the area. But, the Kentucky delegation was not promoting the site that eventually became the location for Fort Campbell—much of which actually is in Tennessee. Instead, they were pushing for the use of an 18,000-acre federal game preserve known today as Pennyrile Forest State Resort Park, according to John O'Brien, Fort Campbell's official historian and author of *A History of Fort Campbell*.

It didn't take the Army very long to reject the Hopkinsville chamber's proposal since the site in North Christian County, near Dawson Springs, was too hilly, and more importantly, too small for an Army armor camp. Officials had far more interest in the rolling farm acreage in South Christian County, near the Tennessee border, because it was favorable for training purposes

In June 1941, about six months before Pearl Harbor and with about 250 possible camp locations identified around the country, the Army secured funds from Congress to perform some site surveys. The Kentucky-Tennessee location was among those making the final site selections list. The fieldwork began on July 30, 1941, with the survey taking place in a cornfield at what is now the intersection of U.S. 41A and Gate 6-Morgan Road, near Campbell Army Airfield.

Congress authorized the funds for what, at the time, would be known as Camp Campbell in early January 1942. Construction began the next month, and the first Army unit was assigned to occupy the camp on July 1, 1942. The activation of the unit took place just 2 ½ months later, according to published reports.

Although originally named Camp Campbell, Clarksville, Tennessee—in honor of Colonel William Bowen Campbell, commander of the 1st Tennessee Volunteer Regiment in 1846—the name was almost immediately changed to Camp Campbell, Kentucky…Don't be surprised if someone's political clout (Maybe Kentucky Senator Alben W. Barkley, then the Majority Leader in the U.S. Senate) had something to do with it. To justify the "Kentucky" location, most folks pointed to the fact that the post office and the headquarters complex were on the Bluegrass State side of the massive military reservation.

On April 14, 1950, about a year after the 11th Airborne Division was moved to the camp, it was re-designated a permanent Army fort: Today's modern FORT CAMPBELL officially was born.

The 101st Airborne Division replaced the 11th Airborne Division as the fort's main occupant in 1956. Ever since then, the Screaming Eagles have called Fort Campbell their home, with the exception of the five years (1967-1972) that the division was deployed to Vietnam. A few years after re-deploying to Fort Campbell, in October 1974, the division was re-designated as the 101st Airborne Division (Air Assault). This designation changed the mission of the 101st from operations by masses of paratroopers to troops assaulting from helicopters. Two other major tenant units operate from Fort Campbell nowadays—the Green Berets of the 5th Special Forces Group, and "The Night Stalkers" of the 160th Special Operations Aviation Regiment (Airborne).

Through the years, with the Army post's mission growing in importance by leaps and bounds, Fort Campbell has become a frequent stopping point for national and world figures. On July 23, 1966, the fort received its first-ever presidential visit when Lyndon B. Johnson came to the post to meet with troops of the 101st Airborne Division, which was still in the process of deploying to Vietnam. Over the next five decades, five more presidents—Ronald Reagan, George H.W. Bush, Bill Clinton, George W. Bush, and Barack Obama—made trips to Fort Campbell to visit with soldiers and their families.

The big occasions usually involved tragedy—Reagan consoling the families of 248 fort soldiers killed in the December 1985 Gander air crash—or a victory during war— President Obama and Vice President Joe Biden presenting medals to 160th helicopter crews for their role in hunting down and killing Osama bin Laden in May 2011.

The Army has not been the only branch of the service to serve at Fort Campbell in the more than 70 years of its existence. Air Force, Navy and Marine Corps personnel also have been assigned and worked jobs at the post—some involving "Top Secret" projects—in the past and through the present day.

From 1947 to 1959, the post included a U.S. Air Force installation— Campbell Air Force Base. Now known as Campbell Army Airfield, the facility takes care of hundreds of Army helicopters every day. The airfield is capable of accommodating Air Force One, and its long runways were among the few places large enough in the country to land a Space Shuttle during an emergency back in the days before that program was ended.

Fort Campbell also played a major role in the Cold War, with that mystery only unraveling in recent years. Most people in the local communities, for decades, were unaware that within the Fort Campbell installation was 2,620 acres of land protected by an electric fence and Marines with shoot-to-kill orders.

The U.S. Navy operated "Clarksville Base" from 1948 through 1969, with the naval facility designed to transport and store about one-third of the U.S. nuclear weapon stockpile during the Cold War. It was among 13 facilities in the country that were built to handle America's nuclear arsenal. Also known as "The Birdcage," the base—at its peak—had hundreds of buildings, storage units and transport tunnels.

Bob Connelly, a Navy Brat who graduated from Fort Campbell High School with the Class of 1966, was someone who knew the secrets of

Clarksville Base. His family was stationed at Fort Campbell twice—once in the mid-1950s and the second time for four years in the early 1960s.

"My Dad was a nuclear weapons specialist as were many of the Dads that worked out at Clarksville Base," explained Connelly, a resident of Riverton, Wyoming, who enjoyed a successful career as a broadcast engineer/manager and pastor.

The Cold War secret presented some unique problems for the dependents of those who worked on Clarksville Base, according to Connelly.

"Our housing area was a restricted area and when we had friends from the post come over to visit, we would have to call the base and let them know who was coming so the Marines who guarded our housing area would let them in," he said. "When I turned 16, and could drive the family car inside the Clarksville Base compound, I had to have a background investigation and a secret clearance."

In the immediate years after Clarksville Base was shut down, Fort Campbell's Teen Club—with lovable Lucy Shaw in charge—began operating at the former Top Secret site, entertaining the sons and daughters of soldiers at one of those super-secret buildings of long ago. No doubt, secret goings-on persisted at the secluded site for many more years, thanks to the many mischievous and high-spirited teenagers like the author, who attended FCHS from 1972 through 1975.

During the 1960s, before moving out to Clarksville Base, the Teen Club operated from various buildings near the on-post schools and housing areas.

Of historical significance, a new paratrooper arrived for duty at Fort Campbell in May 1961, and within a year, he and his band were playing at Teen Club dances for Military Brats. One lucky Brat, Kathy Lord, even got to sing with the soon-to-be-famous soldier's band, and there's actually a photograph out there in cyberspace to prove it.

Believe it or not, the young soldier's name was Jimmy Hendrix. Of course, the sensitive and somewhat shy soldier later changed the spelling to "Jimi" and became arguably the best guitarist in rock history. Heck, he even has a "Forever" commemorative postage stamp nowadays.

Fort Campbell schools trace their beginnings to Congress' passage in 1950 of Public Law 814, which provided money for construction and maintenance of schools on federal land—if the need existed.

In the early days, before there was a high school at Fort Campbell, there was just one football team on the Army post—The Cherubs. The team made up of junior high school students played during the late 1950s through 1961. In the above photograph is action from a game in December 1959, when future FCHS principal Bill Perry was coaching the team. (Courtesy of Sam Green)

The first school to open its doors was built with the new public funding on the Kentucky side of the Army post, near Gate 6. When the facility was constructed in 1951, in what was then known as the Wherry Housing Area (later renamed Lee Village), it went by the name of Wherry Elementary School and initially was for students in kindergarten through Grade 6.

Like the Army, which eliminated segregation in 1948, Wherry Elementary School was racially integrated along with every other post school to follow it. This, for sure, was a rarity in the Jim Crow South. Public schools in Clarksville and Hopkinsville, for example, remained racially segregated well into the early 1960s.

During the mid-1950s, there were two expansions at Wherry Elementary School that added additional school buildings in the immediate area. The expansions made it possible for a realignment of the student population at the school. Eventually, Wherry began educating only fifth- and sixth-graders, while students in grades K-4 attended classes across the street on Polk Road in a facility known then—and until it was closed in the spring of 2016—as the Lincoln Elementary School.

Around this same time, Southside Elementary School (K-6) was built on the Tennessee side of the post, near the three officers' housing areas—Turner Loop, Drennan Park, and Cole Park.

In those early days, the children of enlisted personnel attended Wherry and Lincoln, while the dependents of officers went to Southside.

Barkley Elementary School is now on the site where Wherry once stood on Polk Road. The old Southside Elementary, near 1st and Alaska Avenues, eventually was torn down and replaced by Jackson Elementary School, which opened on nearby Mississippi Avenue in 1958. However, at the time, Southside remained in operation for four more years—until Marshall Elementary School was built in 1962—to accommodate an overflow of sixth- and seventh-grade students.

Fort Campbell Junior High School originally was constructed in 1957 for grades 7-9, but the facility on Forrest Road—near Hammond Heights, the old post hospital and Gate 5—soon expanded and added high school students while a permanent facility for them was being built to open sometime in the late 1960s.

It was the fall of 1962 when Fort Campbell High School officially opened and began educating high school-age dependents of post soldiers at the expanded junior high school facility. Before then, these students had been bussed to high schools off post. Not surprisingly, it reportedly was the unhappiness with racial segregation that led to the creation of a high school on post.

The junior high school/high school facility consisted of the main building and a back extension with two corridors that easily accommodated both groups of students.

Above is an aerial view of Fort Campbell Junior High School—located on Forrest Road, near Gate 5 and the original post hospital—in the late 1950s. An extension later was added to the building to accommodate high school students with the opening of FCHS in the fall of 1962. (Courtesy of Fort Campbell High School)

Fort Campbell's very first, brand-new high school was eventually built just inside Gate 4 on South Carolina Avenue, near Stryker Village. It opened for the 1968-1969 school year. With its opening, the old high school building reclaimed the name of Fort Campbell Junior High School.

Today, the former junior high school is known as Wassom Middle School—named in honor of Brigadier General Herbert M. Wassom, a native of Spring City, Tennessee. Wassom was killed on August 17, 1988, when an airplane on which he was a passenger—along with the President of Pakistan (Mohammed Zia-ul-Haq) and the U.S. ambassador to Pakistan

(Arnold L. Raphel)—exploded in mid-air, apparently the result of a terrorist act.

On a personal note, as a young newspaper reporter in Hopkinsville, I got to know General Wassom a few years before his death when he was assigned to Fort Campbell. His daughter, Tara, even worked as a summer intern for my newspaper while a student at Western Kentucky University in Bowling Green, Kentucky.

It took another 17 years before the tremendous growth at Fort Campbell resulted in the construction of another new high school—the third in the post's history. The 500-student facility was opened for grades 9-12 in September 1985 on Bastogne Avenue, near Drennan Park and Gate 2,

As previously noted, the old high school near the fort's Main Gate was converted into a middle school in the mid-1980s and renamed in June 1989 to honor the late General Fred Mahaffey.

The fourth high school in Fort Campbell's history is now under construction at the same location as the existing high school near Drennan Park. It is being built to accommodate 800 students. The approximately 184,000 square-foot facility will cost $59.3 million to build, according to post officials.

The current high school will remain in operation and become a middle school. Between the two schools the U.S. Army Corps of Engineers plans to construct a soccer field, running track, field house and lighted tennis courts, creating a middle school/high school campus. According to officials, the entire project is expected to be completed sometime around April 2017.

In early November 2015, military officials announced plans to shut down three Fort Campbell elementary schools—Jackson, Lincoln and Barkley. The schools closed in the spring of 2016, after students completed the academic year.

A new Barkley and renovated Marshall Elementary were scheduled to open in their place for the 2016-2017 school year,according to a Department of Defense Education Activity (DoDEA) news release.

Marshall Elementary School, operating for more than 50 years on the Army post, closed its doors at the end of the 2014-2015 school year. Plans for the replacement school call for a state-of-the-art facility—with classroom space for about 650 elementary students. It will be on the same 27-acre site on Texas Avenue.

The "Falcon House" provided locker rooms, showers, and a place to store equipment for FCHS athletic teams. The facility was used from 1962 to 1968 at the very first high school on the Army post that today is known as Wassom Middle School, located on Forrest Road, near Gate 5. (Courtesy of Fort Campbell High School)

Fort Campbell High School opened in 1962 and graduated its first class of 22 seniors the following year. Above is a portrait of the Class of 1965, which was the third graduating class at the school on the Army post. (Courtesy of Fort Campbell High School)

CHAPTER 3: THE EARLY FALCONS

The legend of Marshall Patterson began in the fall of 1962 when Army officials at Fort Campbell, Kentucky, decided the time finally had come to open a high school on the post to educate the sons and daughters of soldiers.

The powers-that-be at the fort, with the verdict, immediately started working on plans to build a new state-of-the-art high school on the Kentucky side of the sprawling military reservation. In the interim, the decision was made to consolidate the high school and junior high school populations under the same roof in an existing facility on Forrest Road, across from the old post hospital near Gate 5. The building, which had originally opened in 1957 and operated as Fort Campbell Junior High School, was expanded to accommodate the older students that now would be attending classes there.

Marshall Patterson – a relatively new and young teacher, with just two years under his belt– was assigned to teach physical education at the new high school and promoted to athletic director and head football coach. Before assuming his new duties at the high school, he had taught at the junior high school and coached the junior high football team—taking over from Bill Perry—for two seasons, compiling an overall record of 13-1.

Even at the very beginning of his career, Coach P was establishing a reputation for taking a keen interest in the young men who played football for him.

The Early Falcons, the ones there at the very beginning, were witnesses to the birth of a coaching legend.

Sam Green played quarterback for the two seasons that Marshall Patterson coached the junior high school football. As Coach P's starting signal-caller, Green also served as the co-captain of the 1960 and 1961 teams.

When Marshall Patterson launched the football program at Fort Campbell High School in the fall of 1962, Sam Green—a 15-year-old sophomore—was the starting quarterback for the Falcons. (Courtesy of Sam Green)

With the launch of the high school football program in the fall of 1962, Green, then a 15-year-old sophomore, became the first-ever starting quarterback for Fort Campbell High School. He also played basketball, baseball and ran track that school year, a practice not unusual at small high schools where athletes participate in multiple sports to fill the rosters.

Green arrived at Fort Campbell in the late summer of 1958 as a sixth-grader after his father was transferred to the Army post from Germany. He said he would never forget the first time he met Coach P, a man who would impact his life forever.

"When I first met him in 1960 as my football coach, I kind of wondered if he knew anything about football," Green admitted, with a chuckle. "Of course, I didn't know at the time he had been an All-Stater in high school and All-Conference at Tennessee Tech…Boy was I wrong."

Coach P, in racking up his 13-1 record at the junior high school, showed everyone he knew a thing or two about football, according to Green. "Caldwell County was the only blemish on our record, and that was in my eighth-grade year," Green said. "We beat them 47-6 at home, and when we went to Princeton, we played their second- and third-string high school team instead of their junior high team…and lost 19-14."

When the Fort Campbell Junior High School football team took the field, the players wore Navy blue jerseys that had white shoulders with red stars and white numbers. Helmets were Navy blue, with a white stripe down the middle. Navy blue or grey pants and black, high-top cleats completed the uniform. The team nickname was "Cherubs" to reflect the legacy of the 11th Airborne Division, the first storied Army unit to occupy Fort Campbell.

"The nickname for the 11th Airborne was Angels, so we were the Cherubs, which are Baby Angels," Green explained.

It didn't take very long for Green and the other players on the 1960 junior high school football team to gain a deep respect for their new, 25-year-old coach, who stood 6 feet, 2 inches tall and weighed a solid 210 pounds. "Coach was a quiet and gentle giant of a man who knew football and people. He taught me so many things that would help me through my adult years," Green said.

Even as a young man, Coach P displayed a habit—whenever he was deep in thought—that would become a trademark throughout his coaching career and into retirement.

"I don't know where he got the habit of rubbing his head, but he was doing that during junior high, too," Green quipped.

Patterson's love of a good chew of tobacco also was evident in those early days. "You would never see Coach without a chew in his mouth during practice, but never would he chew during a game," Green said.

Green, a retired golf course architect and superintendent who now lives in McAlester, Oklahoma, attended Fort Campbell schools through 1963. The family then moved off post to Clarksville, Tennessee, when Green's father was sent to Korea, and he eventually graduated from Clarksville High School in 1965.

Nevertheless, Green, throughout his lifetime, has bled the blue and grey colors of FCHS, and always taken a leadership role in reunions and other affairs of the Falcon Nation. Over the years, he has even made it his personal mission to track down alumni and keep them informed about developments at Fort Campbell.

"Though my experiences were brief at FCHS, the changes in my life were helped along by the tutelage of some of the best teachers in the teaching profession and some of the best coaches, that not only taught me the sports, but also how to be prepared for the future," Green said.

John Bianchini, who has known Green for most of his life, was among the rarest of Military Brats, living at Fort Campbell from 1952 to 1965. He attended Fort Campbell schools during those 13 years, starting with kindergarten and ending with his high school graduation.

Bianchini, like his old pal Sam Green, played football for Coach P for two years on the junior high team, and was a reserve halfback on the Falcons' first high school team in 1962, playing behind seniors Joe Manning and Chuck Muller. He was a starting halfback during the 1963 and 1964 football seasons. In those early years of the FCHS football program, Bianchini scored more than 20 touchdowns as a fleet-footed running back on the varsity squad.

Remember the mention earlier in this book of General Westmoreland's disastrous division parachute jump in April 1958 that killed five soldiers and injured 137? Well, John's father was one of those paratroopers who got hurt in the incident.

Now a retired pharmacist living in Franklin, Tennessee, Bianchini credited Marshall Patterson for preparing him to meet the challenges and difficulties of life. Coach P was fond of restating that famous expression that basically nailed his philosophy of life: *"When the going gets tough, the tough get going."*

Well, John Bianchini was tough, and he got going, thanks to Marshall Patterson. After high school, Bianchini attended Murray State University in Murray, Kentucky, for one year before joining the Army and becoming a Green Beret. He served for four years and was seriously wounded in combat while with the 5th Special Forces Group in Vietnam in 1969. Today, almost five decades later, Bianchini walks with a noticeable limp, a constant reminder of the wartime sacrifice of this gallant hero who is proud to be called one of "Marshall's Boys."

Coach P was a disciplinarian and taught his players by setting the example, according to John Bianchini, whose life has been tested by more than his fair share of adversity over the years.

Bianchini joked that Coach P always had his hands full when it came to him. "I was a hard guy to control," he quipped. "I was always getting after the quarterback in the huddle to call my play—Right 25."

Bob Connelly—introduced in an earlier chapter of this book as a Navy Brat whose father worked at Clarksville Base—also played on the 1961 junior high school football team with Sam Green and John Bianchini.

"Coach P was one of the most influential men in my life," Connelly said.

It was Coach P who tracked him down—as he so often did in his search for promising athletes throughout his years as a coach—in his eighth-grade year and got him interested in football, according to Connelly.

Their relationship bloomed from there. Just before the start of Connelly's sophomore year at the new high school, Patterson—the recruiter extraordinaire—called Connelly to his office to talk him into trying out for offensive center on the varsity football squad. Connelly, who had played on the high school junior varsity team during the 1962 season, said he was told the first team would need a good center that fall, and if he practiced and put his mind to the task, he had a good chance to get the job and start on the offensive line as a sophomore.

Small in stature and more interested in a position that might make newspaper headlines, Connelly said he balked at the invitation. However, Patterson was relentless in his recruiting efforts.

"In the end, Coach P won out and I agreed to learn to snap the ball. Coach P gave me a brand-new regulation varsity football and spent some time showing me how to deep snap and then gave me a practice routine for the summer," Connelly reflected. "When fall camp came in 1963, I could put the ball through the tire almost every time. The long and short of the story is that I went on to be the only sophomore starter on the offensive line….if you can imagine a 150-pound center."

Connelly said Coach P had an uncanny ability to size up athletes and put them in the perfect position to strengthen the team.

"I ended up never missing a quarter for the next three years and was the starting offensive center in 1963, 1964 and 1965," Connelly said. "In 1965, I was selected to the Class "A" Western Kentucky Conference team and was the first Fort Campbell High School Falcon ever selected to the All-State team."

Connelly—like his old teammates Sam Green and John Bianchini—said he never forgot Coach P or the confidence that this remarkable man had in him.

"Coach Patterson had a profound impact on my life. He showed me that through hard work and persistent effort, I could achieve difficult goals," said Connelly, who graduated from FCHS with the Class of 1966.

While at FCHS, Connelly also was a member of Coach P's first wrestling team in 1964, and ran track every year that Marshall Patterson coached that spring sport.

"I was not a gifted athlete. In fact, it was difficult for me to run and chew gum simultaneously," he joked. "A good coach can take a good athlete and help him to become a better athlete. It takes a great coach to take an awkward self-conscious teenaged boy and help him not only achieve remarkable success as an athlete, but also develop into one of the team and class leaders."

Stan Nelson, a member of the Class of 1965, played football for Patterson during his junior and senior years, and also was a member of the first wrestling team at the high school. During the 1964-1965 school year, he served as the president of the Student Body.

A civil engineer, who lives near Birmingham, Alabama, Nelson—in echoing the other Early Falcons—said he had many fond memories of his relationship with Patterson.

"Coach P met with my mother and asked her to fix me special meals so that I would put some weight on…It worked because I went from 168 pounds during my sophomore year to 205 pounds when I graduated from high school," said Nelson, who played fullback on the FCHS football team.

Patterson always kept his athletes and students on task when it came to schoolwork and citizenship, taking the time to mentor and mold them.

"Whenever I was to get an award or honor at school, Coach P would let my parents know in advance so that they could come to school and watch from out of sight at the back of the room," Nelson said.

Stan Nelson was thinking about joining the Army after leaving high school. However, Coach P argued he should go to college and try to play football.

Patterson convinced his old college football coach, Wilburn Tucker, to recruit Nelson as a walk-on after his graduation from Fort Campbell High School in the spring of 1965.

Nelson spent five years in Cookeville, Tennessee, at Tennessee Tech, but he played football for the Golden Eagles only during his freshman year, deciding to end his football days after Coach Tucker lost his job.

"I'm sure Coach P was not happy with my decision," Nelson said. "But Tech was the perfect school for me and granted me a very good education in civil engineering…If it had not been for Coach P, I would have never gone to Tech."

In addition to his college degree in civil engineering, Nelson left Tennessee Tech with a commission in the U.S. Army Corps of Engineers—a wonderful jump-start for his successful career.

At Fort Campbell High School, Nelson not only discovered his future, but he also found the girl he ended up marrying, and the guy who was his best friend for life.

"I met my wife, the former Barbara Scharn, on my first day at Fort Campbell on October 2, 1962, as she came out of chemistry class. I can still remember what she had on," Nelson said. "An hour later, I met Alan Plaisted, who would become my best friend until the day he died."

Years after graduation, during a reunion, Patterson showed former players some old game films of their exploits on the football field. "He then gave me one of his favorite films where he thought I had played especially well," Nelson said.

At the reunion, Marshall Patterson and his wife, Rebecca Patterson, also invited Nelson and Plaisted—as well as their wives—to their home in Clarksville to show them Coach P's prized collections of old leather football helmets, English Blue dishes, Bone China tea cups, falcon statuettes, and prints of sports-oriented covers of *The New York Times Magazine*.

"He was so proud of his tea cups that he wouldn't let his wife dust them for fear she would break them," Nelson said, with a laugh.

Rebecca Patterson, who enjoyed going "antiquing" with her husband, knew for a fact that, next to football, Coach P was most serious when it came to his china. And, she had a fantastic story to back it up.

Near Greensboro, North Carolina, there is a business—located in 500,000-square-foot facilities, the size of eight football fields—that boasts the world's largest collection of old and new dinnerware, including replacement china. The inventory totals about 12 million pieces in more than 400,000 patterns, some over a century in age.

Marshall and Rebecca Patterson visited the huge warehouse on one occasion, and Coach P saw a collectible that captured his heart—a piece in the shape of a falcon. Because it cost a pretty penny, there was some hesitation in buying it—especially on Rebecca Patterson's part. However, because her husband wanted it so badly, Mrs. Patterson allowed him to make the purchase and treat himself.

A pleasant young man—working in the back of the store—was given the task of packaging the prized bird while Coach P and his wife waited up front in the showroom.

"There's only one person in the world that would spend this kind of money for a falcon," the china store employee remarked to a co-worker, with a chuckle. "This has got to be for Coach P from Fort Campbell."

With the permission of his boss, the employee brought the packaged falcon into the showroom to see if he was right about the identity of the buyer. When the young man saw Marshall Patterson standing there, he broke out into a big grin, ear to ear, and yelled out, "Hey, Coach P!"

Hard as it is to believe, the young man working in the china warehouse in North Carolina had once attended Fort Campbell High School and played football for the legendary coach of the Falcons. Rebecca Patterson could not recall the young man's name. "But, Buddy remembered him," she said. It's a small world, indeed.

Stan Nelson and Bob Connelly apparently were among the few students who knew that Coach P worked a part-time job in the early days of his FCHS career. Patterson, for a few years, sold World Book Encyclopedias to supplement the income from his teaching and coaching jobs.

Of the four Early Falcons, only Sam Green (No. 11) and John Bianchini (No. 22) played on Fort Campbell High School's first football team when it took the field for an abbreviated schedule during the 1962 season. By the time FCHS had decided to play football that year, many of the schools already had their schedules filled up, according to Green.

"Plus, not many schools would play us because we were integrated, and segregation was at its peak," he added.

There were five black players on the FCHS roster when the 1962 season got under way in late September. Joe Manning (No. 13)—a 5-foot, 4-inch, 145-pound halfback—was one of the stars for the Falcons, starting in the offensive backfield with fullback Bernard Williams (No. 39). At some point in the year, James "Tex" Allen (No. 23) cracked the starting lineup as a halfback or fullback. The two remaining black players were Phillip Patterson (No. 19), who was Sam Green's backup at quarterback, and Roland Youngblood (No. 12), who was a reserve halfback.

Patterson's assistant coaches on the gridiron that historic first year included Houston Mills, William Leech, and Gayle Spurlock. Coach P had particularly special relationships with Mills and Leech. He always called Leech by his nickname, which was "Bubba."

Mills, who taught physical education at the junior high school, spent his entire 25-year coaching career—right up until his death in the late 1980s—on Patterson's coaching staff.

Leech was at FCHS for about one year, leaving his teaching and coaching career to pursue post-graduate studies that included a law degree from the University of Tennessee. He had played college football with Patterson at Tennessee Tech and actually was drafted by the Chicago Bears to play professional football. However, after graduation from Tennessee Tech, he instead served two years in the Army before reuniting with Patterson at Fort Campbell High.

From 1978 to 1984, Leech served as the attorney general for the state of Tennessee. He later returned to private practice as a senior partner with a prestigious Nashville, Tennessee, law firm, working until his death in June 1996.

The 1962 football team played just seven games and finished with a record of 2-5. "We weren't supposed to win any games," Green reflected.

Chuck Muller and Paul Pavlick, co-captains of the first FCHS football team, discuss game strategy with head coach Marshall Patterson (right) and his assistant, William Leech, during the 1962 season. (Courtesy of Fort Campbell High School)

But, like a Hollywood movie, FCHS made history when it was victorious in its first-ever high school football game, beating Warren County at Bowling Green, Kentucky, 18-0, on Friday, September 21, 1962. On only the sixth play of the game, Falcon halfback Chuck Muller (No. 20) burst through the left side of the line and galloped 60 yards for a touchdown. Muller's long run with the pigskin was history in the making, too. It represented the first touchdown scored by a Fort Campbell High School football team. The Falcons never looked back after the early score, with Muller later scoring again on a 6-yard run and halfback Joe Manning putting up the final points of the night for FCHS with a 22-yard run into the end zone. In their very first battle on the gridiron, the Falcons rushed for 288 yards, compared to 40 for the Dragons.

Warren County and four other FCHS football opponents—Hopkinsville High School, Stewart County (Tennessee), Christian County High School, and Franklin-Simpson High School—fielded all-white teams during the 1962 season.

Green said he played sparingly in the Warren County contest, suffering from a strained calf muscle. The only other win that first season came at Fryar Stadium during the homecoming game when FCHS faced the Henderson-Douglass Bisons—an all-black high school, and one of two played that year—and defeated them, 19-7.

Halfback Chuck Muller and tackle Paul Pavlick (No. 49)—the co-captains of the 1962 FCHS football team—were the heroes of the game, which was played on Saturday, October 27, 1962. Muller scored two touchdowns on runs of 5 yards and 1 yard, and Pavlick—the biggest player on the FCHS roster at 6-foot, 5-inches tall and weighing 220 pounds—blocked two punts. Tom Nicholson (No. 24)—a future West Pointer, Class of 1970— recovered both of the blocked punts, including one in the end zone for a Fort Campbell touchdown.

The rest of the Falcons' first season on the gridiron was just as exciting for the military community at Fort Campbell. But, before taking a look at the other games that year, let's first explore the history of the high school's "Falcon" nickname and mascot.

It's another interesting story that involves two Military Brats who were among the Early Falcons walking the halls of Fort Campbell High School during Sam Green's glory days.

Before there was a high school, there had been only one football team on post, and that team was the Fort Campbell Junior High School Cherubs.

But, when FCHS opened its doors and started playing football and other sports, there was an immediate need to pick a school mascot. So, in the weeks before the first-ever varsity football game in 1962, there was a contest at the high school. Bill Tidmore, a junior who was on the football team, submitted the winning suggestion that ultimately was endorsed by the entire student body—"FALCONS."

Of course, with the 101st Airborne Division occupying the Army post, it's kind of odd that EAGLES didn't get the nod. There might have been a good reason, but no one is really sure. Maybe the answer is with Sam Green's excellent memory.

According to Green, the contest to pick the nickname for the high school's athletic teams was only the launch of what was supposed to be a high-flying campaign to promote Fort Campbell's first football team. Another student, Pat Hunt, who years later would become an assistant football coach at FCHS, volunteered his talent as an artist and drew the sketch of the Falcon mascot. (The original drawing is proudly displayed at the Patterson home on Brandywine Drive in Clarksville.)

"Something else was to transpire," Green said. "Bill Tidmore had a pet falcon. The plan was—before each home game played on Saturday afternoon—for the falcon to be released and fly around the field."

Green said the idea for the flying falcon spectacle called for it to look similar to what fans down in Alabama see on game day at Auburn University with their War Eagle mascot.

"The week before our first home game against Hopkinsville High School, the falcon got other ideas, escaped and was never seen again," Green said. "It sure would have been interesting to have seen this go off without a hitch back in 1962."

If the falcon had shown up at the first home game ever played at Fryar Stadium, the bird most certainly would have been the highlight of the day for FCHS fans. Hopkinsville High School—with its heralded coach, Fleming Thornton, a future member of the Dawahares/Kentucky High School Athletic Association Hall of Fame—pounded the Falcons, 47-0.

It was no contest. According to published reports, Coach Thornton alternated his first-, second- and third-string units during the game, playing 60 Hoptown youngsters—35 in the first-quarter alone. The game—played on Saturday, September 29, 1962, and covered by area media, including the daily newspaper in Hopkinsville, Kentucky, the *Kentucky New Era*—remains etched in Sam Green's memory to this day.

Hoptown's Herb Covington, a preseason All-State pick in 1962, racked up 91 yards rushing on five carries and had three touchdowns in the game—one on a 68-yard punt return. Covington, although the hero of the game, actually spent more time that day riding the bench than carrying the pigskin against what *Kentucky New Era* sports writer Joe Caldwell called a "small-but-scrappy" Fort Campbell squad.

"What a nightmare of a game. We couldn't do anything right," Green recalled. "Coach Thornton had a great team that year. They were bigger, as most of the teams were, and faster. I was just coming off a leg injury when we played Hopkinsville and that slowed me down a lot."

Green completed five of 17 passes in the game for a total of 73 yards. He also threw two interceptions, including one to a huge tackle for the Tigers—Herman Turner—who then lumbered 62 yards for a touchdown. No doubt, Coach P was rubbing his head after that particular play.

The football game marked the beginning of a long friendship between Herb Covington and Sam Green—both of whom were recognized as among the top athletes at their respective high schools.

On a historical note, and a sign of the times, the mood was anything but friendly down in the state of Mississippi the weekend of the Fort Campbell-Hopkinsville football game. The forced enrollment of the first black—James H. Meredith—at the University of Mississippi in Oxford led to rioting that resulted in two deaths. Only three days after that first high school football game at Fryar Stadium, 4,200 paratroopers from Fort Campbell—some likely the fathers of FCHS football players—were deployed to Mississippi to help U.S. marshals maintain order on the college campus.

The Mississippi riots made national headlines. But, what readers apparently failed to see in their newspapers that fall was the story of what was happening in the Commonwealth of Kentucky, where Fort Campbell's Marshall Patterson and his integrated high school football team were fighting the war against segregation on the football field and in the classroom.

One week after the loss to Hoptown—on October 6, 1962—the Stewart County Rebels from neighboring Dover, Tennessee, invaded Fryar Stadium. Although the Falcons were on top for most of the first half in their third game of the season, Stewart County rallied to take an 18-12 victory. Falcon halfback Chuck Muller accounted for both of the Fort Campbell touchdowns—one on a 22-yard run and the other after he caught a pass from quarterback Sam Green and scampered 23 yards into the end zone.

The Falcons, in the following weeks, played two other football teams from Hopkinsville—Christian County High School, which opened in 1959 to accommodate students from several community high schools that had been closed, and Attucks High School. FCHS lost both contests. Christian County High School came to Fryar Stadium on Saturday, October 13, 1962, and drilled FCHS, 33-14. Six days later, in a Friday night game at Tiger Stadium in Hopkinsville, the Falcons played the Attucks Wolves, losing to the all-black high school, 20-6.

In the Christian County game, Sam Green had a pretty good day at quarterback for the Falcons, completing 5 of 11 passes for 142 yards and one touchdown—a 54-yard strike to halfback Chuck Muller. Joe Manning accounted for the Falcons' other touchdown with a 6-yard run. But, despite playing the visitors tough, FCHS simply was outmanned. The team's two starting tackles—Tommy "Randy" Darnell (No. 42) and Paul Pavlick—had been injured in the Stewart County game. A reserve tackle, James Stockwell (No. 27) was hurt, too. If FCHS had been healthy, the Colonels probably would have had their hands full with the young, improving Falcons. Darnell, a junior, was a two-way starter at tackle for that first FCHS football team. A few years after his graduation from FCHS in 1964, he joined the Hopkinsville Police Department and retired 23 years later in March 1990 as the chief of police.

In the Attucks game, Fort Campbell's only highlight of the night was Joe Manning's 14-yard touchdown run. It capped off a 58-yard drive. After that early score, the Wolves dominated the game and improved their record to 6-2 with the victory.

Fort Campbell closed its inaugural football season with a 20-6 loss to Franklin-Simpson High School. The game was played on Friday, November 2, 1962, in Franklin, Kentucky. The Falcons played a tough game against the Wildcats, but two fourth-quarter touchdowns by the host team put the game away.

Few students probably felt like singing after Fort Campbell High School's first football team finished the season with a losing record. But, a junior, Sharon Elizabeth McCoy, looked to the future and was inspired enough to write the school's alma mater.

A FCHS graduate and member of the Class of 1964, Sharon McCoy was a cheerleader during her senior year. In 1982, she died at the age of 36.

Her words still resonate, decades later: *"Hail, oh hail, to dear Fort Campbell, School of faith and pride; Loyal friends of thee forever, Always by your side. Proudly standing past and future, Looking towards the sky; We'll remember you forever, Dear Fort Campbell High!"*

Now, there was something else really special about 1962 and the birth of Fort Campbell High School and its football program. A pretty 14-year-old freshman destined for fame and fortune was making her mark on a student body that came to know her as a good student and popular cheerleader.

The cheerleader's name was Lenore Kasdorf. She left Fort Campbell before her sophomore year and later graduated from the International School of Bangkok (Class of 1966) after her father, an Army Colonel, was transferred to Thailand.

Lenore, in adulthood, became a noted television and movie actress. She is best known for her six-year role as Nurse Rita Stapleton Bauer in the popular soap opera, *Guiding Light*, and for her performance in the 1997 movie, *Starship Troopers*.

During her acting career, Lenore Kasdorf also starred with Chuck Norris in 1984's *Missing in Action*, and has had guest-starring roles on *Coach, The A-Team, Knight Rider, Murder She Wrote, Barnaby Jones, 21 Jump Street, The Six Million Dollar Man, NYPD Blue, Beverly Hills, 90210, Magnum P.I, Star Trek: The Next Generation, Streets of San Francisco,* and *Babylon 5.*

Jenny Ahn-Wangoe, a retired flight attendant who now lives in Washington State, said she and Lenore Kasdorf were classmates for two years, meeting in the eighth-grade at Fort Campbell Junior High School. "She was popular, talented, and sweet. So, it was no surprise she would become an actress," remarked Jenny, who was a majorette for the FCHS Band and member of the Class of 1966.

For Military Brats, especially those who were there, Fort Campbell High School's first year of football was memorable for another reason—The Cuban Missile Crisis.

In October 1962, for 13 terrifying days, the world teetered on the brink of nuclear war after an American U-2 spy plane confirmed the Soviet Union was building nuclear missile sites on the island of Cuba—just 90 miles from Key West, Florida.

Remember—even though few people knew it at the time of the world crisis—nearly one-third of the country's nuclear weapons were being stored in underground tunnels at Clarksville Base, located on the Fort Campbell installation. This fact alone almost guaranteed that the area would be among the Soviet Union's top targets—if nuclear war broke out.

In the end, President John F. Kennedy made Soviet premier Nikita Khrushchev blink, and the missile sites were dismantled.

"I remember there were a few TVs set up in certain classrooms at school, so we could watch and see what was going on," Green said.

It was a time when football, and just about everything else, was put into the proper perspective, according to the old quarterback.

"I know that Coach was looking at it very closely because, if my memory serves me correctly, he may still have been in the Army Reserve so I guess there was a possibility of him being called back to duty," Green noted. "Those were some scary moments for all of us."

Stephen Patterson, Coach P's son, gives the FCHS homecoming queen—June Smith—a kiss during festivities before the football game at Fryar Stadium in 1963. (Courtesy of Fort Campbell High School)

FCHS halfback John Bianchini (No. 22) bulls his way toward the Falcon end zone at Fryar Stadium during a game against Christian County High School in October 1962. The visiting Colonels won the game, 33-14. (Courtesy of Fort Campbell High School)

CHAPTER 4: TWO OLD QUARTERBACKS

Make a fast forward in the glorious history of the Falcon Nation, from 1962 to 2012. Fifty years had passed like the blink of an eye—from the birth of a high school and the beginning of an iconic coaching legend to a brave new world of technological wonders.

Military Brats, who had once called Fort Campbell, Kentucky, their home, were planning to return to the area in masses to celebrate the milestone and the best years of their lives. Reunion planners anticipated a large turnout for the homecoming, thanks to the Internet and social media, which had made the task of contacting alumni so much easier than had been the case in the past.

Despite the passage of time, Americans in 2012 still lived in times that were scary, with our country at the very pinnacle of its War on Terror. Those dark days had begun on September 11, 2001, when Middle East terrorists, in hijacked planes, killed nearly 3,000 Americans by toppling the Twin Towers of the World Trade Center in New York City, crashing into the Pentagon and hurtling a jetliner into a field in rural Pennsylvania.

Only 3½ months before the terrorist attacks, the FCHS community had mourned the passing at age 71 of retired high school principal Bill Perry— the man who hired Marshall Patterson. A former Marine and veteran of the Korean War, Perry served as the principal at Fort Campbell High School for 28 years.

In the closing months of 2012, Coach P, who had been retired now for more than a decade, was nearing the sunset of his life. The sons and daughters of soldiers who had attended Fort Campbell High School and lived through a half century of transformation were now responsible adults—older, much wiser and ever grateful to the coach who steered them down the right path in life.

The world had changed, but FALCON PRIDE was still as strong as ever. Falcon alumni everywhere expected, even demanded, a big celebration to mark the 50-year anniversary of the birth of the high school and football program. It would come that fall during the school's homecoming celebration, when multiple FCHS classes hosted reunion activities throughout the community.

The earliest Falcons—the graduating classes of 1963 through 1976—came together for one of those grand reunions. Hosted and coordinated by the FCHS Class of 1972, it took place at The Quality Inn on Wilma Rudolph Boulevard in Clarksville, Tennessee, from Friday, October 19, 2012, through Sunday, October 21, 2012. The Reunion Committee was steered by six members from that 1972 class known for their spirit and can-do attitudes: Joanne (Nagrod) Bryant, Steve Bryant, Mike McNair, Tina (Barnett) Moberly, Greg Reniker, and Sharon Waters.

On an interesting note—reflecting the times—one of those Reunion Committee members, Joanne Bryant, had had a front-row seat on "The Day America Changed Forever." Joanne, on September 11, 2001, witnessed the carnage at the Pentagon, where she was working as a budget analyst for Secretary of Defense Donald Rumsfeld.

No one should have been surprised by the revelation.

In all likelihood, Joanne was not alone in this life experience. Just like the days of Vietnam, there likely were many sons of soldiers— plenty of daughters, too—that once had been mentored by Coach P and the FCHS faculty before marching off to wars in Afghanistan and Iraq to serve their country in the 11 years since the 9/11 terrorist attacks, some never to return home again.

In the Military Brat World, after all, it's not uncommon to end up in the thick of things. Look at any war memorial anywhere, and it will include the names of Military Brats. As an example, at least three Fort Campbell students of the 1960s—Ed Rykoskey, Kenneth Albritton and Glen Ivey— are among the more than 58,000 servicemen honored on the Vietnam Veterans Memorial in Washington, D.C. In all likelihood, there probably are many more names of former Falcons on that memorial wall and others around the country.

Joanne (Nagrod) Bryant and Steve Bryant pose in front of their class portrait at the 2012 FCHS Reunion. The Bryants—"FALCONS FOREVER"—were high school sweethearts. They now live in Virginia. (Courtesy of FCHS alumni)

After more than three decades at Fort Campbell, Marshall Patterson understood, and appreciated, the sacrifices of military life. And, by this stage in his life, even one of his seven grandchildren—Taylor Patterson,

Stephen Patterson's grown daughter—was fighting for her country, serving in the Air Force and performing dangerous missions in Afghanistan.

With the appropriate theme of "Fifty Years of Falcon Pride," alumni participated in a variety of activities at the 2012 reunion. But the highlight for the long homecoming weekend—particularly for those who had rarely returned to the area since their graduation—was the opportunity to revisit Fort Campbell and attend the Friday night football game, under the lights at Fryar Stadium, where alumni hoped to meet up with Coach P and their favorite teachers.

Four of "Marshall's Boys" from the 1973 football season—(from left) Ed Overcash, Bruce Yuhas, Rick Zielinski, and Earl Linton—walk the football field at Fryar Stadium during the 2012 FCHS Reunion. (Photo by Rob Dollar)

At this point in time, multi-class reunions had been occurring every two years for a decade or more. Usually, at the reunions, the returning graduates visited with Coach P and other FCHS faculty at the football game and maybe even during the Saturday night dinner and dance, where the coach and teachers were toasted as honored guests.

Marshall Patterson, since ending his days as a football coach and teacher, had become a permanent fixture at Fryar Stadium on game nights, sitting in the top row of bleachers, very close to the Press Box. The trek up the bleachers to thank him for making a difference in their lives had almost become a religious ritual for many former Falcon football players and wrestlers who returned for homecoming.

But on Friday night, October 19, 2012, when the reunion group of more than a hundred arrived in two buses at Fryar Stadium, they quickly discovered Coach P was not at the game and would not be attending the dinner and dance the following night at The Quality Inn due to health problems.

Among the disappointed alumni on that beautiful autumn night was Mark Brown, a member of the Class of 1975, who was attending his very first FCHS reunion since leaving high school. "I wanted to have the opportunity to shake his hand again," said Brown, who wrestled for Patterson and had quite a reputation in high school for being a top-notch weightlifter.

What Brown and many FCHS graduates did not know at the time was that Patterson had been suffering from the effects of Alzheimer's disease for several years, and he would have his good days and his bad days.

Although Coach P had managed to make it to the football game two years earlier during the 2010 reunion, it was evident then he already was having severe memory problems. Patterson—who, in his prime, was admired for having a mind like a steel trap—failed to recognize several of his old football players. His ever-loyal wife, Rebecca Patterson, had to tell him their names as they approached them in the bleachers and looked into the familiar steel blue eyes of their beloved coach.

By the time of the October 2012 reunion, Marshall Patterson's mental state had deteriorated to the point that Rebecca Patterson decided it was not a good idea to take her husband to the game or the reunion dinner. And, as it turned out, there would be no next time. Two years later, when the 2014 reunion rolled around, the beloved football coach of the Falcon

Nation already had gone home and to his final resting place in Clarksville's Riverview Cemetery.

Coach Marshall Patterson demonstrates a blocking technique to players during a practice at the high school in the early 1970s. During his 32-year career as the head football coach at FCHS, Coach P won 227 games, including three state championships in 1976, 1978, and 1979. (Courtesy of Fort Campbell High School)

The 2012 reunion turned out to be one of the better—and more memorable—gatherings for Falcon alumni, bringing home for a rare visit many sons and daughters of soldiers who had roamed the hallways during the days that the author attended Fort Campbell High School.

It got off to a good start with the Falcon football team clobbering the Heath High School Pirates, 68-13, in the Friday night homecoming game. The contest was so ugly there was half-serious talk at half-time about taking several of the old Falcon football players out of the bleachers and sending them into the game to give the other team a sporting chance. Maybe people were kidding around, but Sam Green—the first-ever FCHS starting quarterback—got so excited he started warming up, tossing a pigskin back and forth with another alumnus, who, like him, already had 65 birthdays under his belt. Unfortunately, or maybe fortunately, "QB 1" and the other Early Falcons never got their chance to suit up. So, after the game, it was back to the hotel for a different kind of workout—a "Happy Hour" that lasted well into the next morning.

There were quite a few new faces at the 2012 reunion. The cut-ups referred to them as the' "Shock and Awe" Falcons—class favorites who suddenly exploded on the scene, out of the blue, after seemingly disappearing from the face of the Earth for far too many years. This group of legendary characters—just to name a few—included alumni like Steve Reed, Steve Mollohan and Steve Cleghorn from the Class of 1976; Mark Brown, Terry Roberge, Alan Garcia, and Theodius Oates from the Class of 1975; Sabrina (McBrayer) Alls, Vycke (Shen) Horback, Rick Zielinski, Bruce Yuhas, Ed Overcash, and Bernard McCarthy from the Class of 1974; Joni Trusty, Mary (Riddle) Staples, and Randy Rhea from the Class of 1973; and Hermann Harris from the Class of 1972.

For Falcon alumni of the 1970s, Bernard McCarthy had to rank as the biggest mystery that former classmates hoped to solve before their days on this Earth ended.

Now, it's no secret every high school in America has a Bernard McCarthy—that unforgettable classmate who is remembered by everyone for being one of a kind. Bernard was very intelligent during his school days, but he marched to the beat of his own drum. He always carried a box of Kleenex with him in high school—apparently for allergies—and rode his bicycle everywhere he went on post. Although he was often teased relentlessly, Bernard actually figured out in high school just what he wanted to do with his life, and as it turned out, he was among those lucky enough to achieve and live their dream.

Strange as it may sound, Bernard McCarthy, as a teenager, was obsessed with roads. He was interested in safe streets as well as the efficient and effective movement of people and goods on improved highways. He apparently studied the subject so well at the University of Kentucky in Lexington that, after four years in college, he went straight to work for the Kentucky Transportation Cabinet.

At the time of the 2012 reunion, Mr. McCarthy still was employed by the Transportation Cabinet, busy as ever improving the roads in the Commonwealth of Kentucky. And, he still was carrying his box of Kleenex....Like I mentioned, Bernard is, and probably always will be, a bird of a different feather. But there's no one in the Falcon Nation who loves Fort Campbell High School, and the beautiful women who once walked the halls there, more than Bernard McCarthy. Not only is he still doing the work he loves to do, but he's been giving back to the community for more than two decades, working on nearly 360 Habitat for Humanity houses in Kentucky and other states.

Charles Edward Overcash, a former Navy pilot now living in Georgia and flying commercial jetliners for Delta Airlines, stirred another memory for me. Mr. Overcash was a teammate of mine on the 1972 and 1973 Falcon football teams, playing end and defensive back.

It seems like only yesterday when he showed up at summer football camp on a hot August afternoon in 1972. Coach P brought the young man with long sideburns into a classroom, where we were studying our playbooks, to introduce him to the team.

"This is Charles Overcash," Marshall Patterson said. "He's a transfer student, and I think he'll be able to make a contribution to this team."

Coach P then glanced over at the newest Falcon and shot him a get-to-know-you question. "What do your friends call you, son...'Chuck'?"

"No sir," replied Overcash. "They call me 'Ed.'"

"That figures," responded Coach P, who then, with a scowl on his face, rubbed his head. The room erupted in laughter, and Ed Overcash—having made quite a good first impression—was welcomed with open arms into the Falcon Brotherhood. I think he may have even given Coach P a break and spilled the beans about his middle name.

Bruce Yuhas, one of Ed Overcash's running buddies throughout high school, played two seasons for Coach P and probably was one of the greatest linebackers in FCHS football history. Nowadays, he works in the real estate and property management industry in Columbus, Ohio. Bruce's younger brother, Brian Yuhas, played split end and defensive back for three years. He was one of my pals and a member of the Class of 1975.

When the two Yuhas brothers showed up as transfer students at Fort Campbell High School—also during the summer of 1972—they looked like rock stars with their long hair. Of course, the girls swooned over the two good-looking guys with the beautiful locks.

Not so with Marshall Patterson. He was happy to have them on the football team, but he made it clear in no uncertain terms they had to conform to team policy and get haircuts. Coach P might have even rubbed his head when he gave them the bad news.

Thank God, the Yuhas brothers loved football more than their black manes. In the end, they cut their hair, played football and dated cheerleaders. The Falcon football team went 8-2 that year.

When Bruce Yuhas and Ed Overcash reunited at the 2012 reunion, they made up for lost time and entertained their classmates with an unforgettable jig out on the dance floor, most certainly fueled by adult beverages. Talk about male bonding….

Like me, Steve Cleghorn—another Falcon teammate—thoroughly enjoyed the "Bromantic Moment" between the two old friends. It had been nearly four decades since I had seen Mr. Cleghorn, now a resident of sunny Florida. Steve was at the reunion with his older brother, Michael Cleghorn. Coincidentally, Michael, who never attended Fort Campbell schools, ended up marrying one of our FCHS classmates—Sandy Bailey (Class of 1975), who died of breast cancer on June 28, 1999. She was 41 years old. God bless her beautiful soul.

Steve Cleghorn, a character who just couldn't help but make everyone around him laugh until it hurt, hadn't changed a bit since high school. He, too, like me, had tried his best back in the day to play football for Coach P, but without much success. There always will be those guys, I suppose, who just have a hard time walking and chewing gum at the same time.

In talking about the old days, Mr. Cleghorn recounted in vivid detail his memories of football practice, with Coach P nervously pacing back and forth while chewing tobacco and spitting out the juices in every direction. He said there were times when he often felt like a human tobacco spittoon.

"Man, I was always getting hit," Cleghorn joked.

Former Falcons with a knack for making reunions—any reunion, mind you—also showed up in full force for the festivities at The Quality Inn. I had my own special name for these always reliable guys and gals: "The Forever Young" crowd. The group included yours truly and best pal Preston Owens from the Class of 1975; Earl Linton, Liz (Johnson) Kelker, Collette (Garrett) Gales, Dale Kesterson, Debbie (Teague) Kesterson, and Pam Busby from the Class of 1974; Debbe (Jones) Gifford, Vicky (Craig) Coleman, Sally Solis, Susie Chambers, Carla Warren, Susie Gilmore, Debra (Estes) Slater, Jennifer Jones, Ed Ritter, and Jimmy Thomas from the Class of 1973; and Dennis Fendler, Alan Boyd, Ken Shuttlesworth, Rick Evans, Pat Hoyem, Sharon (Cunningham) Hunt, and Sherri (Crowder) Swickard from the Class of 1972.

The 2012 reunion was bittersweet, not only because of Coach P's absence, but also for a special tribute to honor former students and faculty who had passed away over the years. Two of those tragic losses had occurred earlier in the year with the sudden deaths of Falcon Greats Mike Brown (Class of 1973) and Anita Jones (Class of 1975).

Mike Brown—who was a football and wrestling star at FCHS, and the older brother of Mark Brown—collapsed and died on May 13, 2012, while cycling near Willimantic, Connecticut. At the time of his death, he was 56 years old and worked for the Mohegan Tribe after 30 years of active and Reserve duty in the Army and retirement with the rank of colonel.

Anita Jones, a former Army captain, died of cancer on February 14, 2012, at her home in Beaufort, South Carolina. She was 55 years old at the time of her death. Recognized as one of the greatest female athletes in the history of Fort Campbell High School, Anita later ran track for Western Kentucky University and then competed in track and field as an Army officer. She would have represented her country in the women's 400-meter hurdles at the 1980 Olympics had the United States not boycotted the event because of the former Soviet Union's invasion of Afghanistan.

Scores of sympathy messages were left on the website of the funeral home that handled final arrangements for the woman who was named Miss Fort Campbell High School in her senior year.

Among them was one from an old friend who had coached Anita Jones at FCHS—Ed Davis, now retired and living in Hopkinsville, Kentucky. *"Anita was a great person and athlete. She ran for Fort Campbell's Track Team and was a nine-time state champion (individually) in track. She led Fort Campbell to its first state team championship. I had the pleasure of being her first coach...She was a fierce competitor and a great teammate. I will always remember her awesome smile..."*

Ed Davis missed the 2012 reunion due to a prior commitment. Several other former FCHS teachers were missing, too, since they had long passed away.

One of the dearly departed—Rosemary Pace, always a big favorite with the football team for her "Falcon Chocolate Cakes"—was the subject of many conversations at the reunion. The legendary home economics teacher—she taught at FCHS for 18 years, retiring in 1973—died in March 2003 at the age of 88. She was from the Hopkinsville area, and for years after high school, I would see her on occasion at the fair or some other event, wearing one of her fancy hats and enjoying her retirement years. Folks in Christian County, in fact, knew Mrs. Pace as "The Hat Lady."

Even with so many beloved teachers absent, the turnout of FCHS faculty at the reunion was decent. Many of the teachers had since retired after long and distinguished careers. Among those who reunited with former students were: Kathy Carver, Carolyn Jones, Mary Davis, Sherrie Pennington, Rita (Chaney) Cardenas, Patsy Pendleton, Linda White, Roy Medlock, Frank Davis, John Pyle, Tom Morgan, and David Kerr.

It was at the 2012 reunion, where the author perfected what has become a reunion tradition of charming some of his most favorite teachers—like the former Miss Chaney, who had been single and still looking for love in the days when she tried her best to teach chemistry to me and a few other boneheads in her class; Patsy Pendleton, who helped inspire me to develop my writing skills and love of literature; and Sherrie Pennington, who scarred me for life by giving me those B's in her typing and bookkeeping classes. (Just kidding, Mrs. Pennington!)

Yours truly, in pleasant and convincing conversation, confessed to his beautiful teachers that they looked exactly as I remembered them back in high school—more than 40 years ago. Of course, I meant every word of the praise about them finding The Fountain of Youth and keeping the secret to themselves. After all, in my mind, I still was that same teenage boy thirsting for attention. Time had stood still—at least for me.

Funny thing. A few years later, I tried to lavish Dr. Gary Stewart—who had been one of my junior high school teachers before he eventually replaced Bill Perry as FCHS principal—with the same praise and got royally chewed out. He wasn't buying it.

"You better get your eyes checked, Mr. Dollar," barked Dr. Stewart, who is now a professor at Austin Peay State University in Clarksville.

Although Dr. Stewart wouldn't bite, the compliment certainly delighted the lovely lady teachers. I'm fairly sure they had me pegged as their favorite student of all time until old football teammate Alan Garcia—a senior superlative in the Class of 1975, who four decades later still was "Best Looking"—got them all googly-eyed at the Saturday night banquet with tales about his fascinating career as an air traffic controller and hiking of the Appalachian Trail.

No way could I ever compete with this tall, good-looking teller of adventures in the wild blue yonder and wilderness, so I did the next best thing and turned my attention to some of the still fine-looking former cheerleaders at the reunion—Debbe (Jones) Gifford, Vicky (Craig) Coleman, Sally Solis, Sabrina (McBrayer) Alls, Vycke (Shen) Horback, and Mary (Riddle) Staples. It was my duty as a gentleman to declare to each of them—not at the same time, of course—that they had been my favorite cheerleader back in high school. It really wasn't stretching the truth. I liked all the cheerleaders. There were even a handful of my favorite cheerleaders missing from the 2012 reunion – Linda McCormack, Joanie Fendler and Cheri Horan-byard from the class of 1975, Marilyn

76

(Crutcher) Gratz of the class of 1973, and Mavis (Broderway) Thomas of the class of 1976. Heck, I think the only reason I ever went out for football in the first place was to get on the radar screen of the cheerleading squad.

In what could only be called a cruel twist of fate, Mike Brown was supposed to be at the 2012 reunion. He had been talked into coming to the event by classmates, who had not seen him in decades. He was excited and looking forward to his return to Fort Campbell that fall. His unexpected death only months before the joyous occasion just about crushed the spirits of the Falcon Nation.

Mike's brother, Mark, my old classmate, had not planned to come to the reunion because he had recently gotten married and his life was just too busy for a trip down Memory Lane. His brother's death, however, changed his mind. Mark decided to come in his place—with new wife, Mary—as a tribute to his late brother's memory.

While coming of age at Fort Campbell, the author enjoyed special friendships with three classmates that stretched back to our early days of junior high school. Mark Brown was one of those friends—the other two were Preston Owens and Mike Hellums—who made the same journey with me from sweet and awkward junior high teenagers to know-it-all high school graduates.

Coach Houston Mills, one of Coach P's earliest assistants on the football team, was our physical education teacher at Fort Campbell Junior High School. If it hadn't been for him, and Mike Hellums egging me on, I might never have gotten the hang of climbing a rope. Rope-climbing just happened to be a skill that had to be mastered to pass Coach Mills' gym class. It was important, too—for anyone thinking about a career in the circus. In addition to introducing his gym students to "The Tree" and "The Twig"—long, punishing runs that ended in near exhaustion and buckets of sweat—Coach Mills, in his silly way, taught students a thing or two about the social graces. Hee-haw!…The sons and daughters of soldiers at the junior high school were forced to learn the art of square dancing, with some "persuasion" from this big man with the big heart and another PE teacher, Shirley Bell, wife of another of Patterson's football team assistants, Ronnie Bell. Decades after those foot-stomping days in the junior high school gym, the commands—"Allemande left" and "Promenade"—still echo in my head....If I ever end up in a square dance, I know for sure I'm ready, and I'll never make a fool out of myself...I can still "Do-si-do" with the best of them.

The stories at the 2012 reunion—some folks call it swapping lies—about the good, old days in junior high and high school flowed just as smoothly as those adult beverages that were going down the hatches. At one point, while giddy and enjoying the company of my two friends with the fuzzy memories—Mark Brown and Preston Owens—I reminded them about their membership in "The Spy Club" back in the early days of junior high school. The half-dozen members of the notorious club assumed the name of a 1970s television or movie good guy—usually a detective, spy or law enforcement officer—who fought the good fight and always won the hearts of the ladies...Someone in the club was "Joe Mannix"—I think it was me—and someone else was "James Bond." There was even a "Jim West" and a "Steve McGarrett" running around the neighborhoods on post.... The best I can remember, the club never stumbled across any national secrets or saved the world from anything or anybody, but it was pretty adept at the science of girl watching. The club kept close tabs on a few of the junior high school foxes who had captured our fancy—with their pigtails, braces, and interesting conversation...They probably wondered, at the time, what those silly boys were doing, hiding behind bushes with binoculars. Eventually, a few telephone numbers were exchanged in the great fight against evil in the world. It also was true that a few fathers got awful nervous and lost sleep when they found out "The Spy Club" was interested in their daughters. It was a sad day, for sure, when a blonde-haired beauty I had my eye on suddenly left Fort Campbell. The Army dispatched her father—a lieutenant colonel—to Ohio to rebuild the ROTC program at Kent State University. Although there may have been rumors, "The Spy Club" had absolutely nothing to do with the colonel's new assignment, which came about two years after a deadly riot left four students dead and nine wounded on the Kent State college campus in May 1970.

Not surprisingly, Preston Owens—who claims to have no memory whatsoever when it comes to his teenage years—couldn't remember a thing about spying on our sweethearts back in junior high school. Mark

Brown, on the other hand, reacted like a political candidate. Ever cautious of the potential evil eye from his new bride, Mark would neither confirm nor deny the stories of his scandalous "Puppy Love" days at Fort Campbell.

Regardless, "The Spy Club" most certainly had an impact on his life. It may have even influenced him in his initial career choice: Mr. Brown was a longtime police officer in Connecticut before taking off his badge years ago. He left the law enforcement profession to serve as a council leader in the Mohegan Tribe after it gained federal recognition in the mid-1990s, leading to the development of the world-famous Mohegan Sun resort and casino.

Mark Brown and his younger brother, Kevin, are, and have been for years, members of the governing council that runs the tribe's financial empire based in Uncasville, Connecticut. Heck, former President Bill Clinton even showed up at Mark's house as a dinner guest sometime after he left the White House, and my old classmate had the audacity to interrogate him about the Monica Lewinsky affair. From what I've heard about the encounter, "Bubba" just danced around the topic. (You know... It just depends on what your definition of is...is.)

Back in high school, I really thought I knew everything there was to know, but I sure missed the boat with the Brown brothers—Mike, Mark and Kevin. I had no idea they were Native Americans and direct descendants of the renowned Mohegan Chief Matahga. I guess the subject just never came up.

The Class of 1975—Preston Owens, Mark Brown, Theodius Oatts, Terry Roberge, Alan Garcia, and the author—spent a great deal of time at the 2012 reunion talking about our missing classmates. Ears were probably burning around the world.

As is usually the case, family and work commitments prevented many of our classmates from attending the event. Also, it should come as no surprise that some people in this world liken reunions to living in the past so they're never anxious to take that walk down Memory Lane. The many excuses given for missing the reunion were appreciated, anyway. They sure helped three former student leaders—Mr. Owens (Student Council president and Mr. Fort Campbell High School 1975), Mr. Brown (Student Council treasurer), and Mr. Dollar (Senior Class president)—feel better about their leadership skills.

Our class graduated 122 seniors so just about everyone was missing from the fun and festivities—including my own sister, Adele, who had been secretary of the Class of 1975. Like me, she lived in Hopkinsville—where she worked as the branch manager for a staffing company after a 20-year career with General Electric Aviation Systems—but I just couldn't convince her to show up. The same was true for a handful of other graduates still living in the Clarksville area. Go figure...

The only MIAs from the Class of 1975 truly accounted for, I guess, were the classmates whose memories now made us melancholy. I'm talking about the dearly departed: Charles Cunningham, Sandy Bailey, Anita Jones, and as some found out only on the night of the reunion banquet, Steve Falcon. Rest In Peace.

Although I wouldn't bet my life on it, I believe the Class of 1975 was the only class at Fort Campbell High School to ever have a "Falcon" in it. Steve Falcon arrived at FCHS as a senior, and after high school, worked in the supermarket/grocery industry for more than 30 years. He died of cancer at the age of 51 in June 2007, while living in San Antonio, Texas.

Like many reunions, where old friends get together and time seems to stand still, the 2012 event proved to be an overwhelming success. A good time was had by all, with classmates swapping stories and memories until the cows came home. As might be expected, "Marshall's Boys"— former wrestlers and football players who played, or tried to play, for the legendary coach—were having a grand time, tossing down adult beverages and reliving their glory days as high school athletes. Try to imagine the TV character Al Bundy of the old sitcom *"Married...with Children,"* and the picture should come into sharp focus.

During the reunion festivities at the hotel, FCHS alumni eventually got wind of the elephant in the room. Someone—I'm not sure who gets the credit—made mention of the Dawahares/Kentucky High School Athletic

Association (KHSAA) Hall of Fame and the fact Coach Marshall Patterson still wasn't in it. The revelation—it was a bombshell for most former Falcons, who lived in other parts of the country—spread like wildfire through the hotel.

The bomb got dropped on me as I walked into the hotel's Hospitality Room and got buttonholed by Jimmy Thomas and Steve Bryant, who were in the middle of a serious conversation.

A 1973 graduate of FCHS, Jimmy Thomas had been a celebrated halfback on the football team and a champion track star. For a time—after his graduation from Western Kentucky University in Bowling Green, Kentucky, where he also played football—he even worked as an assistant coach for the Falcon football team while grooming himself for a career in the financial services industry. The Thomas name carried considerable clout at Fort Campbell High School since Jimmy's younger brother, Demetrius Thomas, was employed there as the assistant principal. Tell me Jimmy wasn't one proud Falcon.

Steve Bryant, a retired Army major and member of the Class of 1972, wrestled for Coach P in high school and was a member of the 1971 wrestling team that won the state championship. A longtime high school wrestling official, he married his high school sweetheart, Joanne (Nagrod) Bryant, after high school and was now living the good life in Virginia.

"Why hasn't Coach P been inducted into the Kentucky High School Hall of Fame?" Jimmy asked me matter-of-factly. Of course, my old friend believed a career newspaperman who still lived in the Fort Campbell area most certainly would have the answer to his question.

Surprised, but mostly embarrassed because I had been caught with my pants down, the words—really just a flimsy excuse—slid out of my mouth.

"Gee, I didn't know he wasn't in the Hall," I responded. "I guess, all these years, I just *assumed* he was a member." It was the truth, after all. For sure, as a seasoned newsman, I knew everything about local, state, national and international events. But, over the years, I hadn't really paid too much attention to the world of sports since the days of my youth.

Now, Jimmy Thomas and Steve Bryant were among the truest disciples of Marshall Patterson, and I still considered them upperclassmen—my superiors—even though four decades had passed since our high school days.

They flinched when I uttered that word—*assumed*—and I realized as soon as it came out of my mouth that I had committed a cardinal sin in The World According to Coach Marshall Patterson.

One of Coach P's many life lessons—his "Never Assume" speech— suddenly hit me like a ton of bricks. In fact, the suddenness of it kicked my butt. I could hear his booming voice: *Gentlemen, I want you to look at the spelling of the word assume—A-S-S-U-M-E....Never, ever, assume anything..... If you do, you most likely will end up making an ASS (A-S-S) out of you (U) and me (M-E).*

OK. Guilty as charged—I was an ass for not knowing our beloved Coach P had been left behind by the powers-that-be in the Kentucky sports world.

Before assuming anything else, I promised Jimmy Thomas and Steve Bryant that I would get to the bottom of the matter and do everything I could to try and right the wrong of the Hall of Fame forgetting Marshall Patterson. I knew better than to moan, "We *can't* do anything about it."

The word *can't* was not going to come out of my mouth because I had not forgotten it was a word Coach P hated more than *assume*—a word he could not stomach nor tolerate. Heaven help the poor soul who ever uttered the word in his presence.

Coach's "Can't" speech, I guess, must have left a lasting impression on me: *If you tell me you can't do something, it means you won't ever do it.*

Well, with that lesson in mind, I had now volunteered myself to do something about this injustice and so had another former football player who was at that 2012 reunion—Sam Green of the FCHS Class of 1965. Although Sam hadn't seen Coach P since his senior year in high school, he never forgot his old coach—the "Father of The Falcons," who was now suffering from Alzheimer's disease.

Remember, Sam had the distinction of being the first quarterback in the history of the Fort Campbell High School football program. Unlike this author, a backup quarterback who rode the bench his entire career, Sam actually took the field and played most, if not all, of every game in the 1962 season.

If anyone understood the terrible toll that Alzheimer's disease takes on a person and their family, it was Sam Green. His mother, Wilma Lee Green, suffered from the illness, and Sam was her primary caregiver for five years until her death in 2011.

At the 2012 reunion, Sam was doing the thing he does best—promoting Fort Campbell High School and our wonderful lives as Military Brats. He partnered with Jenny Ahn-Wangoe (Class of 1966) to put together a Memory Book, complete with a salute to our military fathers.

Sam, Jenny and some of the other elders of the Falcon Nation—like C. Ray Metts (Class of 1969)—made me proud to be a Fort Campbell Falcon. There was little doubt, for those paying attention, that the most loyal and passionate of the FCHS alumni were the Early Falcons from the classes of 1963 through 1971.

The 2012 reunion was packed with alumni from the high school's first nine graduating classes (1963-1971). Among the attendees were: Jim Yost, Vicki (Allan) Neese, Ed Bassingthwaite, Janice (Ginter) Adams, Shirley (Shastid) Rogers, John Hutson, Josie (Merina) Oakes, John Bianchini, Steve Cook, Carol (Pavlick) Kendrix, Rose (Ashby) Albert, Kay (Woods) Lloyd, Stan Nelson, Barbara (Scharn) Nelson, Bob Mitchell, Euford Herring, Bob Connelly, Barbara (Kennedy) Harper, Carol (Elrod) Pogue, Lee Hamilton, Patricia (Simmons) Campbell Persinger, Frank Fleming, Christina (Kuhns) Murphy, Billy Bolen, Robert Kerr, Sharon (Ozment) Haynes, Naomi (Estes) Baker, Ronnie Johnson, Judy (Ginter) Jones, Theodore Arnold, Mary Lou (Harston) Sellers, Mike Christian,

Jesse Owens, Jerry Weesner, Tammy (Spitzer) Rookstool, Joncie (Wilson) Powell, Margie Bryant, Bev Gray, Consuelo "Cheat" Solis, Karen (Greening) Smith, Dana (Jett) Rand, Debbie (Monaghan) Chapman, John Ignacio, Mitch Waters, Ronnie Chapman, Gay (Arnold) Wanstrath, Donna (Garner) LaPee, Carl Dremann, Danny Betancourt, and Patty Evett.

Jim Yost, a member of the Class of 1963 who ran track and cross country, was recognized at the reunion as Fort Campbell High School's first All-State athlete. As a senior, he won titles in the mile and 880-yard runs during the state track tournament in Lexington, Kentucky, on May 18, 1963.

For old friends who hadn't seen Yost in years, the gathering definitely would be one for the memory books. It would be the last high school reunion for Yost, an Army veteran of the 82nd Airborne Division and former Green Beret who served in Vietnam. Just months before the 2014 reunion, which he also planned to attend, the Falcon great and Seymour, Illinois, funeral home director—still as adventurous as he was in high school—was killed in a tragic accident. Jim Yost died at the age of 69 doing what he enjoyed most in life besides running—parachute jumping from an airplane. At the time of his death, he was participating in a World War II Airborne Demonstration Team's semi-annual jump school in Frederick, Oklahoma.

There also would be no future reunions for two other early, and proud, Falcons—Patricia (Simmons) Campbell Persinger and Tammy (Spitzer) Rookstool.

For Patricia, retired after working for 38 years as a secretary in the Fort Campbell school system, the 2012 event was her first and last FCHS reunion. At the affair, she was confined to a wheel chair and battling cancer. Less than three weeks later, she died at the age of 63 at her home in Clarksville. A member of the Class of 1967, Patricia had been a popular cheerleader and first runner-up in the high school's "Miss Flame" contest.

Tammy, a retired special education teacher who graduated with the Class of 1970, died at her Clarksville home less than nine months after dancing the night away with Ray Metts and other old friends at the 2012 reunion. She was only 60 years old at the time of her death.

The overwhelming turnout of Early Falcons at the 2012 reunion was reason enough for the younger alumni at the event to show respect for their elders. That might sound funny coming from an almost sixtysomething-year-old guy like me, but when an upperclassman opened his or her mouth that weekend, old and graying Rob Dollar—still a young teenager in high school, at least in mind and spirit—was all ears. It was time to listen, not speak.

With the listening and learning came new friendships.

If anyone was in their element at the 2012 reunion, and the reunion that followed two years later, it had to be Ray Metts, a happy-go-lucky fellow who couldn't help but be the life of the party—any party. Now a resident of Ridgeville, South Carolina, Mr. Metts is the owner and operator of a sign company. Although officially retired from the ministry, the former Southern Baptist pastor has never stopped working for God.

On Saturday night, Ray was the Falcon with the nifty moves on the dance floor, almost as good as the suave steps of Fort Campbell High School's dancing machine—Danny Betancourt (Class of 1971). He kept the alumni of the Falcon Nation dancing all night long to the rock music of our high schools days. The big guy leading "The Train" across the dance floor was a sight to see. And, there probably are some folks out there, like me, who still to this day can't get that James Brown song—*"Get Up Offa That Thing"*—out of their head.

Now, Ray Metts' reputation as a master barbecue chef and the world's greatest bacon lover was well known to his classmates. So, it came as no surprise that his old friends at the reunion got quite a kick out of teasing— maybe "ribbing" is a better word to use—him for his culinary skills and big eating habits. When the former Falcon footballer and his buddies weren't talking about great food and clean fun, the conversation always turned to Coach P and the best days of their lives at FCHS.

Metts initially attended high school in the junior high facility on the Army post and then he was among the first students to go to the new high school—now known as Mahaffey Middle School, near Gate 4—after it was built and opened for the 1968-1969 school year.

While at FCHS, Metts (No. 60) played football for Coach P for three seasons as a tackle, guard, center and linebacker. He also starred on the track team, earning medals in two events—the discus and shot put. "Beyond being team captain, I never really did anything worthy of state or conference honors," Metts said. "But no one ever loved FCHS any more than I did."

According to Metts, Marshall Patterson was a big fan of legendary Alabama football coach, Paul "Bear" Bryant, and the Falcons often rolled with many of the same offensive formations as The Crimson Tide. "Coach P would also quote Coach Bryant quite regularly," Metts recalled.

As one of the relatively few football players who developed a strong bond with Marshall Patterson, Metts—while in high school—even helped him coach a Little League baseball team that included a young Stephen Patterson.

Metts said his fondest memories at FCHS, and fiercest loyalties, will always center on Coach P and two other Falcon favorites he's never forgotten—Assistant Coach Houston Mills and Lucy Shaw.

Houston Mills was the longtime physical education teacher at Fort Campbell Junior High School and assisted Coach P as the line coach for the Falcon football team for 25 years.

In the 1960s, Lucy Shaw was employed as the cafeteria manager at the junior high/high school, supervised the concession stands at home football games, and was in charge of preparing the meals for the football team's home and away games. Knowing this bit of history, it wouldn't surprise me in the least to learn that Metts may have gotten his huge appetite for good food and life from "Miss Lucy"—as she was affectionately known to football players and students.

It was Coach Mills who introduced Ray Metts to a few of the thrills in a Falcon athlete's life—like running to "The Tree" or "The Twig." As for Miss Lucy, whenever it snowed and there was a need for someone to clear the sidewalk and driveway at her Clarksville home, she always hired Ray Metts for the job and paid him $5.

86

"She insisted…Shaw, as she called her husband, was too weak (from health problems) to do it," Metts explained. "And, $5 would fill my gas tank back then."

Ray Metts said he considered himself one of the luckiest people in the world to have had role models like Coach P, Coach Mills and Lucy Shaw in his life.

"When I look back, I can't help but notice a pattern of closeness between Coach P, Coach Mills, and Mrs. Shaw," Metts said. "I know that they shared a passion for ministering to us kids and frequently coordinated and supported each other's efforts on our behalf."

Houston Mills died on November 7, 1987, at the age of 48, while Lucy Shaw—later the director of Fort Campbell's Teen Club in the 1970s—passed away about one month later on December 10, 1987. She was 67 years old. The two FCHS favorites may have been long gone, but they certainly were not forgotten by the Early Falcons of the Falcon Nation.

Now, Ray Metts— "The Galloping Gourmet" of the Falcon Nation—has a big heart that is, and always will be, in the right place. About two years after the 2012 reunion, and only three months before FCHS graduates gathered for their next multi-class reunion at The Riverview Inn in Clarksville, Ray—arguably the "heart" of the Falcon Nation—had a brush with death. It resulted in open-heart surgery and some lifestyle changes. Nevertheless, old Ray—much leaner and with a new outlook on life—still managed to show up for the 2014 reunion and took his place out on the dance floor when they started playing that song that inspires everyone to get up and dance like a fool…You know the one… *"Get Up Offa That Thing."* At that next reunion, he also made it his personal mission to remember and celebrate the life of his late friend, Tammy (Spitzer) Rookstool. Thanks to Ray's generosity, the toasts to Tammy's memory with those potent "fireballs" never seemed to end that night. The "fireball therapy" made the hotel bar a lot of money and kept the poor bartender busier than a one-legged man in a butt-kicking contest. With his new lease on life, Ray—always ragging me for frowning in photographs—even tagged me with a new nickname in the hope of keeping a permanent smile on my face. So, thanks to my new friend, Ray Metts, the author now is known to friends and strangers as "Smiley."

All smiles aside, at the time of the 2012 reunion, the final chapter of Coach P's life story was far from being written by the powers-that-be in the Kentucky sports world. Not surprisingly, alumni were demanding *THE HAPPY ENDING*—Marshall Patterson, the "Father of The Falcons" riding off into the sunset and taking his rightful place in the Hall of Fame.

A salute to Marshall Patterson was long overdue, and now—with Sam Green and yours truly behind the center to take the snap—the Falcon Nation prepared to march the length of the football field, from our goal line to the Hall of Fame's end zone, for a score for our beloved coach.

After some digging, it didn't take long to determine that Marshall Patterson had already been nominated for the Dawahares/Kentucky High School Athletic Association Hall of Fame.

The Hall, located in Lexington, Kentucky, was created in 1988, and through the end of 2012, it had already honored 403 athletes, coaches, officials and contributors to interscholastic athletics in the Commonwealth of Kentucky.

Nominations to the Hall are usually made by school officials, colleagues and others associated with the KHSAA. Each year, at least eight honorees are invited to join the prestigious fraternity of sports heroes and legends.

Scott Lowe, who played football for Coach P at FCHS and later served as one of his assistant coaches, filled out the three-page nomination form on Patterson's behalf and signed it on September 15, 2009, around the time he was sharing the FCHS athletic director's duties with Kenneth Jankowski. A close examination of the Marshall Patterson file, however, revealed there had been no activity on his nomination for more than three years. It basically had been languishing in a No-Man's Land—without any letters of recommendation and support materials that would have accelerated a KHSAA review.

Even more appalling was another discovery. According to KHSAA rules and policies, Coach P, with his credentials, apparently could have been nominated for the Hall as early as October 1999 when he turned 65 years old, even though—at the time—he was in his next to last year of coaching the Northwest High School football team in Clarksville. So, an entire decade may have passed before someone familiar with his career finally got around to nominating him for the high honor.

The revelation initially led to some anger and finger-pointing, with the most passionate of the Falcon Nation wanting to know who—if anybody—had fumbled the football and caused Coach P to be left behind on this field of battle.

After all, when it comes to Halls of Fame in anything, everyone knows the sooner an application is considered, the better the chances for success—mainly because contemporaries are still around to ensure that the most deserving are not forgotten.

In fairness, it should be pointed out that, by the time Coach P was nominated for the Hall of Fame, 14 years had passed since his retirement as the longtime athletic director at Fort Campbell High School. In those years after his departure, the school and its athletic programs grew by leaps and bounds and the athletic director's job changed hands on several occasions for various reasons. Therefore, an argument might be made that perhaps there was no steady hand in the office or enough help to take care of additional administrative tasks like nominating a deserving coach to the Hall of Fame. The lack of continuity in the leadership at the high school might also help explain the noticeable absence of top FCHS sports stars in the Hall of Fame. Hard as it is to believe, through 2015, there were NONE in the Hall despite the fact FCHS has produced many world-class athletes—male and female—since opening its doors in 1962. But again, there's no getting around the bottom line: There won't, and can't, be an induction into the Hall of Fame without someone in the KHSAA sphere of influence—like a school administrator, coach or referee—nominating a coach or athlete and then doing the follow-up work that pushes the nomination through the process. No nomination, no induction. It's that simple.

Who are some of the greatest Fort Campbell High School athletes missing from the Hall of Fame? Several names readily come to mind. Anita Jones (Class of 1975), who was invited to jump hurdles for the United States team in the 1980 Olympics, stands out as a shining example in Kentucky girls' track. Alan Boyd (Class of 1972) and Ronnie Chapman (Class of 1971) can stake their claims as top-notch wresters. Both won back-to-back individual state wrestling championships in 1970 and 1971. Andre Offutt (Class of 1978) also was a state wrestling champion, winning titles in 1977 and 1978 and later starring on the University of Kentucky wrestling team. Mike Cassity (Class of 1971) was a state wrestling champion in 1971 and probably Coach P's first blue-chip football player. He was recruited and starred in football as a defensive back for the University of Kentucky Wildcats in the mid-1970s, and for the past forty years, has been a successful assistant college football coach. Darrell Wallace, a star running back on the 1981 and 1982 Falcon football teams, rushed for 2,607 career yards as a member of the University of Missouri Tigers. He was inducted into the school's Athletic Hall of Famein 1997 and later played in the Canadian Football League. Marcus McClinton, who graduated from FCHS in 2004, made the All-State football team as a senior playing wide receiver and safety. He later starred for the University of Kentucky Wildcats, and in 2009, became the first Falcon ever to participate in a National Football League (NFL) combine. FCHS, in its history, also has produced two football players who were recognized as the best of the best and named Kentucky's "Mr. Football"—Micah Johnson (2005) and Antonio Andrews (2009). Johnson and Andrews later enjoyed great careers at major colleges and were good enough to play professional football. On September 27, 2015, in Nashville, Tennessee, Antonio Andrews—who, in his high school career, was 29-0 as the Falcons' starting quarterback—became the first Fort Campbell High School graduate to score an NFL touchdown. As a reserve running back for the Tennessee Titans, the former Falcon had an 8-yard score against the Indianapolis Colts. The Colts won the game, 35-33. Later in the 2015 season, Andrews became the Titans' starting running back.

Cooler heads eventually prevailed in the Coach P matter, and in the weeks after the 2012 reunion, the two old quarterbacks—Sam Green and yours truly—got busy and launched a multifaceted campaign to get Marshall

Patterson the recognition he deserved for a lifetime of taking care of the sons and daughters of soldiers.

With the financial backing of John Bianchini—the retired pharmacist and member of the Class of 1965—and many other Early Falcons, Sam Green commissioned the sculpting of a bronze bust of Coach P for the trophy case at Fort Campbell High School.

Together, Sam and I also worked area newspapers and social media to encourage former Falcons everywhere to write and send letters of support for Marshall Patterson's induction into the Hall of Fame. With Coach P's health deteriorating rapidly, the Falcon Nation was working feverishly to convince the KHSAA to honor him while he was still alive to see and appreciate the accolades.

The very first letter to go into his nomination file—stamped December 14, 2012—was from me and included an essay that made a passionate appeal for Coach P to be honored for a career of teaching, coaching and mentoring thousands of Military Brats over three decades.

Here is the essay—it featured the headline, "A Hall of Fame Coach"—I wrote that helped kick off Coach P's fight for his rightful place in the Dawahares/KHSAA Hall of Fame:

The angel Clarence Odbody has a memorable line in the classic holiday movie, "It's a Wonderful Life."

"Strange, isn't it?" he remarks to George Bailey. "Each man's life touches so many other lives. When he isn't around, it leaves an awful hole, doesn't it?"

Back in the mid-1980s, on a chilly fall Friday night, that very thought was dancing around in my head as I walked across the field at the football stadium in Russellville. At the time, I was a journalist working for a Hopkinsville newspaper, and I had been drafted to help out the Sports Department that night by covering a high school football game between the Fort Campbell Falcons and Russellville Panthers.

I'm sure the fact I knew the legendary coach, Marshall Patterson, had something to do with the assignment. After all, I had played football for him during the 1972, 1973 and 1974 seasons, and it was at Fort Campbell High where I picked up a nickname for life—"Broadway Joe." As a brash, young, long-haired quarterback who knew everything, I could throw a football a country mile just like my idol of the time, Joe Namath of the New York Jets. Of course, it also was true I couldn't run and chew gum at the same time, which was the reason I rode the bench my entire playing career.

It had been more than 10 years since I last saw the giant of a man I knew as "Coach P." As I approached him and the same assistant coaches— Houston Mills, Ronnie Bell and Rocky Cobb—who had terrorized me during my playing days, I felt butterflies in my stomach. I didn't know what to expect. Yeah, I was one of "Marshall's Boys." But, I had never been a gem when it came to playing high school sports. Most of the time, I was an angry young man, blaming coach for not playing me. If there was anyone he might want to forget, it was probably me.

As the team went through its pre-game warm-ups, Coach P paced back and forth, staring down at the ground. Then he lifted up his head and spied me walking toward him. A big smile of recognition broke across his face. And then I heard that familiar booming voice: "Hurry up, Joe. Go suit up. We might need you tonight." It was like I had never left high school.

As it turned out, FCHS didn't need me that night, which was a good thing. They beat Russellville like a drum, and Coach P was in a good mood when I conducted my after-game interview. The man had not changed at all...It was still all about playing as a team...It was "WE" and not "I"....

It was another 20 years before our paths crossed again, this time at a FCHS reunion of the 1975, 1976 and 1977 classes. Coach P had since retired from the Fort Campbell Dependent Schools and also from coaching football at a Clarksville, Tenn., high school for several seasons. I made it a point that night to thank him for being such a positive influence on my life and the lives of thousands of other classmates.

As Military Brats, many of us had fathers who were away from home far too often...When our dads couldn't be there for us, Coach P always was...He willingly filled the void and guided our lives in the right direction. He made a difference.

There are countless FCHS graduates around the country who owe who they are today, in part at least, to Coach P's mentoring and success as a role model. They are serving in the military, teaching, building homes and skyscrapers, and working for the government... Some are even Captains of Industry. But no matter what these former Falcons do for a living, all are making a difference when it comes to making this world a better place.

Many are at the very top of their professions like Major General Jeff Jacobs, commander of the Army's Civil Affairs & Psychological Operations Command (Airborne) at Fort Bragg, North Carolina. At 55, Jeff is still jumping out of airplanes. If my memory serves me correct, it was Coach P all those years ago who helped Jeff meet the physical fitness requirements that allowed him entry into West Point.

Dave Blackwell, the dean of the University of Kentucky's College of Business & Economics, was another Marshall Patterson success as were Ed Overcash, a former Naval "Top Gun" aviator and current pilot for Delta Airlines, and Mike Cassity, who has been a college football coach at the University of Kentucky and several other major universities for more than 35 years.

Coach P often lectured his players that the game of football was just like life...You always had to leave everything on the field and never give up....I'll never forget the day in August 1974 when the Watergate scandal forced President Richard Nixon to resign the presidency...Coach P called the team together in a huddle before practice. He wanted everyone to understand what a sad day it was in America, while still reinforcing the important lesson that there is no gray area when it comes to right and wrong.

Over the course of his career at FCHS, Coach P won a state wrestling championship and took his football team to four state championship games, winning three of them in 1976, 1978 and 1979. Those were the days before everyone, including teams with losing records, automatically made the state playoffs every year, and average athletes got trophies or honors just for showing up for a sport. Upon his retirement, Coach P ranked No. 14 in wins among Kentucky high school football coaches.

As the school's athletic director, Coach P also oversaw the development of the girls' sports program at FCHS, which resulted in several other state championships.

His accomplishments are even more amazing if you consider he spent nearly his entire career as a coach on an Army post. Because of the transient nature of the military, Coach P had to rebuild his teams from scratch during most, if not all, of his years of coaching...And, despite this incredible handicap, he still managed to produce winning teams year after year.

In October 2012, FCHS graduates from the 1960s and 1970s gathered to celebrate the 50-year anniversary of the founding of Fort Campbell High School. Coach P was the first football coach at the school, so a lot of time was spent by some old and graying men, reliving our glory days on the football field.

It was at this reunion that many of us were stunned to learn that our great coach had not yet been inducted into the Kentucky High School Athletic Association's Hall of Fame. For whatever reason, Marshall Patterson is not among those legendary Kentucky sports icons who have been forever honored in the Hall since the induction of the inaugural class way back in 1988.

Coach P is now in the sunset of his life, plagued the past few years by serious health problems that have kept him at home. He was unable to make it to the recent reunion to see the many members of the Falcon Nation who still love him. I'm sure it broke his heart. But, for those of us so influenced by this great man, the bigger heartbreak belongs to us as we try to make sense out of this great travesty. How is it even possible for there to be a KHSAA Hall of Fame, when Marshall Patterson isn't in it?

"Winning isn't everything; it's the only thing" is a well-known quotation in sports. So is "A winner never quits, and a quitter never wins." If you were one of "Marshall's Boys," you never forgot either of those commandments.

Coach P is a winner who deserves to be in the KHSAA Hall of Fame. Somehow, somebody along the way dropped the ball, and what this great coach and human being did during his lifetime was forgotten.

Without Marshall Patterson, a man who molded the lives of thousands of Military Brats, the Hall will never be anything more than a sad joke. That is a fact.

The KHSAA can count on one thing: There won't be any quitting in the Falcon Nation until the day when Coach P rightfully takes his place in the Hall of Fame.

The floodgates had now been opened, and letters on Marshall Patterson's behalf began piling up at the KHSAA office in Lexington during the 2013 calendar year. Alumni of the Falcon Nation really got personal when the Christmas holiday season rolled around that year. They communicated their great love for Marshall Patterson and his family by sending scores and scores of Christmas cards to the Patterson residence in Clarksville. Norm Miller, who played on the 1976 state championship football team and graduated from FCHS in 1978, came up with the idea for the Christmas card campaign so that Coach P would know he had not been forgotten. No one knew at the time that it would be the last Christmas for the former Falcon football coach, who would die peacefully at his home the following month.

By the spring of 2014, Marshall Patterson's Hall of Fame file had swelled to more than 50 letters and support materials. The dramatic change likely prompted the Hall of Fame's Induction Committee to screen, review and debate his career for the very first time that April—unfortunately, about five months after his death at the age of 79.

However, when officials announced the Hall of Fame's new class of inductees in June 2014, Marshall Patterson's name was not on the list. The

Falcon Nation, for sure, didn't agree with the decision. But, Coach P's Military Brats also knew better than to criticize the decision-makers and moan that they had been unfair to a great football coach.

No one was ready to give up despite the disappointment. "Marshall's Boys" were nowhere near the point of throwing in the towel. The KHSAA had not heard the last from the alumni of the Falcon Nation. That was as certain as death and taxes.

The KHSAA snub brought home to me another memory of Coach P and a life lesson very appropriate to the situation at hand for Falcons everywhere. It was Marshall Patterson's "Care" speech—the one he always gave during demanding practices that sometimes resembled one of the nine circles of Hell in Dante's Inferno.

To the best of my recollection, it went something like this: *Gentlemen, don't get upset or worried if I get in your face and yell at you for not doing something or for doing something wrong. It doesn't mean I don't like you or think you can't get the job done…It means I care about you, and I want you to get it right so you can be the best…Now, if you want to worry about something, then worry about the day when you don't do something or do it wrong and there's no reaction from me…If that ever happens, you'll know I've given up on you.*

Of course, anyone who knew Coach P would tell you in a heartbeat that he never gave up on anybody. He cared for every single one of his Military Brats and was always ready and willing to fight for them.

Surely, there was someone connected with the KHSAA—someone who had known Coach P—who was familiar with his divine rules for life and what likely was to follow from the caring and loving alumni of Fort Campbell High School, scattered around the globe.

The mere thought about the possible consequences of the KHSAA snub put a huge grin on my face…The suits up there in Lexington—they weren't the media but still Spiro Agnew's famous words came to mind, *"Nattering Nabobs of Negativity"*—were about to learn what happens when thousands of Military Brats get together to raise holy hell.......

At least one person in the KHSAA office should have had a good idea of what was coming—Darren Bilberry, an assistant commissioner who had joined the organization in February 2007.

Bilberry was a Military Brat, too. He had attended Fort Knox High School, where he was a star football player for the Eagles before graduating in 1985. An All-State running back, Bilberry later played under Coach Jerry Claiborne—a Hopkinsville native—at the University of Kentucky from 1987 to 1989.

The selection process for Hall of Fame inductees takes place behind closed doors. So, there's really no way to know the position taken by Bilberry on Marshall Patterson's nomination when the KHSAA Induction Committee met in the spring of 2014 and considered it for the first time.

But the author of this book is quite certain of one thing: Mr. Bilberry was very familiar with Coach P's reputation on the football field since he actually played against Marshall Patterson's Fort Campbell Falcons back in high school—at least twice, in the annual Army Bowl rivalry.

During the 1983 football season, Fort Knox, in a home game, thrashed the Falcons, 35-0, in the 11th meeting between the two Army high schools. Bilberry ran for a 19-yard touchdown in the victory. The Eagles ended the 1983 season with a 15-0 record and won the Class AA state championship.

In 1984, the Army Bowl was played at Fort Campbell's Fryar Stadium, and Bilberry—then a 6-foot-3, 192-pound senior—led Fort Knox to a 38-12 victory. The game—played on Friday night, October 5, 1984—turned into a nightmare for the Falcons, with Bilberry rushing for 176 yards on 31 carries. He scored three touchdowns in the game—including one that came after he intercepted a pass and then ran 61 yards into the Fort Campbell end zone.

Bilberry definitely made an impression on Marshall Patterson. In a post-game interview with Hopkinsville's daily newspaper, the *Kentucky New Era*, Coach P—still shaking his head after the terrible beating that the FCHS team took at Fryar Stadium—admitted that Darren Bilberry was the key to the game, and he had done everything that night except sell popcorn to the fans.

Through the remainder of 2014, the campaign to get Coach P inducted into the Hall of Fame was the top priority of the Falcon Nation. And, when the multi-class reunion rolled around that year, many more letters of support were collected for the KHSAA as well as petitions that contained hundreds of signatures.

The love and respect for Marshall Patterson, no doubt, helped boost the attendance at the mid-October reunion held this time at The Riverview Inn in downtown Clarksville. The usual suspects, of course, were there to raise a ruckus. Faithful alumni who had missed the 2012 reunion—like the author's Hopkinsville neighbor, Debbie (Russell) Rager, a world-class operating room nurse, who had been the president of the Class of 1974, and her basketball-star classmate, Phil (Baush) Labat—also got back into their high school groove and returned for another walk down Memory Lane with former classmates.

New faces, as well, showed up for the 2014 reunion to renew old friendships and join the fight to right the wrong done to Coach P. The party was coordinated by the Class of 1974, with Liz (Johnson) Kelker and Earl Linton, who was another of Marshall Patterson's old quarterbacks, running the show.

Several more of "Marshall's Boys" made it to town. Art Shemwell (Class of 1973), a retired Army colonel who now lives on an island in the Caribbean, was there with his younger brother, Eric Shemwell (Class of 1974), a triathlete in the Atlanta, Georgia, area, where he works as an operations manager for a leading international producer and marketer of beer, wine and spirits. Both Shemwell brothers played football and wrestled for Coach P in high school.

Ken Baker (Class of 1974), who was a teammate of mine on the 1973 Falcon football team, surprised his old friends by appearing unannounced at the Saturday night banquet and dance. Now a highly-regarded environmental engineer in Nashville, Ken and I roomed together for a semester at Western Kentucky University in Bowling Green, back in the fall of 1975. At the time, fresh out of high school, I was trying to "find myself" after getting lost in the real world.

The Class of 1975 cheered the return of two former cheerleaders who showed up for the 2014 reunion—schoolteacher Joanie Fendler and "Super-Grandma" Cheri Horan-byard, known for spoiling eight grandchildren—and welcomed first-timers Ed Horan, Janet Ward, and Donnie Thomas to the party. From the Class of 1973, Barry Cunningham, Bridget Fendler, and Greg Storey joined old friends in reliving some of the best years of their lives, (Donnie Thomas—another of Jimmy Thomas' younger brothers—and Barry Cunningham were starters for the FCHS football team in the early 1970s.)

Lastly, two stars from the 1976 state football championship team—Mike Moats and Frank Balkus—made a triumphant return to their old stomping grounds to make new memories with their Class of 1977 peers: Kathy (Russell) Mitchell, a former mat maid, Diana (Camp) James, a former cheerleader and track/basketball star, and the marathon-running Pamela (Hicks) Brisendine.

At the Friday night homecoming football game, a trio of old but still young-at-heart Falcons—Sam Green, John Bianchini and Rob Dollar, the author of this book—proudly made a pitch from the Fryar Stadium Press Box to those at the game and in the radio audience for more letters and petitions on behalf of Coach P's induction into the Hall of Fame.

Donny Caver was one of the other folks in the Press Box that night, applauding the cause of the Falcon Nation. Caver, who graduated from Fort Campbell High School in 1984, played for Marshall Patterson for two seasons as a backup quarterback. After he left high school and stayed in the area, Coach P talked him into keeping statistics for the FCHS football team. At the time of our visit, Caver was well into his 31st year as Fort Campbell High School's official football and basketball statistician.

During a half-time ceremony at the football game—with Rebecca Patterson in the crowd, flanked by her two daughters, Jeanann (Patterson) Pardue and Marsha (Patterson) Anderson, and their families—the bronze bust of Marshall Patterson was unveiled and presented to coaches and administrators for display in the trophy case at the high school. It was a good night, indeed, for the alumni of the Falcon Nation.

On a side note, a second bust was made and given to Rebecca Patterson a year later to keep in her home. Sam Green delivered it personally to Mrs. P who broke out into tears of happiness.

The 2014 reunion marked the first official gathering of former Falcons since Coach P's death earlier in the year. As a result, the program for the Alumni Dinner/Dance included a special tribute to him that was penned by the author of this book—on behalf of the Falcon Nation.

With the title, "Remembering Coach Patterson," the tribute read:

In each of our lives, there are people we never forget, no matter how much time passes. The person is always someone special, someone who cared and someone who made a difference.

Marshall Patterson was such a man for thousands of men and women of Falcon Nation. For more than 30 years, he excelled as head coach of the Falcon Football Team while also serving as wrestling coach, teacher, mentor and athletic director. Over the course of his career at FCHS, "Coach P" and his Falcon teams won a state wrestling championship and appeared in four state championship football games, winning three of them in the 1970s. As athletic director, he oversaw the development of the girls' sports program at the high school, which resulted in many other state championships.

But make no mistake about it, this great man's talents and compassion were not limited to athletic contests. As Army Brats, many of us had fathers who were away from home far too often.....And, when our Dads couldn't be there for us, Coach P always was...He willingly filled the void and guided our lives in the right direction. He helped make us who we are today, and for that, we will forever be grateful.

Coach P passed away in January 2014 after a wonderful and remarkable life...a life the Falcon Nation will never forget.

Although he was someone who never chased honors or recognition during his lifetime, no one is more worthy of a place in the Kentucky High School Athletic Association's Hall of Fame than Marshall Patterson. There will be no quit in Falcon Nation until this great man is recognized for his amazing achievements in high school sports and his life of doing good for his fellow man.

The Falcon Nation was on a mission to right the wrong, and it was full throttle ahead. Maybe, just maybe, the following year—2015—would be the year when Coach P received his overdue invitation to join the fraternity of the best of the best in Kentucky high school sports.

Until then, Falcons everywhere had no choice but to play a game of wait, hope and pray that the KHSAA would come to its senses and do the right thing.

Fort Campbell High School alumni celebrate at the 2014 multi-class reunion, which was held in mid-October at The Riverview Inn in Clarksville, Tennessee. Many who attended the event signed a petition that asked the Kentucky High School Athletic Association to induct Marshall Patterson into its Hall of Fame. (Courtesy of FCHS alumni)

When Marshall Patterson's days as the head coach at Fort Campbell High School ended after the 1993 season, he had posted 227 victories over a career that spanned more than three decades. As of December 2015, Coach P was ranked No. 24 on the Kentucky High School Athletic Association's career wins list for football coaches. (Courtesy of Fort Campbell High School)

CHAPTER 5: VOICES FOR COACH P

When the word got out that Marshall Patterson had been forgotten, it didn't take very long for those who knew and loved him to raise their voices across the country and make the case that, if anybody deserved to be in a Hall of Fame, it most certainly was the "Father of The Falcons."

Kentucky High School Athletic Association (KHSAA) officials in Lexington, Kentucky, received more than 50 letters and support materials on Patterson's behalf from December 2012 through early November 2013.

Additional letters of recommendation—the number is unclear—and petitions in support of Coach P's induction into the Hall also were collected during the 2014 calendar year and became part of his KHSAA file.

Patterson advocates—in the letters, the majority written prior to his death in January 2014—included top Army officials, college administrators, community leaders, school superintendents, coaches, teachers, sports writers, and most importantly, the sons and daughters of soldiers who benefited from his stern, unwavering hand over the years. The earliest letters written on Coach P's behalf—just like the materials of other Hall of Fame nominees—were available for the public to view on the KHSAA's web site.

Marshall Patterson, during his career, was highly regarded as an educator and coach. He could have written his own ticket and worked anywhere in the country, at any level, but he chose to stay with his Military Brats at Fort Campbell, Kentucky.

Ray Metts (left) and Walter Williams lead the FCHS Falcons onto the field for the second half of the 1968 homecoming game at Fryar Stadium. Many of Coach P's former football players and wrestlers wrote letters on behalf of his induction into the Dawahares/KHSAA Hall of Fame. (Courtesy of Fort Campbell High School)

One of those letters in his KHSAA Hall of Fame file—written in the fall of 2013 by Johnny Miller, the former athletic director at Austin Peay State University in Clarksville, Tennessee—revealed the telling story of Patterson's loyalty to Fort Campbell High School.

In the letter, Miller wrote:

This letter is in reference to the consideration of Coach Marshall Patterson for the KHSAA Hall of Fame.

I have known Coach Patterson during his entire tenure at Fort Campbell High School and have followed his success very closely. I was football coach at Clarksville High School in Montgomery County, Tennessee, several years, and even though we did not compete, I had great respect for his success.

Later, as Athletic Director at Austin Peay State University, I interviewed Coach Patterson for the head coaching position. This certainly indicates my trust in his abilities. He preferred to remain at the high school level, which I respected.

I know of no one in your state more deserving than Coach Patterson. He coached with the highest standards and lived his life the same way.

Another fine tribute to Coach P came from a former Falcon football player, Josh McKillip, who, in the spring of 2015—about 18 months after he wrote his letter—was named the new head football coach at Fort Campbell High School.

If Marshall Patterson had been living, he surely would have been smiling with the announcement about the hiring of McKillip, who coached the FCHS track team to two state championships and also served as an assistant football coach for two of Coach P's successors.

Josh McKillip—in his October 29, 2013, letter—made a compelling argument that his old coach was Hall of Fame—by any book.

McKillip wrote:

My name is Josh McKillip, and I am currently the assistant head football coach and defensive coordinator at Fort Campbell High School as well as a 1993 graduate of FCHS. I am writing this letter in support of the nomination of Marshall Patterson into the Kentucky High School Football Hall of Fame.

I'm sure that at this point in your selection process you are already aware of Coach Patterson's win-loss record, years of service to the military community, multiple state championships in multiple sports, national-ranked team, and his accomplishments as athletic director. It is not my purpose to restate these facts, even though it is my opinion that those alone merit induction into the Hall of Fame.

My purpose is more to relate the impact Coach Patterson has had on my life, as well as the impact on countless other Military Brats like myself, and to advocate for his induction into the Hall because I know he is and always has been too humble to advocate for himself.

I can honestly say that other than my father and my grandfather, Coach Patterson has been the male role model that has influenced my life the most. He was a steadying force in my life when my world was extremely unpredictable. As a military dependent, my father was deployed for two of the four years that I was in high school. My most impressionable years had my father, the person charged with shaping my development into a young man, serving his country in multiple war zones. The person who stepped in to fill this void was Coach Patterson. He was very in-tune with the needs of the military child, and he treated us as if we were his own children. When we could have taken the easy route and run with the wrong crowd, Coach Patterson instilled self-confidence in us all and steered us towards positive influences. When we could have been easily swayed towards drugs and alcohol, Coach Patterson made sure to let us know his high expectations for us and that those activities would not benefit our lives. When we easily could have blown off academics because of all the distractions in our lives, Coach Patterson made sure that we were students before we were athletes and that making excuses for our behavior was unacceptable. I say "we" and "us" because I know that

Coach Patterson not only did these things for me personally, but he did it with all of my teammates and previous teams as well. Probably the greatest compliment that I heard during those times came from my father who said the reason he could feel comfortable and at peace to leave and do his job as a soldier was because he trusted Coach Patterson with us.

It was no surprise to anyone who knew me and was familiar with the influence that Coach Patterson had on me, that I would enter the teaching and coaching profession. Over the years, I have found myself relating so many of the lessons that Coach Patterson taught to us about football and life in general to my students and athletes. I have found a way to give back to my community what Coach Patterson gave to me, which is extremely rewarding.

In conclusion, at the end of each football season during our awards banquet, it has been my pleasure to present the Marshall Patterson Coaches Award to one of our players. The award is a reflection of honesty, integrity, dependability, and reliability. Basically, the recipient is the player that chooses to do the right things in life, not just when it is easy or convenient, but all of the time. I choke up each year when I talk about the award's significance and the impact that Coach Patterson had on my life. It is one of the most prestigious honors that a player can get, and it is a great way for us to honor our legendary coach. Each year, I also say what a crying shame it is that Coach Patterson has not been inducted into the Hall of Fame.

With this letter, I feel that I have at least done my part to right this situation. Please help me rectify this crying shame by inducting our legendary coach, Marshall Patterson, into this year's Hall of Fame Class...

What follows is a sampling of some of the other letters—or excerpts from letters—written on Coach Patterson's behalf that helped make the case for his induction into the Dawahares/KHSAA Hall of Fame.

Again, all of the letters were sent to the KHSAA the year before Coach P's death.

Dr. Gary Stewart, former FCHS principal and now a professor at Austin Peay State University in Clarksville—in his letter—described his working relationship with Coach P and praised him for his commitment to the school and its students.

Stewart wrote:

I am Gary Stewart, and I am writing this letter of support for Coach Patterson in an effort to have his name placed in the KHSAA Hall of Fame. In addition to myself, I am also writing this letter posthumously for my predecessor, Mr. Bill R. Perry.

Bill was the principal for Coach Patterson's early years in coaching, and he and I both shared in the Kentucky state championships he brought to Fort Campbell High School. Additionally, from 1977 until 1999, I had the privilege and distinction of working with Coach Marshall Patterson at Fort Campbell High School. I was the principal there for the better part of those years, and Coach Patterson served as the head football coach, head wrestling coach, athletic director and later as my administrative assistant.

To enumerate the accomplishments of this man would take more than a few pages, perhaps even a small journal. During my tenure with Coach Marshall Patterson, the things that impressed me and caused the student athletes to revere him was not his won-loss record, as remarkable as it was. Students, teachers, administrators, parents and friends were awed by the value he placed on building character and developing young people to become the leaders of our society. He never viewed a single individual as beyond being worthy of his very best. The lives he touched on the athletic fields of Fort Campbell, Kentucky, the Greater Clarksville area and even the world is his greatest achievement and his legacy. The students and parents who had the privilege of his coaching and his teaching have carried those same lessons throughout their lives and are now sharing those lessons with their children, their grandchildren, and other young people they work with.

It was an honor working with Coach Patterson. My friend, Bill Perry, would agree with me, if he were still alive, that Coach Patterson deserves this award not because of what he did in athletics but what he did in the lives of the athletes and non-athletes he was associated with. I was proud to be a Falcon for 33 years because of such people as Marshall Patterson. Coach Patterson and I talked a great deal about life and what we should be teaching in school, on the football field, on the court, on the mat, in life. We were in agreement on every point. Coach Patterson will forever be Mr. Football at Fort Campbell High School. He will forever be the greatest coach and the greatest Falcon to walk the halls of Fort Campbell High School.

He was and will always be my friend. He was and always will be one of those few people I will admire, respect and revere because of what he gave the students and the families and community members at Fort Campbell. He gave them all the greatest memories of their lives and he is still giving those same memories to others through the lives of the men and women he coached and coached against as the head football coach and head wrestling coach of Fort Campbell High School.

I am hopeful that Coach Patterson will be honored with admission to the Hall of Fame. However, he has already received his greatest award. He is Coach Patterson; he is Coach "P" to thousands of former students and even to their children and grandchildren. His legacy is forever etched in the minds and hearts of countless Falcons from around the world...

Chuck Henderson, president of the *Kentucky New Era* newspaper in Hopkinsville, Kentucky, and a Civilian Aide to the Secretary of the Army, directed his case for Coach P's induction into the Hall of Fame to the top man at the KHSAA—Commissioner Julian Tackett.

Henderson's letter to Tackett, a friend, read:

Dear Julian:

I am writing you to recommend that Mr. Marshall Patterson, the coach at Fort Campbell High School, be included in this year's class of inductees to the KHSAA Hall of Fame. I am one of the very few who can recommend Coach Patterson from the perspective of a player and football referee.

You know I have been a licensed KHSAA high school official since 1969 (44 years) and a player at Hopkinsville High School (1965-1969), which included state championships. During my high school days, I recall that Coach Patterson and Fleming Thornton (already in the Hall of Fame) were close friends yet both were very competitive. The one virtue both of these great coaches had besides the desire to win was building character in young men. I also worked as a baseball umpire with Eldridge Rogers for 22 years and interacted with Coach Patterson as the athletic director, where every detail was in place down to food, towels and hot showers, if desired.

Coach Patterson, no doubt, was a great winning coach, evidenced by his 227 wins in football and 27 state championships in various sports while also serving as athletic director at the school for 33 years. He was the epitome of what a coach should be in his coaching, mentoring of players and treatment of game officials. We certainly could use people of his character today in all of our high school sports. Besides his outstanding record, do you realize that this was achieved at a high school on a military post?

In addition to my career running newspapers, I also do work as the Civilian Aide to the Secretary of the Army. In this position, I understand better than most just how incredible his accomplishments were. His coaching career was at a time when the Army never let a soldier stay at one post more than two or three years, which meant he never had the time to build a steady stream of players he could count on. He had to play and win with whatever families lived on the post (only 4,400 houses on post) as military that lived off post were not eligible to attend on-post schools.

There have been many legendary football coaches from Western Kentucky (already inducted in the Hall of Fame) to include Fleming Thornton, Ken Barrett, Joe Jaggers, Jack Morris, Fred Clayton and Al Giordano, to name a few. I do not know why Coach Patterson is not already in this elite group, but it is time that Marshall Patterson joins the ranks of these others. Time gone by can be a terrible thing as people who have done great things get lost on younger decision-makers who never knew of them...

Retired Army General J.H. Binford Peay III served as the commanding general of the 101st Airborne Division (Air Assault) and Fort Campbell in the early 1990s.

Now, the superintendent of the Virginia Military Institute in Lexington, Virginia, the general noted that Marshall Patterson met the challenge when the Army needed him the most.

He wrote:

I write to endorse that of many supporting Coach Marshall Patterson for induction into the Kentucky High School Hall of Fame. I observed him during two separate assignments at Fort Campbell, the latter being 1989 through 1991 and the 101st Airborne Division's deployment to Desert Shield/Desert Storm.

Coach Patterson was a real hero during this period when many service parents were absent for a long year during the Gulf War. He, in many ways, was a substitute parent, counseling hundreds of young people and clearly he had a major impact on their lives. His game-winning records are legendary in the region...especially noteworthy when one considers the continuing yearly turnover of players on his teams, as their parents were with regularity transferred to new stations.

Coach Patterson represented Fort Campbell High School and the Command so well. He was recognized as a true gentleman, a role model for many to emulate...and a legendary winning coach.

Retired Army Colonel Thomas E. Skrodzki, former garrison commander at Fort Campbell, reinforced—in his letter—many of General Peay's observations.

The colonel wrote:

I would like to strongly support Mr. Marshall Patterson for induction into the Kentucky High School Hall of Fame. He is a most deserving candidate. His record speaks for itself not just for his winning percentages and titles as a coach and athletic director, but for himself the person and man he was to so many families and youths of Fort Campbell's soldiers. His tenure spanned the decades of Vietnam, and up through Desert Shield/Desert Storm and other deployments.

During all of those periods of turmoil, he became a second father for countless sons and daughters who spent their early years at Fort Campbell High School while fathers and mothers were away in service to our country.

His winning ways are hard to imagine despite the turnover of students who constantly rotated in and out of the installation. He had to compete against feeder systems available to other coaches in more stable conventional hometown environments, yet he produced winning teams year after year.

Marshall Patterson is a gentleman in every respect. He did everything proper and by the book while treating his students of the game with the utmost dignity.

I spent my last seven years at Fort Campbell and both my children graduated at Fort Campbell High School, each lettering in several sports. I was the Booster Club president for two years and had an up-close experience with Coach Patterson. I was also the garrison commander responsible for the installation schools. I was a witness to how he represented the high school and the Fort Campbell community every day. He is a most deserving candidate…Please induct him this year.

Lee Elder, a former journalist and public affairs officer for the U.S. Army Recruiting Battalion in Nashville, Tennessee, voiced his disappointment that the KHSAA had not already inducted Marshall Patterson into its Hall of Fame.

In his letter, Elder wrote:

I would like to add my voice to those already being sounded about admitting former Fort Campbell High School Coach Marshall Patterson into the KHSAA Hall of Fame. Frankly, many of us had assumed that

Coach Patterson had already been given this honor, and I feel remorse that we didn't follow up until now.

I worked many years in the media covering the Clarksville/Fort Campbell area during Coach Patterson's tenure at Fort Campbell High School and later at Clarksville Northwest High School. During my decade at the Nashville Banner, The Leaf-Chronicle and the Fort Campbell Courier, I was able to see Coach Patterson in action.

His exploits as a football coach, starting a new program and building it to a perennial champion, are legendary along with his stellar work as an athletic director. However, what impressed me most with Coach Patterson was his stellar character and the way he was able to impart it to so many of his players and fellow coaches

I've met many of Coach Patterson's former players over the years, many of whom proudly serve in the U.S. Army. To a man, when they mentioned they played football at FCHS, I've asked, 'So you played for Coach P?' It's then that their chests puff out and their voices fill with pride and they reply, 'Yes Sir!'

Coach Patterson will be remembered for many things during the course of his life. However, the difference he's made in the lives of young people over the years is perhaps his crowning achievement.

It is my sincere hope that being a member of the KHSAA Hall of Fame can be another accolade. It is certainly most deserved and long overdue.

Josephe' Williams, a former student-athlete and member of the FCHS Class of 1981, reminded the KHSAA, in his letter, that Marshall Patterson was much more than a football and wrestling coach.

Williams, who played on two of Coach P's state championship football teams, wrote:

It was brought to my attention that there is a current campaign to get the Kentucky High School Athletic Association to induct Coach Marshall "Coach P" Patterson into the Hall of Fame.

As an alumnus of Fort Campbell High, Class of 1981 and a member of the state champion football teams of 1978, 1979, and state runner-up in 1980, in my opinion this honor is long overdue.

Not that winning games or leading a team to the state championship game in two different divisions in back-to-back years should be a requirement for this honor, but I believe Coach P ended his career with a 227-120 record. And please don't overlook the fact that unlike most other high school coaches, Marshall Patterson started every year with basically a new crop of players. Coaching for a DOD (Department of Defense) school on a military installation presented some unique challenges to say the least. With every transfer in and out of Fort Campbell, some of the talent that Coach P cultivated the year before moved to a different team, in a different state or country. What is an amazing tribute to his talent as a coach was that during the spring and summer leading up to the football season Coach P was not only adept at assessing the talent that he had on hand, but he was very skillful in finding ways to solidify this group of individuals into a team. Again not only a team, but a team that competed evenly against teams that for the most part have known each other all twelve years of their schooling, but also to excel and win championships against some of the powerhouses in Kentucky High School football.

While this event would be to recognize Coach Patterson for an athletic association honor, Coach P was and in many ways still is more than a football coach. Speaking from my personal experience, the football field was just the classroom Mr. Patterson used to teach us life's intangible lessons like, integrity, stick-to-itiveness, brotherhood and the visible and not so visible rewards of hard work. Mr. Patterson has influenced my decisions far beyond the football gridiron. One question he asked us, "Do you stop at a stop sign in the middle of the night when you are the only one on the street?" This wasn't a Driver's Ed question as many of us "may" have had only our learner's permit....It was an integrity question. What he really was asking was, "Will you do the right thing even when no one is there to watch you?" I hear Coach P challenging me to do the hard right thing even today.

Not only has this lesson lasted me and influenced my choices, but I used this as a teaching point when mentoring my soldiers. Also, I have tried to instill this life lesson in my sons. This is just one of the many lessons Mr. Patterson taught me, not only through words but actions, that have lived on in my life and I am sure is multiplied in many of the young men and women who passed through his sphere of influence.

Beyond question, Marshall Patterson has made extraordinary contributions and has had superb accomplishments in Kentucky high school sports. He is worthy of statewide recognition and set an example that others still strive to emulate.

Joanne (Nagrod) Bryant, a retired federal government employee and member of the FCHS Class of 1972, credited Coach P with her husband's success in life.

In her letter, she wrote:

...I am sure that you have received numerous letters of glowing recommendations from previous athletes—products of Mr. Patterson— who have gone on to become very successful men, many who have become coaches themselves. While, I never knew what it was like to be coached by this amazing man, I was privileged to witness, firsthand, the impact of his coaching.

You see, 38 years ago I married my high school sweetheart, Steve Bryant—one of those products of Mr. Patterson. I watched from the sidelines as this "gentle giant" coached, mentored, and molded my husband into the man he is today. Steve was coached by Mr. Patterson over a four-year period in wrestling and was fortunate to be part of the FCHS 1971 wrestling team that took first place in the state. I witnessed Coach Patterson, as he guided Steve, not only giving him the skills he needed to be successful on the wrestling mat, but providing him with lifelong lessons that he turned to many times over the years.

Growing up as a Military Brat, on military installations all over the world, in the shadow of our parents was, at times, a very daunting experience. After all, we were expected to be a reflection of our parents. However, for many of us, especially during the Vietnam days, our fathers were missing from our lives during our very formative years. Our teachers, counselors and coaches of FCHS became our surrogate parents. We looked to them for more than just our math, English and social studies: Sometimes we needed someone to confide in; someone to lean on; someone to provide those important life lessons—a gentle push in the right direction.

There is no doubt in my mind that Coach Patterson played a very important role in my husband's life. After graduation from FCHS in 1972, Steve went on to graduate from Austin Peay State University and was commissioned into the Army. Steve had a successful 20 years as an Army officer, pursued leadership roles in his post-retirement career and helped raise three prosperous children. Steve has demonstrated those important qualities of dedication, honesty, and loyalty he learned from Coach Patterson throughout his life.

Over the years, since Coach Patterson's retirement, he and his wife return to FCHS during the homecoming game, which is the highlight for our alumni. It's our chance to once again thank this great man for all he has done for us. I recognize that Coach Patterson's coaching record would be reason enough for him to be inducted into the KHSAA Hall of Fame. Take it from a woman who has seen firsthand the impact this man has had on my husband's life and the lives of so many other FCHS athletes—he walks the walk and talks the talk and exemplifies the true meaning of "Coach" in every sense of the word.

Mike McNair, a resident of Woodland Heights, California, and member of the FCHS Class of 1972, reflected on Marshall Patterson's innovative coaching methods and told the KHSAA that he was a master of creativity.

McNair wrote:

I was a high school wrestler for Coach Patterson in both 1971 and 1972. I loved wrestling and though I was competitive and always gave the varsity guys my best shot, I just couldn't crack the starting lineup. Let me tell you about a creative way Coach Patterson dreamed up to give all of us JV guys a chance to earn a varsity letter, and to stay fully committed to be the best we could be, whether it was pushing the heck out of the varsity guy, or being prepared for our fifteen minutes of fame in case our first-team guy was injured.

He would form two FCHS teams, alternating a varsity and JV wrestler, and each team would wrestle two local teams back-to-back at our gym. He called them "double-dual" wrestling meets. Through this format, I obtained a varsity letter by beating varsity guys wrestling for Christian and Caldwell counties (I'll never forget the teams, believe me), and he did this more than once over a period of years before costs and injury concerns eliminated his dual meets. Few coaches have the creativity to do something like that, to get all the JV guys to push, and to strengthen the team two or three places deep at every weight class. That varsity letter, earned on a Kentucky state championship team, is still very special today.

Some twenty years later, the letter jacket I wore with pride for so many years started to mysteriously shrink. I'm sure it wasn't me, and I called Coach Patterson, engaged in small talk hoping he might remember me, and asked if I could buy a current model of the FCHS letter jacket as a replacement. He replied that he would be happy to order one for me, and without skipping a beat asked if he could include the wrestling and golf icons on the jacket. I was surprised he would remember my varsity sports after all these years, but Coach Patterson always invested himself in all of his athletes and P.E. students so I shouldn't have been surprised at all.

I'm certain you have all the documents and other records to support his coaching chops, but I wanted to add a personal note. Please give him the full Hall consideration he deserves.

Steve Shafer, a member of the FCHS Class of 1966, described Coach P as a gentleman who always stood up against what was wrong in society.

Shafer, in his letter, wrote:

I graduated from Fort Campbell in 1966. I wrestled under Coach Patterson for two years, 1964-1965 and 1965-1966. He was a great coach, but even more he was a great person.

I hope this short story will illustrate: My senior year we were traveling to the state wrestling championships in Louisville. We were in two vehicles. We arrived at the outskirts of Louisville about the time for supper. We pulled into a small restaurant and began to unload. It was raining fairly hard. I was in the first group to enter the foyer of the restaurant, and both of our black wrestlers were in my group.

The manager met us at the inner door and stated we were not able to enter due to the black wrestlers being in our group. Coach Patterson arrived then and asked what was wrong. Of course, he was outraged. This was the only time I ever saw him visibly shaken by the situation. But he quickly got himself under control, and like the gentleman he was, he politely told the manager that we would gladly eat elsewhere. He was the most dedicated coach I ever experienced.

Larry Schmidt, former sports writer for *The Leaf-Chronicle* in Clarksville and *The Paducah Sun* in Paducah, Kentucky, lauded Coach P's professionalism and reputation among the high school football coaches in the region.

In his letter to the KHSAA, Schmidt wrote:

I am writing this letter to recommend Marshall Patterson for the Hall of Fame. To be honest, I am rather stunned that he has yet to be inducted but hope I am not too late to recommend one of the finest men and football coaches I have ever known. During my career as a sports writer for The Leaf-Chronicle (Clarksville, Tennessee) and The Paducah Sun, I wrote about his teams and his athletes over a 20-year career.

The fact alone that he won three state championships at Fort Campbell is a solid resume in itself, but how he did it was even more phenomenal. He built the FCHS program literally from the ground floor up. It was truly a rags to riches story. Jack Morris, the legendary football coach at Mayfield High School, always told me how much respect he had for Coach Patterson. And when the two schools were in the same classification, their annual clashes were games of prep football lore. To appreciate what he did, you need to appreciate the environment of being the coach at a military post. Because of the changes in duty stations,

Patterson's team was at the mercy of the Army. Returning lettermen were a luxury and rebuilding took on a different meaning. Some say when the right commanding general was at the post, he had more luck with that issue than others. And there was some pride on the line when Fort Campbell and Fort Knox met annually in the Army Bowl.

Patterson turned boys into young men. They respected him and he very seldom had to raise his voice to get their attention. He was as gracious a loser as he was a winner. He was committed to the principle that football allowed for life lessons. He was a class act.

When he retired from Fort Campbell, he coached at Clarksville Northwest, a school that was truly at the bottom on the food chain for football. He made the Vikings a contender, as well, before he completely retired from the game.

When I think about Hall of Fame coaches in Kentucky football, I know that there has been one huge oversight. I urge you to correct that and induct Coach Patterson into your Hall of Fame.

Gene Washer, former sports writer and Publisher Emeritus of *The Leaf-Chronicle* in Clarksville, applauded Marshall Patterson's character and integrity, and he made it clear to the KHSAA that there was no finer coach—anywhere.

Washer wrote:

During a 17-year career as a sports writer at The Leaf-Chronicle in Clarksville, I have had the honor and pleasure of writing about many famous and great athletes and coaches, but none any finer than Marshall Patterson.

Not only was he one of the finest football coaches, but he excelled as a wrestling coach, too. When you think of Coach Patterson, there were more important things than his won-lost records in both sports, when he didn't know year from year if his players would ship out with their military families.

He was a man with superior character and integrity. He left a positive mark on all those he coached, those with whom he coached, parents and certainly a lasting impression on a young twentysomething-year-old sports writer. It was an honor to have been around him and to report on his achievements...

Van Stokes, deputy director for the Directorate of Family and Morale, Welfare and Recreation at Fort Campbell, Kentucky, told the KHSAA that Coach P's leadership was invaluable to the military community at the Army post.

He wrote:

...I have known Coach Patterson since 1985 when I became the Director of Sports for the 101s Airborne Division (Air Assault) and Fort Campbell, Kentucky. Throughout my career I have never known another high school coach who has exemplified greater character and leadership than Coach Patterson. As a coach and athletic director in a military community, Coach Patterson served as a beacon of values for the entire community. The record books provide results of programs and competitions. But the record books cannot begin to capture the impact Coach Patterson has had in the lives of soldiers and their families. He has stood beside young athletes as their parents have gone forth and served our country. He coached people first and the sport second. Very few people have had such a positive and lasting impact on the lives of families in this community. He has been a pillar of commitment and discipline.

Having worked with coaches on the collegiate and Olympic levels, I have not known another coach for whom I have more respect. I am strongly convinced that Coach Patterson is highly deserving of this honor and I highly endorse his nomination.

Martha P. Speake, a counselor at Fort Campbell High School, remembered Marshall Patterson as an educator who loved kids and knew how to motivate them.

In her letter to the KHSAA, she wrote:

...Coach Patterson was certainly an excellent football coach and athletic director. He had the ability to motivate students to reach their highest potential. He was a gifted athlete himself and he understood not only the skills needed to excel on the playing field but also the psychological factors needed to be successful. In the classroom, he was a joy to watch. He loved his work. He loved kids. It showed in every interaction he had with students, parents and fellow teachers.

Yet with all those superior qualities, Coach P was much more. He was a role model for his students. Many of our students had fathers who were not at home and were in active combat zones. Coach Patterson taught these young men how to make wise decisions and grow into men who would be respected contributing members of society.

His beliefs and morals were unquestionable, and he lived by a code of ethics that I wish everyone could copy. I don't believe I can think of a finer man and one who is more deserving of this honor. The win/lost records for Coach P's teams are certainly impressive, but the commitment and love he showed to the students in our school are lasting.

Hopkinsville Mayor Carter Hendricks—who penned his letter while he was serving as the president and chief executive officer of the Hopkinsville-Christian County Chamber of Commerce—told the KHSAA that he gained great respect for Coach P during his football-playing days at Christian County High School.

Hendricks wrote:

...As a Kentucky native and former KHSAA athlete at Christian County High School, from 1987-1991, I have long been proud of the KHSAA and the athletic competition in the Commonwealth. I participated in football, track, power-lifting, and wrestling throughout my high school career.

It was through football that I would come to know Coach Patterson. Granted, I never got to know Coach Patterson well. I did get to know his teams well as we competed against them frequently during summer scrimmages. His teams were always tough, fast, and disciplined. They never beat themselves with penalties or foolishness.

It'd be easy to dismiss Coach Patterson's impact because he coached at Fort Campbell. We want to assume that this provided him with some sense of utopian school. It's actually quite the contrary. Coach Patterson had to essentially rebuild his team every year as he'd lose players because of troop movement and duty assignments...I respect the KHSAA and the Hall of Fame selection process. I urge the KHSAA to honor Coach Marshall Patterson with induction into the KHSAA Hall of Fame...

Sam Green—the McAlester, Oklahoma, resident who was Marshall Patterson's first starting quarterback in 1962—insisted there was no better role model than his old football coach.

Green, in one of the earliest letters to the KHSAA, wrote:

...There are countless FCHS students/alumni around the country who owe what they have become, in part, to Marshall Patterson's mentoring and success as a role model. While under his tutelage (teacher/coach), I learned so much about life through sports....Marshall Patterson is a winner to all that know him and deserves to be in the Kentucky High School Athletic Association Hall of Fame. To many whose lives were molded by him and the accomplishments that he achieved, the Hall of Fame would be the ultimate reward to a great man...

Debbe (Jones) Gifford, a member of the FCHS Class of 1973, described Coach P's positive influence on a younger brother, Mike Jones, in her letter to the KHSAA.

A former Falcon cheerleader and mat maid, she wrote:

...Not only was Coach Patterson a master of producing results with limited and evolving resources ... he was more importantly a "ROLE MODEL" for all to look up to and work hard to earn his respect and praise.

My brother struggled as a teenager, but with the positive influence of Coach Patterson, he became a great wrestler, leading the way for him to become an All-European champion, after moving to Wurzburg, Germany, in his junior year! As you can see, the influence Coach Patterson had on many has been lifelong and not just during the formative high school years...

Chad Corley, a member of the FCHS Class of 1992, argued that Coach P was different from other coaches because he willingly served as a "father figure" for many student-athletes when their fathers were deployed overseas.

In his KHSAA letter, Corley wrote:

...While I don't discount the impact or value of other coaches as mentors to their athletes, Coach P took that responsibility and commitment to another level. He literally did serve as a father figure to me and many others for months and even years at a time while our fathers were stationed overseas or supporting a military conflict. Beyond making sure we were staying out of trouble, Coach P challenged us to excel in the classroom and on the field while helping our mothers maintain a household in our fathers' absence.

Personally, I played quarterback for Coach P from 1989-1991, a significant portion of which my father was in the Middle East fighting the Gulf War. We didn't win any state championships, but did win a lot of games and I have a lifetime of memories. Without question, I would've preferred my father to be there at times, but the next best thing was having Coach P provide direction and encouragement that helped shape the man I am today. It was a bonus that he transformed a 5' 9", 160-pound marginal athlete into a scholarship college football player.

There are countless other stories like mine from fellow Fort Campbell High School alumni that further exemplify Coach P's selfless character. While each story is unique, they all share a common thread of caring and compassion. Coach P racked up wins and state championships in unusually challenging circumstances, and happened to change lives in the process. How is that not worthy of a place in the Dawahares/KHSAA Hall of Fame? On behalf of all past, current and future Fort Campbell High School students and their families, I implore you to induct Coach Marshall Patterson in the next Hall of Fame class…

John Ignacio, a FCHS golf star and member of the Class of 1971, summed up Marshall Patterson's "greatness" in one of the shortest letters to the KHSAA.

Ignacio wrote:

I have read most of the letters of recommendation already submitted, and there is very little that I can add to them as far as Coach P's accomplishments both on and off the field.

If I had to put his greatness into one category I would have to call it "A Maker of MEN." Coach P took boys and turned them into men.

Jim Stanton, now a Georgia resident in the hotel industry, focused his letter on Marshall Patterson's ability to build character and deal effectively with the challenges of losing key athletes every year.

Stanton, who was one of FCHS's top tennis players from 1974-1976, wrote:

…Coach Patterson was the head coach and director of athletics during multiple state championships in several sports and those results over multiple years and these accomplishments are a matter of public record and certainly speak for themselves.

What is important is how he used sports and competition at the high school level to train young men and women for life. He taught toughness, perseverance and hard work to a transient group of students whose parents were assigned to duty at Fort Campbell for brief periods of time. His students were from diverse backgrounds of varied race, creed and color. He taught respect and decency among his students. In fact, he demanded it.

Students seldom stayed the entire four years at the high school. Their dads were transferred or were sent to war and moved away. Personally, Coach Patterson inspired us to better ourselves and to not accept excuses.

You might wonder how many more state championships Coach Patterson would have got if even half his athletes were to have made it from freshman to senior year...

One of Marshall Patterson's earliest Falcon football players, someone who actually followed him into the coaching profession, contended that Coach P's huge impact on thousands of lives and his school and community should not be overlooked by the KHSAA.

David Bear, a former Army officer who now teaches and coaches at Eisenhower Senior High in Lawton, Oklahoma, poured his heart out in a three-page letter.

Coach Bear, proud to be called one of "Marshall's Boys," wrote:

...It is with a sad heart that, as I write this letter, Coach Patterson is suffering from Alzheimer's and should he be selected, will likely not be able to appreciate and enjoy this honor he so richly deserves. That said there are literally thousands of people, to include former students, players, educators, and even opposing coaches who feel strongly that Coach Patterson's selection for this tribute is long overdue.
Many of these people will not take the time to send letters of recommendation. Unlike the vast majority of coaches whose names you will consider, due to the significant turnover in population at Fort Campbell High School, most of those who would support Coach Patterson's induction, live all over the world. They are unaware of this effort, and in truth, most would imagine, as I did, that he was selected for induction many years ago. A significant number of those who were his contemporaries in teaching and in coaching that would provide strong endorsements, to include several of his assistants, have passed away or are ill. I sincerely hope that you will take these circumstances into consideration when evaluating his nomination.

In the letters you receive, I expect people to discuss Coach Patterson's influence on them directly. Although I intend to do this as well, I think there are many other aspects of his record that should be considered.

During the earlier portions of Coach Patterson's career, particularly the 1960s and early 1970s, the high school population at Fort Campbell was highly transient due to the Vietnam War. Most coaches are concerned about replacing seniors when they graduate or players who are injured, but Coach Patterson not only had those issues, he also had to deal with many of his players leaving in mid-season due to their parents being transferred by the Army. It was not uncommon for a star player to be on the football field or the wrestling mat for the Falcons one week, and be in Washington, Germany, or Japan the next week.

As with most coaches, and I have been one, often it is necessary to take on the role of a parent. This was especially true with Coach Patterson as many of his players had fathers and mothers who were overseas fighting for and defending the United States. In these cases, Coach Patterson frequently assisted not only the student/player, but also the family in coping with the separation. Unfortunately, there were all too many times over his career that Coach Patterson also had to deal with student/players whose parents were killed overseas. These became trying times, not only for the individual involved, but also for the team, the school and the entire Fort Campbell community. Coach Patterson was one of the key elements that helped bind these groups together during these difficult times...

...In August of 1968, I arrived with my family at Fort Campbell, and I wanted to be a football player. I was a sophomore, and although I had never played organized football, I thought I was a pretty good athlete and decided to join the team. It was a typical hot, humid day in Kentucky when I went out for my first practice as a "receiver," and it was almost my last day. I was overwhelmed by everything that was expected (they had been practicing three weeks already), and the weather did not help. To make things worse, the receivers/ends practiced most of the day with the linemen and at 135 pounds, I was one of the smallest. My father encouraged me to stick with it, but after five weeks of the season we were 0-5, and I had only been in on two plays in a junior varsity game...on defense. Coach P was my physical education teacher and since he was

also my football coach, I wanted to impress him in class. One day in class, we were learning "football fundamentals," including passing the ball, good stances, and long punt snaps. With just a little instruction, I quickly was able to perfectly hike the football to the punter nearly every time. Coach Patterson came over to me and said, "David, at practice today I want you to start working out with the offensive linemen as a center." I was "fourth-string" center, the junior varsity season was over, and I obviously was not going to play on Saturdays. Three weeks later, after both the second- and third-string centers had been injured in practice, the starting center got hurt (leg broken) in the first half of the next-to-last game of the year. Beginning the second half of that game, I was the starting center and played 11 more games for Coach P at that position. Prior to my senior year, my father was transferred; however, I became the starting center at 150 pounds for a school easily seven or eight times as big as Ft. Campbell.

I apologize if I bored you with this story, but my life changed that day in Coach P's physical education class. The confidence he showed in me over the next year has stayed with me throughout my life. I am a 1975 graduate of West Point, airborne qualified and 30-plus year teacher and coach. There are other people to whom I could attribute my successes and they certainly contributed; however, Coach Patterson truly instilled in me the qualities, both mental and physical, that have taken me through my life.

Approximately ten years ago, after having no contact with my school, my classmates, or my coach for over 30 years, I was fortunate to attend a high school reunion at Fort Campbell. I cannot express to you how I felt seeing many old friends who had shared with me my two short years at the school. However, on the Friday night when we attended the football game and Coach P was in the stands with us, I have rarely had the exhilaration as I did when I shook his hand. He did not remember the 150-pound center from the 1969 season; I did not expect him to. He had coached hundreds, if not thousands, of others just like me during those interim years. To Coach P, I was "one of his boys" and to this day, I am both happy and proud of that honor.

This year you will look at many nominees to be considered for induction into the Kentucky Coaches Hall of Fame. Although these recommendations are certainly important, it is the impact a coach has had on his players, his school, his community, and the Kentucky football program that is crucial. During the selection process, Coach Patterson's name will come up, and you will ask, "Should we vote for this man?" Maybe the question you should ask is, "What took us so long to realize Coach Marshall Patterson is so deserving of this recognition?" Due to his illness, Coach P will not know that you voted for him and in all likelihood, will not realize the significance of the tribute. However, there are thousands of people whose lives he impacted that will be appreciative and gratified...

Marshall Patterson raises his arms in victory after one of his FCHS wrestlers became the school's first wrestling champion at the state tournament in Louisville in 1969. (Courtesy of Fort Campbell High School)

The Falcon wrestling team returns to Fort Campbell High School after winning the 1971 State Championship in Louisville, Kentucky. Many of Coach P's football players and wrestlers wrote letters on his behalf to the KHSAA. (Courtesy of Fort Campbell High School)

CHAPTER 6: MAKING HEADLINES

Nobody, but nobody, promoted Fort Campbell High School athletics with more passion and purpose than Marshall Patterson.

For more than three decades, Coach P—as head football coach and FCHS athletic director—was no stranger to the news media. He helped make and keep Falcon athletes in the headlines, always doing whatever it took to shine the most positive light on the sons and daughters of soldiers stationed at Fort Campbell, Kentucky.

Although he loved his football and wrestling programs, Patterson—definitely a coach without an ego—never once was accused of favoritism during his career. Coach P treated ALL sports at the high school with an equal hand and promoted each and every one of them with the same fighting spirit.

In what was rare for that time, Patterson's sense of fairness extended to the new age of girls playing high school sports. He encouraged it, and was a cheerleader for equality. The proof was in the pudding. The second and third state championships for Fort Campbell High School—following soon after the first state crown was won in wrestling in 1971—were the result of the school's amazing girls' track team. Those memorable championships in 1973 and 1975—made possible by track greats like Jennifer Jones, Sabrina (McBrayer) Alls, Liz (Johnson) Kelker, Barbara Camp, Carolyn Jones, and the late Anita Jones—came in the aftermath of the Title IX education amendment to the Civil Rights Act. It greatly expanded high school athletic opportunities to include girls, thereby revolutionizing mass sports participation in the country.

Sabrina (McBrayer) Alls, a popular cheerleader and one of the sprinting stars on the 1973 state championship girls' track team, said Coach P always was very supportive of the girls' athletic teams as well as the cheerleaders and mat maids at the high school.

"He always talked to me about staying positive and going after my dreams. He gave me so much encouragement along with Coach (John) Pyle," said Sabrina, who now is living the good life in Georgia, with husband and former soldier, Rick Alls.

Marshall Patterson, according to Miss Sabrina, was genuine to the core and truly cared about the students at Fort Campbell High School. "Coach P was a coach that would ask about your grades, not because he had to, but because he cared," she explained.

When the girls' track team brought home the school's second state championship in 1973, no one was happier than Marshall Patterson, according to Sabrina (McBrayer) Alls.

"He was very proud of our success in becoming state champs," she recalled. "Once when I was walking down the hall at school, he saw me and said to the other students, 'Everyone move…Here comes a state track champion.' I can still see him with his hands behind his back, slightly rocking, and grinning like crazy."

Ironically, the girls' track team is responsible for the greatest share of the state championships earned by Falcon athletes during Marshall Patterson's 33 years as athletic director at Fort Campbell High School. By the time of Coach P's retirement in 1995, the Lady Falcons had won 12 state track crowns.

According to the Kentucky High School Athletic Association (KHSAA), only one high school in the entire state, through 2015, had won more championships in girls' track than FCHS, and that was Paducah Tilghman with 14.

Veteran newspaperman Chip Hutcheson, who, in the fall of 2015, began a 12-month term as the president of the National Newspaper Association, covered Marshall Patterson and FCHS athletic teams while serving as the sports editor of the *Kentucky New Era* newspaper in Hopkinsville, Kentucky, from 1970 through 1976. In later years, Hutcheson was the editor and publisher of a twice-a-week newspaper in Princeton, Kentucky—*The Times Leader* of Caldwell County—formerly owned by his family. He also was an executive with the Kentucky New Era Media Group, serving as the publisher of *The Eagle Post* in Oak Grove, Kentucky.

"In the 1970s, the Pennyrile-area football teams had some extraordinary football coaches — men who established themselves as being among the elite coaches in Kentucky," Hutcheson noted. "Marshall Patterson was in that group, but he certainly would be considered the most 'low-key' of the bunch."

Hopkinsville's daily newspaper—in a tradition that continues to the present day—hosted an annual preseason dinner for the football coaches of the six high schools in the coverage area, and Hutcheson recalled that Coach P was always the "most reserved" of his colleagues at the event, preferring not to toot his or his players' horns. "He developed plenty of outstanding football players, but he was never one to put them in the spotlight before the season," Hutcheson recalled.

Although the transient nature of the military adversely affected his team nearly every year, Coach P never used it as an excuse for a poor season, according to Hutcheson. "He lost a number of quality players in that 1970-1976 time period, but you would never hear him complain. His mantra was ADAPT—not complain."

After Hutcheson left the sports editor's job at the *Kentucky New Era* and returned to Princeton, he did not cross paths with Coach P again until FCHS came to town 17 years later to play Caldwell County during the 1993 football season. At the time, Hutcheson's teenage son was a sophomore defensive end for the Tigers, and that night, the young Hutcheson made the play of the game.

"Caldwell was leading 7-3 in the fourth quarter when Fort Campbell ran an end-around. My son was the only player standing between the Fort Campbell ball carrier and the end zone, and made a tackle for a loss that cinched the win for Caldwell," Chip Hutcheson recalled. "It was with great pride that I told Patterson after the game that it was my son who had made that play. Once again, Patterson was the ultimate example of class—smiling and complimenting him for the play of the game."

Throughout his career, Marshall Patterson was the consummate professional as a high school football coach, according to Chip Hutcheson.

"From my vantage point, he was the high school version of legendary Dallas Cowboys coach Tom Landry. He dressed professionally and always demonstrated a calm demeanor on the sideline — even in situations when another coach would have been exploding at the officials," said Hutcheson, a member of the Kentucky Journalism Hall of Fame.

Hutcheson, as proof, pointed to the 1972 football season. The Falcons began with two losses—one of which was a heartbreaking defeat that ended on a controversial play—followed by eight straight wins. If Lady Luck had smiled, and fate wasn't so fickle, Coach P might have won his first state football championship in 1972 and not four years later in 1976.

The 1972 FCHS team—led by juniors Eric DeLeon, Bruce Yuhas, Eric Shemwell, Dale Kesterson, and Ed Overcash, and seniors Chuck Powell, Mike Brown, Wes Barnett, Jimmy Thomas, Bruce Tibbs, Art Shemwell, Ron Taylor, Del Carr, Lance Morrison, Barry Cunningham, and Charlie DeLeon—went 8-2 for the season and took home the school's first-ever trophy in football by beating the Russellville Panthers in the Tobacco Bowl, 35-6.

The game was played on Saturday afternoon, September 23, 1972, in Russellville, Kentucky, and Chuck Powell   the Falcons' 175-pound fullback and corner linebacker, who played magnificently on offense and defense—was honored with the MVP trophy.

As an aside, Mr. Powell, a Falcon football and wrestling legend during my days at FCHS, was among those lucky classmates who married up in life by taking the daughter of a Fort Campbell soldier as his bride. Chuck's high school sweetheart, Vicky (Cox) Powell, was captain of the cheerleading squad at FCHS and a member of the Class of 1974. Their great love has endured the test of time. In 2015, Chuck and Vicky celebrated their 42nd wedding anniversary. The couple—with three grown children and five grandchildren—resides in the Huntsville, Alabama, area. A Civil Service employee with 32 years in the field of aviation flight testing, Chuck Powell works at the Redstone Test Center. Vicky Powell is a retired daycare operator. Looking back, I guess Chuck—old No. 30— knew what he was talking about when he penned his Senior Quotation for the 1973 Falcon Yearbook. It read, *"Never leave a good thing (ha ha) unless you find something better."*

Now, let's get back to 1972 and a few more comments about the Tobacco Bowl. After the huge victory, and with our coveted Tobacco Bowl trophy in tow, a bus crammed full of proud Fort Campbell Falcons left Russellville and drove off into the sunset. The bus headed south for Nashville, Tennessee, where the team that night attended a Vanderbilt University home football game—a treat made possible by the generosity of Coach P and his assistant coaches.

The contest at Russellville was a rare, daytime road game for Coach P's Falcons. It was played during the early-afternoon hours on Saturday and not on a Friday night like the other on-the-road opponents on the FCHS schedule that year. Back in the 1960s and 1970s, there were no lights at Fryar Stadium, so FCHS home games were always played on Saturday afternoons. Because the majority of Falcon opponents played all, or most, of their games under the Friday night lights, they were unaccustomed to the heat and tired easily. Not surprisingly, the Falcons usually owned the day, thanks to Coach P's emphasis on the physical conditioning of his players.

This great 1972 football team—small in size but lightning quick in speed—was Coach P's 11th varsity squad since starting the program in 1962. Like all Marshall Patterson-coached teams, it was well-disciplined, and there was no grandstanding among the players. The author was privileged to be a member of this "almost-state championship" team and learn from some of the greatest football players to ever suit up for the Falcons.

Of course, the main lesson I learned that year was that "almost" only counts in horseshoe-pitching and hand grenades. Nevertheless, no one who is part of the Falcon Nation can talk about the 1972 season and the state championship that may have slipped through our fingertips without brooding over *"The Fifth Down."*

Decades later, the author still has nightmares about the unhappy ending of what might be considered the most controversial high school football game ever played in Kentucky. It is THAT game that Chip Hutcheson still remembers as the prime example of an instance where Coach P showcased his class, character and sportsmanship for area football fans.

The game took place two weeks before the Tobacco Bowl. It was September 9, 1972—the week after FCHS had lost its first game of the season to Mount Juliet, a larger-sized high school in Middle Tennessee, not far from Nashville. The place was Fryar Stadium and the mighty Fort Campbell High School Falcons — including me (No. 10), a sophomore quarterback who that season spent most of the time on the bench instead of tossing a football— were hosting district foe Trigg County. Back in those days, Trigg County always was the BIG game of the year. In fact, Coach P and his assistant coaches led the players to believe—I'm not sure whether they were serious—that if the team beat Trigg County and lost every other game that season, it was still a successful season.

The Wildcats, regarded in those days as our archrival, were the defending Class A state football champions and most of the 1971 championship team—including all-everything running back Selby Grubbs—took the field on that hot Saturday afternoon. For four quarters, FCHS fought tooth and nail and handed the bad boys of Trigg County a good, old-fashioned whipping. There was just one problem. We beat them like a drum that day, but still lost the game. It happens sometimes.

Marshall Patterson's FCHS football team was winning the game, 7-6, late in the fourth quarter—thanks to a 12-yard touchdown pass from quarterback Wes Barnett (No. 12) to halfback Jimmy Thomas (No. 20), and Thomas' extra point kick. Everything was going Fort Campbell's way, but then lightning struck. With about 3 minutes left, and FCHS driving for another score from Trigg's five, the Wildcats' Henry Martin intercepted a Falcon pass and returned it to the Trigg 20-yard-line. The Wildcats were 80 yards away from a winning touchdown or field goal, and they got right to work. Two big pass plays, from Trigg quarterback Jimmy Mathis to Ronnie Diggs, picked up large chunks of yardage and moved the ball down to the Fort Campbell 9-yard-line, with less than 1 minute left on the clock.

The Falcon defense mounted a terrific goal-line stand and kept Trigg from scoring—four times. Somehow, however, the officials—and apparently both teams—lost track of the downs and Trigg County's Selby Grubbs ran an extra play and punched the ball into the end zone from the 1-yard line. Sonny Thomas' extra point kick was good, and the victory was sealed for the Wildcats.

As the final horn sounded, Trigg County walked off the field and away from the confusion with more points on the scoreboard and a huge district victory, 13-7.

"Trigg wins controversial game over Ft. Campbell" trumpeted the headline on the sports page of the Monday, September 11, 1972, edition of Hopkinsville's daily newspaper, the *Kentucky New Era*.

Chip Hutcheson, who covered the game for the *Kentucky New Era*, led his story with the disputed fifth down.

Hutcheson wrote:

The story of the Trigg County-Ft. Campbell football game Saturday is more like a mystery than a sports story. It's not a "who-done-it" type, but a "who-done-what."

Apparently, no one knows what actually happened in the closing seconds of the ball game. Confusion and controversy still exist over whether Trigg should have been allowed to run the final—and winning—play of the game.

In post-game remarks that appeared in the *Kentucky New Era*, Coach P— always the gentleman—told Chip Hutcheson he believed an official erred when he stopped the clock just before Selby Grubbs bulled his way into the end zone for the game-winning touchdown. *"I honestly thought we'd beat them, and I knew that we had better material. I thought they had five downs, but I was more upset about the official stopping the clock when time would have run out."*

Unless my memory is playing tricks on me, when the Falcon football squad watched the game film the following Monday, FIVE downs were counted during the goal-line stand. However, no protest could be made to change the outcome of the game, so the final score became history.

With the huge win under their belts, the Wildcats marched through the rest of their opponents that season to repeat as state football champions in Class A for 1972.

Although it was not known at the time, the controversial loss effectively put an end to dreams of a state championship season for bench-warming Robert Dollar and his Falcon teammates. No state championship rings for the 1972 season. Just disbelief, heartbreak—and way too many "What if's?"....

Remember, back in those days, one district loss could—and often did— cost a team its opportunity for post-season play. Nowadays, of course, every team—including those with losing records—makes the playoffs. It's probably a money thing. Or perhaps just political correctness and the evil influence of Korporate Amerikan politics.

The Trigg faithful claimed, and always will, that they would have won the game anyway, even without the fifth down. Their argument: If the downs had been counted correctly, Trigg could have always had reliable kicker Sonny Thomas kick an easy field goal for the win.

But, what if he had missed, or the field goal had been blocked? I guess we'll never know.

Not surprisingly, after the game, there was an awful lot of whining that the officials had robbed Fort Campbell's Mighty Falcons and given the game to Trigg County. The bellyaching stopped when Marshall Patterson put his big foot in a few butts and focused attention on one of his favorite life lessons.

He was calm, direct and got right to the point: *Gentlemen, life isn't always fair.* Then, he got angry and hollered out some words—true to the core—at the team that made the hair on the back of my neck stand up: *If you really want to hear the truth, Trigg County didn't win that ball game. We beat ourselves. They never would have scored in the first place, if we hadn't let them march down the field to our goal line.*

That was Coach P, in a nutshell. He didn't like to lose, but what he hated even more were excuses for failure. To this day, those who played in *"The Fifth Down"* game, or saw it, regard it as the stuff of legend. It is a frequent subject of conversations at Trigg and Fort Campbell high school reunions.

Trigg County High School has its own Hall of Fame. Over the years, inductees have included the entire 1971 and 1972 state championship football teams, and as individual sports greats, two All-State players that led those two squads to glory on the gridiron—Selby Grubbs and David Sadler.

Grubbs, a manager at a Hopkinsville factory, still lives in Trigg County, where he has served as the chairman of the local Board of Education. Sadler, who went on to play college football for Paul "Bear" Bryant at Alabama, died of a brain aneurysm in January 2009 in his hometown of Cadiz, Kentucky. He was only 53 years old.

A two-way starter on the offensive and defensive line for the two Trigg County state championship football teams, Sadler earned a scholarship to the University of Alabama. He was a starter and captain on the 1975 Crimson Tide team that beat Penn State in the Sugar Bowl.

According to published reports, Sadler's hospital care, his funeral, and the burial were paid for in their entirety by a trust fund—established by the late and great Alabama football coach to help "Bear's Boys" through the tragedies of life. The financial package included full scholarships for Sadler's three daughters to attend the University of Alabama, if they decide to go to college there.

Sadler was injured and did not play in the controversial 1972 Fort Campbell football game, but he was on the sidelines at Fryar Stadium, cheering on his teammates.

Like David Sadler and FCHS's late Mike Brown, there's at least one other shining star from the legendary, five-down football game who is gone and now only a sweet memory—Charlie DeLeon, a lineman and the big brother of FCHS quarterback Eric DeLeon. Charlie—Mr. Fort Campbell High School 1973—died in May 2014 in a tragic motorcycle wreck in upstate New York. A dentist at West Point, he was 60 years old.

As a third-string quarterback for Marshall Patterson's FCHS Falcons, the author played sparingly during the 1972 football season. By sparingly, I mean I usually got into a game for a few plays only when Coach P's starters had a huge lead and time was running out on the clock. One such occasion was the next-to-last game of the season when FCHS played the Stewart County Rebels in Dover, Tennessee, on Friday night, October 27, 1972. The Falcons won the game in a romp, 40-6, so I know I played in it. But, because I can't remember anything about the game, I'm also sure I didn't do anything worth remembering after all these years.

There's a strong possibility, however, that this old quarterback ran into a future newspaper colleague and friend on the field of battle that night when he finally got into the game. David Ross—then a sophomore, who started for the Rebels in the 1972 season as a strong safety and wide receiver—never has forgotten the night that "Marshall's Boys" came to town.

"I was on the field the whole game," said Ross, who still lives in Dover, but teaches school in neighboring Houston County, where he also is an assistant football coach at the middle school for The Fighting Irish. "I remember the ass-kicking we got that night."

The beating was not anything new. The prior year, in 1971, an awe-struck Stewart County team had come to Fort Campbell for the homecoming game at fan-filled Fryar Stadium, where they watched a soldier parachute out of a helicopter to deliver the game ball on the 50-yard-line. FCHS beat the Rebels like a drum that Saturday afternoon. The half-time score alone was 40-0, and an assistant coach for Stewart County—Philip Wallace—in an attempt to rally his troops, kicked a dressing room locker and broke his foot, according to Ross.

David Ross said the high caliber of Fort Campbell football was well known in the area. "Our coaches told us we were going up against the best-coached football team we would ever play…Everyone had great respect for Marshall Patterson."

The 1972 game in Dover was marked by some ugliness that Coach P stopped as soon as he became aware of it, according to Ross. During warm-ups, FCHS fans—while walking across the football field, on the way to their bleachers—started taunting the Stewart County players, Ross recalled. "We almost had a fight with the fans. Then, when Coach Patterson saw what was happening, he sent one of his assistants over to get the fans away from us."

David Ross said the 1972 game was the last time Stewart County ever played Fort Campbell High School in football. The Falcons were just too good. "We really had no business playing you guys," he noted.

Marshall Patterson was a great football coach. But, so was Joe Jaggers. Trigg County's 1971 and 1972 state championship football teams were coached by Joe Jaggers, who, at the time of his retirement, had 292 victories after 33 years as a Kentucky high school football coach. As of December 2015, Jaggers was ranked No. 10 on the career coaching wins list in Kentucky.

Jaggers—who also won three Class AA state football championships (1983, 1988, and 1990) while coaching at Fort Knox in Central

Kentucky—was inducted into the Dawahares/KHSAA Hall of Fame in 1993. His coaching career included stints at three other Kentucky high schools—Old Kentucky Home, Nelson County and North Hardin.

After going toe-to-toe with Joe Jaggers' Trigg County teams from 1971 to 1976, Marshall Patterson, in his later years, competed against Jaggers' Fort Knox Eagles several times in the Army Bowl—the annual football game between FCHS and Fort Knox that began in 1974. On at least two of those occasions, Joe Jaggers came out on top, with big wins in 1983 and 1984 when Assistant KHSAA Commissioner Darren Bilberry was playing for the Eagles and they won one of two consecutive state championship football games.

In mid-September 2015, the Falcons and Eagles locked horns for the 40th time—there were two years when they did not play each other, apparently due to scheduling conflicts. Fort Campbell won the homecoming game, 43-8. With the victory, the Falcons increased their lead in the rivalry series to 26-14.

Scott Burnside, another former sports editor for the *Kentucky New Era* newspaper in Hopkinsville, covered high school football games in the area from 1978 to 1993. During those years, Burnside had many opportunities to watch Marshall Patterson in action, coaching his heart out from the sidelines. Coach P, according to Burnside, was always gracious in post-game interviews, whether the Falcons won or lost.

However, there was one coach the Falcon mentor just hated to lose to and congratulate, and that was Joe Jaggers. Marshall Patterson, for sure, was no big fan or supporter of Coach Jaggers.

"I don't think he cared much for Joe Jaggers. Sometimes, after a loss, a few choice words might come out of his mouth before he walked across the field to shake his hand," Burnside quipped.

Like many in the Falcon Nation, maybe *"The Fifth Down"* was the reason for Coach P's apparent lack of affection for Coach Jaggers. Something definitely had rubbed him the wrong way over the years.

Burnside's longtime sidekick in the *Kentucky New Era* Sports Department, Ray Duckworth, remembered Patterson as a warm, generous man with a good sense of humor. Duckworth, now living in North Carolina and working for state government, was a sports writer and editor with the Hopkinsville newspaper and the *Fort Campbell Courier* for nearly 15 years in the 1980s and 1990s.

While serving as *Kentucky New Era* sports editor in the early 1990s, Duckworth convinced area coaches to make predictions on the outcomes of the weekly area football games for a column in the Friday edition of the newspaper. Not surprisingly, Coach P—ever the professional—was always thorough and timely in the assignment. And, his picks were generally right on target.

Once when doing the football picks for games that were going to be played on a "Friday the 13th," Duckworth surveyed coaches about their superstitions. The question tickled Patterson, who never was known to carry a rabbit's foot or four-leaf clover on game night.

"Coach P just laughed...He said he was born on Friday the 13th ...Well...sort of," Duckworth recalled. Marshall Patterson, probably with a twinkle in his eye, then had some fun recounting the confusing story of his birth to the befuddled newspaperman.

Born officially on October 13, 1934—which was a Saturday—in Lewisburg, Tennessee, at the family home, Patterson's nervous father apparently took care of filling out the birth certificate while his mother recovered from the delivery. Later, after Mom Patterson was more alert, she discovered, to her horror, disturbing and possibly erroneous details on the birth certificate that effectively made Little Marshall an unlucky baby, at least in her mind. So, like any good mother would do, she marked through the information on the birth certificate that troubled her and changed it to her liking.

What resulted from an apparent Friday the 13th scare, of course, was a good family story and plenty of confusion forever on the exact birth date of Marshall H. Patterson—October 12, October 13 or even October 14 of 1934. (I've personally seen all three dates on a variety of documents and publications.) Whether Coach P was actually born on a Friday the 13th probably is a moot point. I suppose the truth of the matter is there was a Friday the 13th on the calendar that week in October 1934 when he was born, and it was extremely close to the blessed event of his birth. Furthermore, it's an undeniable fact that, every now and then over the years, Marshall Patterson actually celebrated a Friday the 13th birthday every time October 13th fell on a Friday.

Coach P liked to laugh, and he enjoyed good-natured fun and camaraderie. Just like Chip Hutcheson, Mr. Duckworth got quite a kick every year, before the football season got under way, socializing with the area coaches at the annual preseason meal in Hopkinsville. At the event, there would always be plenty of roasting and toasting, but the real fun centered on the coaches playing "possum" by trying their best to lower expectations for their team, Duckworth noted.

According to Duckworth, Coach P—reserved, but a master of dry humor—always set the stage for the tales that might be told at the football coaches' dinner. "He'd step up to the podium and quip, 'It's good to get together and swap some lies,'" Duckworth recalled.

In the 1980s and 1990s, after Fort Campbell began playing in the Class AA Division, Coach P's Falcons gained a new archrival—Mayfield High School. The perennial powerhouse from Graves County in far Western Kentucky—with one of the most storied football programs in the state— replaced Trigg County as Fort Campbell's most hated opponent on the football field.

FCHS and Mayfield would tangle in some epic battles on the gridiron over the years, and the winner usually advanced to play for a state championship. Jack Morris, who coached the Mayfield Cardinals for 24 years, was inducted into the Dawahares/KHSAA Hall of Fame in 1997. During his high school coaching career, he totaled 254 wins—27 more than Coach P—and won four state championships. Coach Morris also had five runner-up teams.

Patterson loved to joke that the City of Mayfield rolled up the sidewalks whenever the football team was playing a home game. "In Mayfield, they don't know *Dallas* is on—on Friday nights," Duckworth remembered him telling fellow coaches on one occasion.

When it came to working, and cooperating, with the news media, there was no better partner than Marshall Patterson. As the athletic director, he always went the extra mile to make sure FCHS sports got the space it deserved on the pages of area newspapers.

Duckworth recalled an incident that occurred during the first Gulf War (Desert Shield/Desert Storm) in the early 1990s, in the months after Iraq invaded Kuwait. Months before the start of the 1991 war, the entire 101st Airborne Division (Air Assault) was deployed from Fort Campbell to Saudi Arabia—the launching point for allied troops—and the Army post was virtually shut down to the public for security concerns.

"We needed to cover Christian County in boys' basketball at Fort Campbell High School, but the Public Affairs Office wasn't going to let us on post," Duckworth said. The newspaper, without hesitation, telephoned Marshall Patterson, and the problem was solved. "Coach P met Scott Burnside and escorted him to the high school for the game."

Duckworth said no coach was better than Coach P when it came to getting game information to the newspaper in a timely manner. As athletic director, he demanded that his FCHS coaches cooperate with reporters. Excuses were unacceptable.

"There was a softball coach who wouldn't cooperate with getting us scores, and he was rude on the phone," Duckworth noted. "Either Joe Wilson or I called Coach P's office. A few minutes later, the coach called me, irate, that he had been told by Coach P to call us." Again, problem solved.

Tim Ghianni, who worked for Clarksville's daily newspaper, *The Leaf-Chronicle,* for 15 years in the 1970s and 1980s, is another authority on Marshall Patterson's coaching abilities and character.

No high school football coach in Kentucky or Tennessee ever walked the walk like Fort Campbell's Coach P, according to Ghianni, who is now a freelance writer and college journalism instructor in Nashville, following a distinguished 33-year career in the newspaper industry.

In the spirit of full disclosure, Tim Ghianni is the author's best friend and his co-author of two books published in recent years. Ironically, when Tim interviewed Coach P for the first time in the summer of 1974—the year his journalism career got off the ground—Falcon quarterback-wannabe Robert Dollar was going through his drills on the same field. About eight years later, I was formally introduced to Mr. Ghianni, then the sports editor, when I interviewed and was hired as a reporter for *The Leaf-Chronicle*.It was the beginning of a lifetime friendship, with one of the foundations of our special relationship being the shared love and respect for Marshall Patterson.

As a professional courtesy, I'm allowing Tim Ghianni, a master storyteller, to tell the readers of this book, in his unique and humorous way, about the Coach P that he knew and grew to love and respect over the years.

Take her away, Tim:

I guess I can't think of Marshall Patterson without thinking about the notorious "chuckle incident" that became Saturday morning, post-game newsroom fodder back in the days when journalists punctuated their comments with deep sucks from whichever one or two cigarettes they were burning in their ashtrays.

But I'll get to that incident eventually, because, well it makes me chuckle. I began my full-time journalism career just as football season was getting under way in the early autumn of 1974.

Gene Washer, then the sports editor at what then was called "The Clarksville Leaf-Chronicle" in old-English newspaper type, had hired me virtually the moment I walked into the building at 200 Commerce Street in downtown Clarksville. The Tennessee bureau chief from The Associated Press in Nashville—where I'd gone to inquire about work—had dispatched me up there that very same day for an interview, as it was kind of an emergency.

The guy who had preceded me as No. 3 man on a three-man sports team— David Jones, who now is some sort of retired stockbroker or empire builder or perhaps some washout somewhere—had departed to take a similar prep-writing job at The Tennessean, a then second-rate newspaper which has now turned into a laughing-stock or embarrassment, at least in Nashville.

I worked for Washer and for Assistant Sports Editor Max "Sounds Reasonable" Moss. I was, at that point, simply a "prep writer," although eventually I became "prep editor" and then "sports editor," assistant city editor, special projects editor and associate editor of the newspaper. It was in the sports editor-capacity that I helped hire the author of this book, Robert Stanley Dollar, who I had actually seen on the football field (or at least the sidelines or bench) as the second-string quarterback for the Fort Campbell Falcons football team.

My first responsibility as No. 3 sports writer was to cover the schools other than the two main schools in Clarksville—which were Clarksville High and Northwest High at the time. Max kept those to himself, I suppose, to limit travel. Sounded reasonable to me as he looked about three times his 40 years of age.

I was dispatched to cover the surrounding satellite schools. I did cover The Clarksville Academy in its infancy as a football program. But, my main schools were Fort Campbell, Erin (now Houston County), Dover (now Stewart County High) and Monkey Central. Well, actually that was Montgomery Central, but I kind of liked the nickname I gave it, and it caught on out at a school surrounded by a lake out in the sticks of Montgomery County. It was there, as a sports writer, that I first encountered Robert Smith, who retired recently from the staff of The Leaf-Chronicle. He was a Montgomery Central High School student at the time who loved photography. I remember Robert shadowing me as I wandered around the field with my own 35mm camera, smiling at me...

I particularly relished the times I was sent out to Fort Campbell, though. As an old hippie, someone who can recite "Alice's Restaurant" by heart and who enjoys singing Country Joe's "Fish Cheer," there was something special about going into Gate 4—the main access point—onto that massive Army compound that straddles the Tennessee-Kentucky line between Clarksville and Hopkinsville. (Well, actually Oak Grove, but that was mostly a town of loose women and corruption back then, so I drove through quickly.)

Despite my liberal leanings and anti-Vietnam War stance, I've always considered myself a patriot, so I got a charge out of being greeted by the MP at the gate and directed to Fryar Stadium. Remember, this was decades before 9-11, so no one searched my car or frisked me and generally didn't even ask for ID.

"I'm from the newspaper in Clarksville and I'm here to cover the ballgame," I told the spit-shine guy at the guard shack.

"Have a good visit, sir," he said, waving me through the gate. Back in the 1970s, Fort Campbell, though large, was easy to navigate. And if you got lost, there were hundreds of soldiers walking around, any of them more than happy to point you to Fryar Stadium, where "Marshall's Boys" were playing football.

My first time at Fryar Stadium was pretty impressive. No, there weren't many folks in the stands. Just proud moms and pops and family members...But they sure made a lot of noise for the Military Brats out on the field.

One of those Brats, it turns out, became my truest friend in life...Who'd have thunk it?

I never liked watching football in press boxes or in the grandstands, so as soon as I parked my 1965 Fort Falcon Futura (I had to cup my hand over the carburetor while someone else turned the ignition key to start that car), I wandered through the gates and onto the sidelines.

The game hadn't started yet. Rob and the rest of the returning veterans on this team—I was the one who coined the phrase that to have returning players at this Army post where families transferred in and out with reckless abandon was about "as common as pink parachutes at Fort Campbell"—were out on the field pretending to prepare for the game

146

They were tossing the ball around and, of course, slapping down on each other's shoulder pads. As a former halfway good, speed-eating defensive end in high school—the leader of the "dingbat" squad of outlaws who didn't make the first string and instead played mid-week games on muddy fields in Chicago—I was familiar with the drill or the drills, rather. Anyway, I approached the fellow who was watching it all, a whistle hanging from his neck, his flattop firmly held into place like a porcupine's needles, a clipboard tucked beneath his arm.

It was, of course, Coach Marshall Patterson. And he was glad to see me. Unlike a lot of the coaches I encountered, he didn't ignore me until the game was over. He greeted me, told me to be careful when taking sidelines photos because sometime the sweeps and screen plays got a little off-course. (I have, as a matter of fact, many times been at the bottom of piles of football players after attempting to take photos of plays coming around end. Probably one reason I'm mentally unstable to this day.)

On that first meeting, Marshall chatted with me about my own background. About football. About life. I immediately was charmed by this guy. He was gruff, sure. But he was a man's man, a guy who liked young people (Remember, I was only five years out of high school myself), and who was glad to see somebody, even me in my bow tie and sport coat, covering the game.

After the game, I let his team either celebrate or whine and pray amongst themselves while I stood on the home team's 40-yard line and waited for the coach.

Since I was the only journalist covering the game, Marshall (He told me to call him that), was more than welcoming.

He answered my ignorant questions with style and grace. He didn't swear (The "f"-word and "GD" were frequent vocal punctuation by most of the coaches I covered), and he described the game, both the good and the bad things he saw from his team.

After football season was over, I did almost the unthinkable in those athletic dark ages. No one covered high school wrestling for any newspaper I knew of. But as a former high school grappler—I'd qualify at 165, but generally fill in the roster at 180 or heavyweight, depending on the competition—I sought out the wrestling team at Fort Campbell. While down in the city to the south, Clarksville, wrestling was relatively innocuous and second-rate, Marshall had a first-rate team of grapplers, quick to go for the first open takedown and then ride the opponent into the ground by squeezing on their scrotums. It was a part of the game. Marshall always was glad to see me there, covering wrestling, because I think he liked that sport even better than football.

It's been a lot of years, several decades even, since those days and I moved off preps after just a couple of years to cover Austin Peay State University in Clarksville and occasionally some larger event, like the Muhammad Ali-Leon Spinks fight in New Orleans in 1978. But I'll never forget the stern dignity of Marshall Patterson, who despite it all was a damn nice guy.

Now, get ready for that chuckle. One day, in a story I wrote about Marshall, I quoted him as saying something and added the word "chuckled," because he did. He was really happy after his team blew out another school. I can't remember the exact quote. It was something like: "We really played well," said Marshall Patterson, with a chuckle.

His wife called me the next morning at the newspaper to voice a concern about the story. No she wasn't upset with coverage. It was, well, to quote her "My husband never chuckles. I've never heard him chuckle at home." The comment left me speechless. Finally, I broke the silence on the telephone.

Jokingly, I asked her whose fault that was…And, then I grabbed a cigarette—and chuckled.

Tim Ghianni, at some point after the telephone call, shared the chuckle story with Coach P, who then apparently shared another chuckle with my funny—or warped, as some claim—friend. No coach has ever had a more caring and supportive wife and partner than "Mrs. Coach P"—Rebecca Patterson—so I'm hoping this great and gracious lady allowed herself at least a half-chuckle over the infamous chuckle incident.

Mr. Ghianni's mention of wrestling provides me with the opportunity to share an emotional back story. Wrestling as a high school sport in Kentucky began in 1964—only two years after Coach P got his job as head football coach and athletic director at Fort Campbell High School. Not knowing much about the sport, Marshall Patterson read a few books and taught himself some basic moves on the mat. And then, he launched the FCHS wrestling program. In only a few years, he had built a solid program recognized as among the best in Kentucky. In 1971—only the eighth season of the new high school sport—the FCHS wrestling team claimed the state championship, just a year after falling nine points shy and finishing runner-up to perennial powerhouse Woodford County.

As a wrestling coach, Marshall Patterson was inspiring and a great motivator. He had the ability to convince his athletes that nothing in this life was impossible—if you just put your mind to it, worked hard and stuck with it.

Coach P made believers out of hundreds of wrestling fans that attended the regional wrestling championships at Fort Campbell High School on Saturday, February 10, 1973. During the tournament, which was won by Hopkinsville High School, Fort Campbell senior Art Shemwell squared off against the top 155-pounder in the state—Hoptown's Kent Parrent. In three previous matches that season, Parrent had mopped the floor with Mr. Shemwell, winning every one of the contests without even breaking a sweat. He was that good. But Art Shemwell—who was co-captain of the FCHS wrestling team—had made matters worse by allowing Mr. Parrent to get into his head.

Before the two wrestlers hit the mat, Coach P got into Art Shemwell's head with a rousing pep talk that was better than the one seen in the *Rocky* movie when it was released three years later in 1976. (Remember that inspiring scene in the movie, where Rocky Balboa's trainer, Mickey "Mick" Goldmill, gets him ready to fight for the heavyweight boxing championship of the world?) The regional wrestling match between Shemwell and Parrent was epic, and as someone who was there, I don't believe I've ever heard more noise in any gymnasium anywhere. Art Shemwell, for sure, was wrestling the best he had ever wrestled, but

Parrent was just too tough and in total control of the match, with a 2-0 lead and time running out on the clock.

And that's when it happened: The Hoptown Tiger wrestler, maybe getting overconfident, made a mistake. Art Shemwell seized the opportunity, and in a lightning-quick move, pinned Parrent to the mat. The gym exploded into a wild celebration, with Art's younger brother, Eric Shemwell, and other Falcon wrestlers rushing to the mat to hug and hoist Art into the air as they reveled in the wrestling miracle. While his wrestlers and FCHS fans rejoiced in a stunning upset that had seemed improbable, Coach P stood off to the side, smiling that knowing smile that always formed on his face when things went right for Fort Campbell High School.

A week later, Art Shemwell and Kent Parrent competed in the 155-pound weight division at the state wrestling tournament in Louisville, Kentucky. Art Shemwell lost his first match and was eliminated from the tournament. Parrent, in an act of redemption, wrestled his way to an individual state championship in the 155-pound weight division. In addition to Shemwell, five other Falcon wrestlers qualified for the state tournament that year— Ron Taylor, Lance Morrison, Wes Barnett, Mike Jones, and Eric DeLeon.

Fort Campbell's heavyweight, Ron Taylor, was the only Falcon to go all the way and claim a state championship in 1973.

In a twist of irony, Parrent would return to the same Fort Campbell High School gymnasium where he suffered the memorable 1973 wrestling defeat—just seven years later, this time as a new health teacher and wrestling coach. He taught and coached at Fort Campbell for about nine years.

Chip Hutcheson, who was sports editor for the *Kentucky New Era* at the time of the 1973 regional wrestling championships, remembered the excitement of that larger-than-life match between Art Shemwell and Kent Parrent. For someone who basically learned the sport on his own, Marshall Patterson turned out to be an excellent wrestling coach, according to Hutcheson.

While at the helm of the FCHS wrestling program, in addition to the 1971 team championship, Patterson led his 1970 and 1978 squads to runner-up finishes at state. He also coached eight individual state wrestling champions—Steve Johnson (1969), Jim Hoeh (1969), Alan Boyd (1970, 1971), Ronnie Chapman (1970, 1971), Mike Cassity (1971), Ron Taylor (1973), Andre Offutt (1977, 1978) and Mike Balkus (1978).

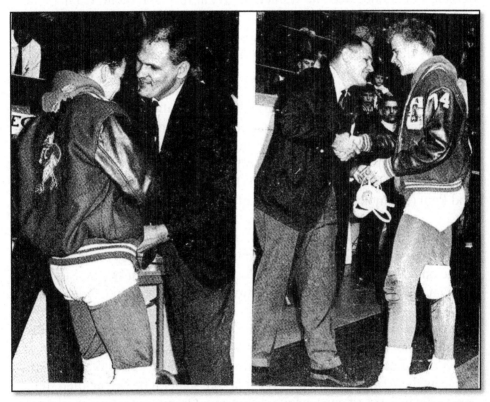

Marshall Patterson, who started the FCHS wrestling program, coached his first two state wrestling champions in 1969 when Steve Johnson (left) and Jim Hoeh (right) claimed crowns at the state wrestling tournament in Louisville, Kentucky. (Courtesy of Fort Campbell High School)

"In the years that followed, my son was a ranked wrestler for Caldwell County, and Coach Patterson always took an interest in watching him whenever he was at a tournament where Caldwell was involved," Chip Hutcheson noted. "It was that interest in young people — regardless of what school colors you wore — that earned the respect of so many people for the legendary Falcon coach."

Near the end of Coach P's career as the head football coach for the Falcons, something most unusual happened at Fort Campbell High School: In 1991—around the time the first Gulf War was ending—a female student decided she wanted to go out for the football team. I'm not sure if Marshall Patterson—then in his 30th year as football coach—chuckled or rubbed his head. Maybe both…Anyway, it became a big story that had reporters running from near and far to cover it. Talk about a media frenzy.

Now, in prior years, girls had had their place on the Fort Campbell football team, but in the capacity of equipment managers and trainers. Among the pioneers were Susie Evans (Class of 1977) and Iris Tomkins (Class of 1975), part of the 1974 football team, and two juniors who were on the following year's team—Julie (Mahaffey) Augeri (Class of 1977) and Pam (Schmoker) Sutton (Class of 1977).

This is not a kiss-and-tell book. And, not to get off the subject, but I can't help but mention that sweet and beautiful Julie (Mahaffey) Augeri likely is the only Falcon who ever dated Coach P's one and only son, Stephen, who, at the time, was attending Northwest High School in Clarksville.

During her Fort Campbell years, Julie was one of the four daughters of then-Colonel Fred Mahaffey and his lovely wife, Jane Ann Mahaffey. As previously noted in this book, Fred Mahaffey, in the years to come, would serve as the Army's youngest ever four-star general before he died in his early-50s in 1986 of cancer linked to Agent Orange exposure in Vietnam. Nine years after his death, Jane Mahaffey collaborated with retired Army General Edward C. Meyer and R. Manning Ancell to write and publish a great book about the military: *Who Will Lead? Senior Leadership in the United States Army.* Regarded as the model Army wife, Mrs. Mahaffey passed away in 2010 at the age of 71 in Arizona. She and her husband are buried at Arlington National Cemetery just outside Washington, D.C

For the record, Miss Julie had been my prom date before my graduation from FCHS in the spring of 1975. Several months later—after I was in college and out of the picture, not that I was ever in the picture—she began going out with Stephen Patterson. He was known as "Steve"—or Coach P's son—to Julie and most of the teenagers he hung out with back in those days. The short-lived romance probably was awkward for Marshall Patterson since Julie was a manager on the football team, and he saw her every day at school and at football practice. She also was a mat maid for the FCHS wrestling team.

A retired Army Reserve colonel now living in the Southwest United States, Julie still remembers in vivid detail an incident that happened while she was dating Steve Patterson. And, it sure didn't leave Coach P in a chuckling mood.

"One evening, I went out with my best friend and her boyfriend, and Coach Patterson's son. We accidently drove the car into a ditch in the backwoods and couldn't get it back out," Julie recalled.

"We ran around trying to find help and, at one point, even faced a shotgun from a suspicious man in his trailer. Somehow the police found us and took us back to the station. Coach Patterson came to get us and wound up delivering me home.

"It was really late, and I was more afraid of facing him in class the next day than I was about my own parents' anger. No one wanted to disappoint Coach Patterson, least of all me. He stared me down throughout the class with those piercing blue eyes. I was so ashamed and never got into that kind of trouble again."

The high school memory shared by Julie (Mahaffey) Augeri—it's the truth, the whole truth, and nothing but the truth—underscores some of Coach P's most endearing qualities as a human being: He was very protective of family and his students, and he was someone that no one ever wanted to disappoint.

Let's return now to 1991 and the story of Fort Campbell High School's first-ever female football player. Up to this point in time, no girl had ever suited up in a helmet and shoulder pads and took the field with "Marshall's Boys."

Before I continue with the story, I feel the obligation to offer a disclaimer, just in case: In light of the strange times we now live in, there's certainly no way I can rule out the possibility that there might have been a future "Caitlyn Jenner" in the FCHS dressing room back in those boring days before the enlightened Age of Political Correctness.

Regardless, I'm willing to bet when Mary Smith walked into Marshall Patterson's office shortly before the start of spring practice in 1991 and told him she wanted to play football, Coach P probably tried to talk her out of it—only because he was worried she might get hurt. When she stuck to her guns, I'm sure she also got the lecture that, if she joined the football team, she would be treated like every other player.

Coach P was a fair man, after all, and treated all of his players with fairness and respect. No one was special. As far as I know, there had never been a player cut from a Marshall Patterson football team. Everyone who showed up for practice, followed team rules, met the physical requirements and gave 100 percent on the field made the squad and got to suit up for games. So, the welcome mat most likely was put out for Mary just like it would have been for any other football-loving student at Fort Campbell High School.

The matter apparently was handled in a most professional manner by the school administration and coaching staff. But, don't try and tell me there wasn't a backlash to this rare occurrence. It was anything but business as usual. I'm sure I'm not the only one who wishes they could have been a fly on the wall of Coach P's office when he surprised his longtime senior assistants—Ronnie Bell and Rocky Cobb—with the news that the Falcons had their first female football player.

If I had to guess, there most likely was a smirk on Coach Bell's face. His smugness often made him an easy target for the slackers and agitators on the football team. As for Coach Cobb—known for his steely eyes, penetrating stare and colorful commands to his defensive backs like "You better stick to him like stink on shit"and"GATA"(Get After Their Ass)— he probably swallowed his trademark cigar, or came very close to it.

For those who spent a lot of time around him, Rocky Cobb was a man of few words. He could be a real Teddy Bear. But, in an instant, he also could turn into a grizzly bear that would eat your lunch. He apparently was very protective of women—particularly his mother. For whatever reason, Mama Cobb was a sensitive issue with him. Back in my bench-riding days at FCHS—when the "Yo Mama" insults were the rage of the country, and sometimes even funny—a prominent FCHS athlete made the mistake of flinging the joke in Coach Cobb's direction. He literally went ballistic, and screamed out some words I'll never forget: "Don't you ever talk about my mother again, or I'll stomp all over you." Everyone was stunned after the loud outburst from the normally quiet and reserved coach. Then, less than 30 seconds later, Coach Cobb got back to business like nothing had happened. I always wanted to ask him whether the incident was real, or just him messing with our minds. But, there's no way I was ever going to bring up the subject of his mother—just in case. As for those "Yo Mama" jokes, they quickly lost their popularity with FCHS athletes after the story about Coach Cobb turning into The Incredible Hulk started making the rounds.

By the time Mary Smith showed up for the 1991 football season, Coach Houston Mills no longer was around at FCHS, barking out orders to his linemen. He had already passed away and gone to his final reward four years earlier in November 1987. So, it's really anybody's guess on what his reaction might have been to a girl joining the football team. What do I think? For someone I remembered as "a real man's man," Coach P's longtime friend and veteran assistant coach probably turned over in his grave—a couple of times.

Remember Jimmy Thomas? Well, my old teammate from the 1972 football team had now joined Coach P as a member of an expanded FCHS coaching staff. Knowing Jimmy Thomas like I know him—always friendly and seeing the best in life—I'll bet a girl football player didn't bother him at all. He very likely adopted the position that works so well for new members of Congress: Keep your head down, keep your mouth shut, and just hope for the best.

When Mary Smith turned up, wanting to play football, Coach P already was very familiar with her twin sister, Kerri Smith, who was serving as a trainer for the FCHS football team. At the time, Rebecca (Wissmann) Milliner, was the equipment manager for the Falcons.

"There were many people who were not too happy she was playing," Rebecca (Wissmann) Milliner recalled. According to Miss Rebecca—a member of the Class of 1993, who now works as a pastry chef in Hornel, New York—the controversy was par for the course. "It's like anything out of the norm... People have many opinions."

Mary Smith made it through the tough three weeks of spring practice, when it's not uncommon for players to quit after discovering football is not their cup of tea, and then returned for summer conditioning and the start of full-contact drills for the upcoming football season.

On Friday, August 9, 1991, Marshall Patterson invited the local media out to Fort Campbell to interview and take photographs of the FCHS football team.

The *Kentucky New Era* newspaper in Hopkinsville gave the assignment to Ray Duckworth, then a young and brash sports writer who still had his hair. Duckworth showed up for the "Media Day" event and interviewed Coach P and some of those on the FCHS team—including the Smith sisters, who were 16-year-old juniors.

Mary Smith told Duckworth she had always liked football and believed she could compete with the boys. *"At first some of them didn't accept me. They thought I was just trying out. Now they've got to realize that I want to play...I enjoy being knocked down. It makes me try harder every time I get knocked down. One of these days, I'm going to knock them down."*

Chad Corley, a senior and starting quarterback for the 1991 FCHS football team, told the *Kentucky New Era* sports writer it was no big deal having the 5-foot 8-inch, 150-pound girl on the squad. *"She gets along with everybody. She's just one of the guys."*

Coach P, in his interview with Duckworth, noted that Mary Smith had earned her spot on the team, like every other player, by meeting the minimum physical fitness requirements that called for completing 50 sit-ups and one pull-up, and running 600 yards in 2 minutes.

Patterson admitted to the Hopkinsville newspaperman that he expected some anxious moments when it came time to put Mary—who was being tried out in the guard spot—through hard-hitting contact drills. *"There's a fatherly instinct in me that I've always had, and I'd have the same for girls. I treat each player as if they were my own son...But, if she were my daughter, she would not be here. That's the fatherly protectiveness in me. I have trouble telling these boys, 'Let's hit her.'"*

Recalling his glory days at FCHS, Terrance Summerhill, who was a running back on the 1991 football team, agreed that the coaches and players accepted Mary Smith as a teammate, and he didn't remember any problems during her time on the team.

"I first met Mary the first day of spring training. She was excited, but you could tell she was a bit nervous. It was the first year in school history that a girl would play for the Falcons," said Summerhill, who now lives in Killeen, Texas.

"Coach Patterson was fair. Everyone got a chance to show off their skills. Mary, to me, was a real tough gal with this 'I'm one of the guys mentality.' Yes, we teased her at times, but it was in fun. She had thick skin and she didn't back down."

According to Summerhill, Mary Smith rose to the occasion and proved she could play with the boys during hard-hitting, two-a-day practices in the hot August heat.

Mr. Summerhill still smiles at the memory of a humbling experience.

Here's his account of what happened: "Coach Bell had us running blocking drills. Well, I had to block Mary. On this day, she seemed fueled by something. She was on defense, and I was in my wingback position. At the first snap of the ball, she rushed in with quickness and knocked me on my butt. It shocked me. This girl is serious I said to myself. Of course, I never heard the end of that from the players who witnessed it. Even Coach

Bell said a few words like, 'You let a girl knock you on your butt, Summerhill.' Let's just say after several more times at the drill, Mary had earned my respect that day."

Of course, with a girl on the team, special accommodations—like a separate locker room for dressing and showering—were necessary. Mary Smith's sister, Kerri, and Rebecca (Wissmann) Milliner helped her get ready for practice and games during the football season. "We used to duct tape her boobs to get her shoulder pads on," Rebecca quipped. "Football at Fort Campbell is among my fondest memories. Those guys and the girl that year were like my family."

Mary Smith (left) played football for FCHS in 1991, while her twin sister, Kerri, was an equipment manager for the Falcon football team. In the above photograph that appeared in the Hopkinsville, Kentucky, daily newspaper, the sisters share a laugh during Media Day at Fort Campbell. (Courtesy of *Kentucky New Era*)

According to Summerhill, Mary played on the line—defensive tackle or offensive guard—and she wore jersey No. 63.

The 1991 football team—with talented athletes like Chad Corley, who earned a scholarship to Austin Peay State University after graduation, Darrell Alston, B.J. Bradford, and future FCHS head football coach Josh McKillip—failed to win a state championship. Nonetheless, the Falcons were a great football team that year, going 9-4. The final loss of the season was to Mayfield, 10-6, in the regional championship game. It was the fifth year in a row that Mayfield had defeated FCHS in a regional championship game and ended hopes for a state AA crown.

But, there was one shining moment in the season that rivaled the best feel-good scene of any Hollywood movie about the game of football.

Think about the popular, true-life movie, *Rudy,* which was about a young man's dreams of playing football for Notre Dame.

Mary Smith was Fort Campbell High School's "Rudy Ruetigger"…She lived Ruetigger's football dream nearly two years before the inspirational movie about his life was released in movie theaters across the country.

The place was Fryar Stadium, apparently during the homecoming game against the Lone Oak Purple Flash on Friday night, September 27, 1991.

Above is the 1991 Fort Campbell High School football team, which included the first-ever girl football player. Mary Smith (No. 63) is the sixth player, from the left, in the third row. (Courtesy of Fort Campbell High School)

Let's allow Terrance Summerhill to describe the scene:

"Mary had suited up for every varsity game that year, but never got into the game. On this particular night, I believe it was homecoming, but I'm not really sure....We were up big, and as the clock was slowly ticking away, the people in the stands started chanting....Mary!...Mary!...Mary!...Mary!...Mary! Then some of the players, including me, joined in....It seemed like the whole stadium was chanting her name.''

According to Summerhill, everyone in the stadium was looking in the direction of Coach P, and as the chanting got louder and louder, the Falcon mentor finally made his decision and sent her into the game.....But, don't try and tell me there wasn't a "head-rub" first...Maybe more than one...

Coach Marshall Patterson welcomed the Falcons' first girl football player to the team during the 1991 season, but never allowed the rarity to become a distraction out on the field. (Courtesy of Fort Campbell High School)

Summerhill continued his story: "The moment she put her helmet on and ran out on the field, the whole stadium erupted in cheers. It was the greatest moment for me, our football team, our fans and our school. I will always tell that story as I saw it. I was happy for Mary on that night. She never gave up."

Terrance Summerhill said he believes Mary Smith played for about 2 minutes, and he said he remembers her making at least one tackle. And, the Falcons won that game, 45-6, with Summerhill making one of the Falcon touchdowns on a 10-yard run.

Today, Chad Corley lives in Atlanta, Georgia. He said, all these years later, he still has fond memories of Mary Smith and that great 1991 FCHS football team. "I don't recall her being very big or athletic, but she gave it her all," Corley noted. The rarity of having a girl on the football team, in the end, was just another feather in Coach P's cap, according to the former Falcon quarterback. "I think Coach P navigated it well, and he didn't allow it to become a distraction."

Now, if there was anyone who knew, for sure, the true feelings of Coach P about the Falcons' first girl football player, it would certainly be his wife and partner in life. Rebecca Patterson said her husband never once made a fuss about it. "He was very accepting of it," she claimed.

Mary (Smith) Hammond, the mother of three young children and the first girl to play football for Fort Campbell High School, died of a heart attack on October 1, 2012, according to her twin sister, Kerri (Smith) Lovelass, who now makes her home in Washington State. Mary's death at age 37 followed an illness that had put her in the hospital for several months.

Just 16 months later, Marshall Patterson passed away, too. It wouldn't surprise me in the least if sweet Mary was waiting for her high school football coach at the Pearly Gates of Heaven along with Saint Peter – holding a roll of duct tape and a list of potential players, both male and female, for a heavenly football team.

Now, there's a divine vision worthy of a "head-rub" and a big chuckle.

Falcon running back Andre Offutt (No. 43) hits a wall of Bellevue defenders after taking a hand-off from FCHS quarterback Ricky Gibbs (No. 12) during the 1976 Class A state championship football game in Lexington, Kentucky. Fort Campbell won the contest, 22-0. (Courtesy of Fort Campbell High School)

CHAPTER 7: THE FIRST TIME

The first time is always the sweetest—especially when it comes to state football championships.

And often, the wait for that great shining moment seems like an eternity. But, when the dream becomes a reality, there is no greater feeling in the world.

In his 15th year as a head football coach, Marshall Patterson—"Father of The Falcons"—was hoisted into the air as a champion and carried off of his "Field of Dreams" in Lexington, Kentucky, by his high-flying Falcon football team after they won the 1976 Class A state championship by beating Bellevue, 22-0.

I knew some of the players on that first-ever championship team since they had been freshmen or sophomores during my senior year at Fort Campbell High School. In the game for all the marbles, two of them— Andre Offutt and Mike Moats—had been responsible for putting 10 points on the scoreboard for FCHS.

But, it was junior quarterback Ricky Gibbs who led the way to victory over Bellevue, a perennial powerhouse, with two touchdown runs of 21 yards and 9 yards.

It's a small, small world for Military Brats. Nearly 30 years after that first state football championship for the Falcons, the author—Rob Dollar—was minding his business during a reception at an Arlington, Virginia, hotel. At the time, February 2005, I was working for the Mayor's Office in Hopkinsville, Kentucky, and had come to town with a delegation of government and business leaders from the civilian communities that surround Fort Campbell, Kentucky. The goal of the trip was to lobby Congress in the nation's capital on behalf of our important military neighbor.

After a pleasant conversation with Holly Petraeus—wife of Army General David Petraeus, a former Fort Campbell commander, who, at the time, was away from his Virginia home, saving Iraq—I bellied up to the bar and got myself an adult beverage. While enjoying my drink, a full-bird Army colonel walked into the room and up to the bar. As he stood next to me, I glanced at the name tag on his uniform. It read, "GIBBS"....I almost dropped my drink. I knew instantly it was Ricky Gibbs, one of "Marshall's Boys." He had made the military his career, and years earlier, actually had been stationed at Fort Campbell as a company and battalion commander. At the time of our encounter, he was assigned to The Pentagon. In later years, Ricky Gibbs—who commanded combat troops in Iraq and Afghanistan—would rise to the rank of brigadier general before he retired from the Army. His service included numerous high-ranking posts overseas and stateside.

Of course, Ricky had never met me before so he was in for the surprise of his life. I looked over at him, introduced myself and then dropped a name: "Marshall Patterson." His eyes lit up, and then two old Falcons shared a good laugh and some great memories.

Ricky and I, with our Falcons Forever bond, enjoyed a nice visit. It was like we were long-lost friends, not just two guys meeting for the first time. Most of our conversation, of course, was spent talking about Coach P and the influence he had on so many FCHS graduates.

During the time he was assigned to Fort Campbell, Ricky Gibbs visited with his old football coach often, and I'm sure they relived the glory years. Coach P, like he had done for many other former players in the past, gave Ricky some game films. The former Falcon quarterback told me they were from the 1976 championship season—one of the best years of his life.

Marshall Patterson's 1976 Falcons ended the year with a 12-1 record, losing only to the Mayfield Cardinals, 22-6, on the road in the second game of the season. That year Mayfield finished as the runner-up in the Class AA state championship game.

Mike Moats and Bruce Baughman were the co-captains of the 1976 team, which, along with Gibbs and Offutt, included such talented athletes as Rick Larson, Norm Miller, Frank Balkus, Doug Loope, Adrian Ashworth, Billy Batchelor, Roger Block, Billy Church, Steve Hellums, George Cottrell, Tom Spinelli, Ahmad Coston, Greg Leehouts, Eugene Walker, Jimmy Curry, Alfred Walker, Charles Buster, Greg Gibson, Erick Murray, Reginald Offutt, and Keith Odister.

Coach Marshall Patterson and his 1976 Falcon football team celebrate the school's first-ever state championship after defeating Bellevue, 22-0, at Commonwealth Stadium in Lexington, Kentucky. (Courtesy of Fort Campbell High School)

Although Ricky Gibbs brought home the bacon, and state crown, with his brilliant play in the Bellevue game, there probably would have been no state championship in 1976 without senior Rick Larson.

Larson and Gibbs shared the quarterbacking duties for FCHS during that dream championship season.

"Actually, Gibbs got hurt in practice right before the first game. He probably would have started the whole season had it not been for that," recalled Rick Larson, a resident of Clay, Kentucky, now retired after a 30-year career as a teacher, coach, assistant principal and principal.

"I started the first seven games and he finished out the year. I remember Coach P calling me into his office after I got benched at halftime of the Todd County game. He told me Gibbs would be starting the next game. He was great about it and told me how important it was going to be for me to be ready as a backup."

Senior Mike Moats (left), a co-captain on the 1976 FCHS football team, helps his Falcon teammates hold the large trophy given to them for winning the Class A state football championship. (Courtesy of Fort Campbell High School)

There are probably only a handful of former FCHS football players who had a special relationship with Coach P over the years, and Rick Larson most certainly was among them.

After his graduation from Fort Campbell High School in the spring of 1977, Larson enrolled that fall at Western Kentucky University in nearby Bowling Green, Kentucky. On weekends, he would return home and keep statistics for the FCHS football team on their game nights.

Eventually, Coach P asked Larson if he would be interested in helping Ken Killebrew with the coaching of the newly-created freshman football team at the high school. "I eagerly accepted and transferred to Austin Peay State University in Clarksville, Tennessee, so I could be at practice every day," Larson recalled.

The former Falcon quarterback not only changed colleges, but he also changed his major to education with the intention of becoming a high school coach just like the most influential person in his life—Marshall Patterson.

"It was a terrible disappointment to me not to be hired as a teacher and a coach at Fort Campbell High School after I graduated from college, but Coach P did what he could do for me," Larson said. "I never considered the prospect of working anywhere but Fort Campbell. That job didn't come so I took a teaching and coaching job at Northwest High School that summer after graduation." As fate would have it, the job in Clarksville would only be a temporary stop on Larson's career ladder.

Sometime much sooner rather than later, lightning struck and Rick Larson found himself in Cadiz, Kentucky, where he was hired as a teacher and assistant football coach at the high school there. "Ironically I ended up at Trigg County High School with the opportunity to coach eventual University of Kentucky running back Al Baker," Larson recalled. "The following year, Coach P approached me at a basketball game and told me they had a position for me if I wanted to join his staff at FCHS. One of the toughest decisions of my life, to that point, was to turn down his offer and stay on and see Al through his high school career at Trigg. The opportunity never came again."

So, for most of the 1980s and 1990s, Rick Larson found himself on the opposite sidelines of his coaching hero whenever Fort Campbell and Trigg County tangled in football. Don't forget that Trigg County, for years, had always been one of the Falcons' most hated archrivals on the gridiron.

Larson, who coached for 17 years, said he never got any grief from Coach P or his coaching staff for taking the job at Trigg County. Not even a "head rub" or a fake chuckle.

"We played Fort Campbell regularly through the years I coached at Trigg and were actually in the same district at times depending on the alignment," the retired educator noted. "The highlight for me personally every year was to greet Coach P, Coach Bell and Coach Cobb before the game and chat about players and the prospects of our respective seasons. Coach P was always so gracious and complimentary before and after games and made me feel like he was proud of me. It was still tremendously important to me to have the validation from Coach P, but it also made me so proud to have him consider me a colleague in an arena in which he was so well respected."

Rick Larson said playing for Coach P, and having his respect as a fellow coach, are honors he has never taken for granted.

Rick Larson, a senior, was one of the two quarterbacks who helped guide Marshall Patterson's 1976 Falcons to a state football championship, the first of three for the legendary coach. (Courtesy of Fort Campbell High School)

"The wins and losses have faded from my memory, but the unique evolution of our relationship is something I'll always cherish," Larson said. "Coach P certainly had as much of an effect on the direction my professional career took as anyone I've ever known. I'm sure I rarely lived up to his standards, but I certainly had the best role model any coach ever had."

After Coach P's retirement, Rick Larson, like other alumni, made it a point to visit with him whenever he was in the area or attending class reunions.He also was among former FCHS football players to attend Marshall Patterson's funeral in late January 2014.

"My fondest memories of Coach P are his idiosyncrasies that made him 'Coach P'…Whenever I think of him I will remember his laugh, that little deep chuckle he had. I'll remember the 'head rub,' the flattop, the little drop of to tobacco spit that was always just hanging from the corner of his mouth but never seemed to move," Larson said.

"I don't remember the yelling and 'coach-speak' so much. I remember a kind face and the kind words he spoke to me. I was never much of a factor in the grand football scheme of things, but I remember when he presented me with the Sportsmanship Award at the football banquet my senior year. He, of course, commented on how I tried and never missed practice….But, he ended by saying I was the best lip reader he'd ever coached. He would always motion me to the hash mark in games and tell me the play from the sideline. He said I never called the wrong play. Who thinks of that? The human side of Coach P, his kindness and empathy for all of us is what I will always remember."

Ricky Gibbs also never forgot the lessons he learned on the football field at Fort Campbell High School. When Gibbs was promoted to the rank of brigadier general—while serving with the 1st Infantry Division ("The Big Red One") at Fort Riley, Kansas, in December 2009—he credited his high school football coach, Marshall Patterson, and principal, Bill Perry, for putting him on the road to success.

At the ceremony, Gibbs said: *"Coach P was not fancy. I heard him raise his voice a couple times, and I think I only heard him cuss one time. He emphasized basics, standards, discipline and teamwork. I think we all know those are characteristics we share in the Army today."*

Now, let's return to that first state championship season. The year before, the 1975 Falcon football team had lost a heartbreaker to Heath High School in a game that cost them the chance to go to the playoffs and chase the dream of a state championship. Again, remember back in those days, post-season play was nearly impossible with even one district loss.

Rick Larson was a member of that 1975 team, and he said the experience set the tone for the 1976 season.

Here is his word-for-word narrative of Fort Campbell High School's first championship season:

I can remember vividly the Heath running back breaking free on a draw play and scoring from 50 yards out to dash our district title hopes, and at the time, playoff hopes since only the champion advanced in 1975.

As the 1976 pre-season workouts began, you wouldn't know by Coach P's demeanor or enthusiasm that he didn't expect as much or more from this team. He had the Trini Lopez and Black Sabbath blaring on the stereo and pushed us through day camp workouts like he was expecting great things from us. Early on, I found it curious that Coach P seemed to believe in us just as strongly as last year's seniors.

I remember how he constantly reminded us of what it takes to win. Things I don't think I understood at the time. Things like "You've got to love the game," and "Giving your best every play is about not letting your teammates down." Perfect execution in practice was non-negotiable. "Run it again!" because somebody didn't step right on the snap. Years later I got it. That's what championship coaches do. Those are their expectations, every year, every practice, every play, every game.

As we got into the season, I don't think I had any idea whether we were going to be a pretty good team or a really good team. Every game, Coach P told us how much he respected our opponent and how we had to play hard and execute to win. We won easily the first week, but we had "made a lot of mistakes that had to be corrected." We lost to perennial power Mayfield the second week and the message was the same, "Keep playing hard, correct our mistakes, get better next week."

I think the turning point in our season happened one week during practice about midway through the schedule. We had won a few games in a row, and I guess we were dragging a little in a drill he called, "Oklahoma's." The offense had to run plays up and down the field 10 yards at a time with perfect steps and execution. The other coaches had all been fussing at us for not sprinting full speed for several plays, but Coach P was just glaring at us. Finally, Coach P told the other coaches to go with him back to the office. He told us if we really wanted to be state champions and were willing to do what it takes, then to come and let them know. "But right now," he said, "you're wasting our time."

I can't speak for the other seniors, but that's the first time I thought, "Dang, he really thinks we can be a championship team." After some strong words and encouragement from a couple of our vocal leaders, we started the drill on our own at a much greater intensity level. I remember we were all yelling every time we came off the ball and sprinted the 10 yards like our hair was on fire. It was actually a lot more fun! I don't remember if someone went and got the coaches and told them we were ready to practice hard or they just came back down on their own, but we ended with one of the best days of practice I can remember.

The rest of the season unfolded just like Coach P told us it would. We beat Heath at Heath for the district title and rolled through the playoffs with not much resistance. When I see those pictures of that first state championship game, I think about those 14 years Coach P showed up every summer with the same expectations, the same enthusiasm, the same blueprint for building a championship team. More importantly to those of us who played for him is the realization that the blueprint for winning championships is real similar to the blueprint for success in life.

The state championship game against Bellevue was played on Friday, November 26, 1976, at Commonwealth Stadium on the campus of the University of Kentucky in Lexington. Built at a cost of $12 million and opened in 1973, the massive stadium seated nearly 60,000 fans at the time.

After arriving in Lexington on Thanksgiving Day, the Fort Campbell football players—just like a familiar scene in *Hoosiers,* a 1986 sports movie about a small-town high school basketball team in Indiana—ventured out to the stadium to take a look at the field where they would compete for a state championship.

Mike Moats, a cancer survivor who now lives in Indiana, said he and his teammates, after walking onto the field and looking around the huge stadium, were simply awe-struck. Sensing the nervousness of his players, Coach P reassured them right there on the spot that they belonged in the championship game. To this day, Moats recalls Patterson's exact words: *"The playing field in this stadium is the same size as our football field."*

It was a bitter cold and snowy day when FCHS and Bellevue took the field to play for a state football championship. When the game ended, it was bedlam for the Falcons and their faithful.

"I really can't remember specific comments after the game, we were all so elated," Rick Larson said. "I do remember, though, we got back to the high school at like 1 a.m., and the gym was packed. We filed in, and the place erupted. Coach P said a few words to the crowd about the support we got and how proud he was of how hard we had worked. That was probably the coolest part."

Norm Miller was a junior lineman on the 1976 state championship team. Nicknamed "Frog," the former Army officer is now a health physicist in Clinton, Tennessee.

At Fort Campbell High School, Miller may have been on the road to becoming one of the school's greatest athletes. He already was the strongest, shattering the school's records for bench press and military press as the only member of "The 600-pound Club." Going into his senior year, Miller was selected to the preseason 1977 All-State football team as an offensive tackle. However, in a scrimmage before the Falcons' first game, Miller suffered a knee injury that ended his days as a star high school athlete. The injury—just like the one suffered by my old friend and former teammate, Preston Owens—ended up costing Norm Miller an appointment to the U.S. Military Academy at West Point.

172

So, although Norm Miller had no way of knowing it at the time, the 1976 football season would prove to be the highest mountain he would climb in his high school athletic career.

"Frog" still smiles when he thinks about one of the greatest days of his life. Just like his old teammate, Rick Larson, there are vivid details etched forever in his mind.

"I remember staying in the hotel in Lexington. It was the first time we ever stayed overnight at a place. I remember the pure joy and eagerness we had to win," Miller recalled.

"The last play I remember was late in the fourth quarter… The Bellevue quarterback hurried his throw and threw an interception. I still remember his eyes when I knocked him to the ground. I knew then we had won because I could see defeat in his eyes.

"I remember the fire truck escorting us back to post when we got close to the base. And I remember the commanding general (Major General John A. Wickham Jr.) and his raucous speech, thanking us. This was a happy day!"

Days after the big victory, Coach P received a congratulatory letter from General Wickham. "Your efforts have brought recognition to this post, and in particular, to the Fort Campbell High School," the general wrote. "You can take great pride in your achievement and are to be congratulated on a job well done."

Earlier that championship season, after FCHS won its first-ever district crown, a colonel who was part of the 101st Airborne (Air Assault) Command Group at Fort Campbell presented Marshall Patterson and his Falcons with a Letter of Commendation. The colonel's name was Colin Powell, a future Chairman of the Joint Chiefs of Staff and future Secretary of State for President George W. Bush. The Powell letter, in the years to come, became one of Coach P's most cherished possessions.

Norm Miller said, before his injury and the loss through transfers of a handful of returning starters, there had been high hopes for the 1977 Falcon football team.

Ironically, a new transfer to Fort Campbell High School—senior Tom Kastner, a future Army colonel, West Point professor and administrator, and superintendent of New York Military Academy in Cornwell-On-Hudson, New York (The same high school that schooled Troy Donahue, John Gotti Jr. and Donald Trump)—beat out senior Ricky Gibbs that season for the starting quarterback's job. Gibbs, the hero of the 1976 state championship team, was moved to the defensive backfield. It was just another example of Coach P making a tough decision—following his head and not his heart—to do what he believed was best for the team.

FCHS Coach Marshall Patterson (second from right) and his assistant coaches (from left) Rocky Cobb, Houston Mills and Ronnie Bell transformed the Falcons football program into a perennial power, winning three state championships in 1976, 1978 and 1979. (Courtesy of Fort Campbell High School)

Despite the setbacks, the 1977 Falcons had a pretty good year, but lost in the playoffs in overtime. If things had jelled, and Lady Luck had smiled, the Tom Kastner-led team also might have been state champions, which would have made it four in a row for Coach P. (FCHS teams coached by Marshall Patterson later won state championships in 1978 and 1979.)

Norm Miller, after his high school graduation in 1978, attended Austin Peay State University in Clarksville on an ROTC scholarship. Although his days as an athlete were over, the former Falcon enjoyed working out, and he still had a reputation as a strong man.

No doubt, he will always be remembered by many in the Clarksville community for his wrestling match with a bear at a once-popular night spot near the downtown area. "I wrestled 'Ginger The Wrestling Bear' at Texas East while I was in college," Miller said, with a laugh. "She was a 750-pound female brown bear. I got her on her back using the wrestling moves that Coach P taught me."

Unfortunately, "Frog" failed to pin the bear and win the $1,000 prize. "It was rigged, where you had to get both of the bear's paws on the ground to win the match," Miller explained.

At Austin Peay State University, Miller was a member of the Alpha Gamma Rho fraternity on campus that included a former teammate from the 1976 state championship team—Cedric "Ced" Perry, the younger brother of Mike Perry, a FCHS football star from the author's days as a Falcon.

With the highest mountain tops, there also are always the lowest of valleys for those on their journey through life. Even for "Marshall's Boys."

On March 21, 1981—just two weeks after celebrating his 21st birthday—Ced Perry died of a self-inflicted gunshot wound, and it was his friend and Falcon brother, Norm Miller, who found the body at the fraternity house. Ced Perry's funeral—with pallbearers Ray Soyk, Bruce Guillry, Wade Hadley, James "JD" Baker, Steve Allen, and Mark Childress—was held four days later at McReynolds-Nave Chapel in Clarksville. He was buried in Greenwood Cemetery

Not long after the tragedy, Norm Miller ran into Coach P, whom he had not seen in years.

"He looked me in the eyes and thanked me for taking care of Ced Perry and the Perry family. Then, he grabbed my hand and shook it. I guess someone must have told him about me finding him," Miller said. "This was a time for me when I needed Coach P's thanks and understanding the most in my life."

Major General John A. Wickham, Jr., commanding general of the 101st Airborne Division (Air Assault) and Fort Campbell, addresses fans in the FCHS gymnasium, shortly after the school's 1976 football team returned home with the state championship trophy. (Courtesy of Fort Campbell High School)

CHAPTER 8: PORTRAIT OF A MILITARY BRAT

When Marshall Patterson decided to teach and coach the sons and daughters of soldiers, he probably had no earthly idea he would spend an entire career on the Fort Campbell Army post.

Fort Campbell, Kentucky, was a different kind of world, after all, compared to the slow-moving and simple lifestyle of his upbringing in rural Tennessee. The challenges of the job also were unique, to say the least, as the young, just-out-of-college educator—soon to become known as "Coach P" for life—found out when he showed up for work at the fort in the summer of 1960.

Marshall Patterson saw that first day on the job that he had put himself into a fast-paced and chaotic environment that was anything but stable. The school system was, and always had been, a whirlwind of change— with students often in class one day and then gone to the other side of the world with their soldier fathers by the end of the same week.

If there was an ironic twist in the situation, and there was, it sure wasn't lost on Coach P and other faculty. In the world of schooling Military Brats, stability was something that only applied to good teachers and coaches that planned to stay around for the long haul. Job security, however, depended on a willingness and ability to adapt to the ever-changing classroom conditions.

To better appreciate Marshall Patterson and the enormous challenges he faced, and conquered, at Fort Campbell High School, non-military folks must understand the unusual students he was tasked to teach and coach for more than three decades.

Military Brats—the children of active-duty soldiers, sailors, airmen and Marines—are widely recognized as a most exclusive subculture. They face challenges on a daily basis that are totally foreign to their counterparts in the civilian world.

At the top of the list, of course, is the turmoil created by a nomadic lifestyle. Brats live the life of a gypsy, rarely staying in the same location for more than a few years. They move from place to place, always leaving old friends behind and then having to start from scratch to forge new friendships.

Published studies show military families relocate 10 times more often in a lifetime than their civilian counterparts—on the average every two or three years—and the typical military school often experiences a turnover rate of up to 50 percent every single year.

The same studies claim that military kids are more disciplined than their civilian peers, although Brats also tend to be more susceptible to emotional struggles, particularly during deployments.

Many researchers and sociologists further agree that Military Brats are much more "worldly" than youngsters in civilian schools, mainly because of their travel opportunities and exposures to different cultures and ways of life. On this point, studies have shown that 80 percent of Brats insist they can relate to anyone—regardless of race, ethnicity, religion, or nationality.

Lastly, there's strong statistical proof that ex-military kids in very high numbers end up pursuing service-related careers such as the military, teaching, counseling, police work, nursing and working overseas for the government.

No argument there. Just take a look at the history of the graduates of Fort Campbell High School over the years. There have been, and probably always will be, many future soldiers, educators, counselors, police officers, nurses and government employees in their ranks—just itching to get out into the world and make their marks.

The same is true of FCHS graduates who dream of careers in the private sector, maybe hoping to become a mogul or Captain of Industry or even the author of a best-selling book.

Today, there are an estimated 15 million Military Brats in the United States. That total, which very likely could be on the low side, apparently includes current and former (or grown) Brats. After all, once a Military Brat, *always* a Military Brat.

On an interesting note, statistics reveal that about 60 percent of all Military Brats live in ten states: Texas, California, Florida, Virginia, Georgia, Colorado, North Carolina, Maryland, Arizona, and Washington. All have one thing in common—they contain large Army, Navy, Air Force or Marine bases.

But, make no mistake about it, Military Brats are everywhere.

When Elvis Presley was in the Army and stationed in Germany in the late 1950s—incidentally at the same time as the author's family, but at a different post—he met a 14-year-old Military Brat at a party. That Brat, Priscilla Beaulieu—now known as Priscilla Presley, an actress and businesswoman—was the step-daughter of a career Air Force officer. She married the undisputed—and long dead—King of Rock and Roll several years later in Las Vegas.

Of course, Elvis' former wife isn't the only noteworthy celebrity who's lived the Military Brat life. I pointed her out only because of our Elvis connection. I like Elvis, too, and only wish I had had the chance to snarl my lip at him in Germany as a 3-year-old Military Brat.

There are many celebrities out there who grew up as Military Brats—Kris Kristofferson, Christina Aguilera, LeVar Burton, Bruce Willis, and Shaquille "Shaq" O'Neal, just to name a handful that come to mind.

They know what it means to make sacrifices for their fathers' careers. Those who serve, or have served, in the military—as the head of a family—understand that a successful career is impossible without the unwavering support of the spouse and sacrifices from the children.

Senior Debbe Jones (third from right) and classmates at Fort Campbell High School watch a wrestling match in the school gymnasium in early 1973. It was Coach Marshall Patterson who talked Debbe Jones into serving as the wrestling team's statistician. (Courtesy of Fort Campbell High School)

This fact often is lost on the non-military community. Although most folks recognize and appreciate what military members do for the love of their country, they seldom think about the sacrifices that Military Brats make while growing up. Brats must endure many hardships, including losing precious time with their Dads or Moms during deployments and the disruptions of moving from place to place every few years.

Military Brats, Inc., a non-profit corporation, is one organization working hard to get Brats their just due. In early 2015, a campaign—hopefully, it will end in success one day—was launched to encourage Congress to declare an official day each year as "Military Brat Day."

Sacrifice certainly was no stranger to the sons and daughters of soldiers who graced the halls of Fort Campbell High School.

Debbe (Jones) Gifford graduated in 1973 from FCHS, where she was a cheerleader, drum major, mat maid, and the older sister of one of Coach P's rising star wrestlers of that era—Mike Jones.

"Like so many other Brats, my family lived in many different places over the years. We lived in Dodge City, Kansas, Colorado Springs, Colorado, Bamberg, Germany, Fort Leonard Wood, Missouri, Casper, Wyoming, Rock Falls, Illinois, Fort Campbell, Kentucky, El Paso, Texas, and Schweinfurt, Germany," she recalled. "You really had to learn to adapt and make friends quickly."

Debbe's late father, Command Sergeant Major Norman C. Jones, was a career soldier. After his retirement from the Army, he developed cancer due to Agent Orange exposure in Vietnam and died at the age of 72 in 2005. Command Sergeant Major Jones and his wife, Evelyn, in addition to Debbe and Mike, raised one other child, Randy, who followed in his father's footsteps and joined the military.

Evelyn Jones, a Kansas resident, celebrated her 80th birthday in July 2015. Known to Fort Campbell Brats as "Mama Jones," Debbe's sweet mother is an honorary member of the Falcon Nation due to her tremendous support for the high school and Army post she once called home. Over the years, she's helped her daughter, Debbe, with numerous reunion-related tasks—like making decorations and name tags.

The Jones family was stationed at Fort Campbell for three years in the early 1970s, according to Debbe (Jones) Gifford, now a telecommunications project manager living in Shawnee, Kansas.

During those days at Fort Campbell High School, Marshall Patterson was someone who, from the start, made a huge impression on her. He carried a lot of weight at the school, in terms of respect and authority, the former cheerleader explained. "I believed his words were Gospel."

She continued: "Coach P had a unique gift for recognizing talent, not only from an athletic aspect, but from a personal aspect as well. In my junior year, Coach P asked me to keep the team stats for all wrestling meets and tournaments. In hindsight, I can honestly say this gave me confidence and a sense of accomplishment. First, that he trusted me to handle the task and secondly, I learned that I had the aptitude and ability to handle so many moving pieces."

A broken romance with her athlete boyfriend—one of "Marshall's Boys"—made Debbe's senior year at FCHS very difficult. And, it was not lost on Coach P despite his busy schedule and many responsibilities at the high school.

Debbe (Jones) Gifford said she was reminded of Coach P's kindness and concern for her in high school while looking through an old Falcon yearbook one afternoon. Before she graduated and left high school, Marshall Patterson had signed it and left her an inspirational message. *"I have enjoyed knowing you and working with you as you supported our teams. Your spirit and dedication to your school have helped to make FCHS the 'best'! Your work to support our team has been the greatest! I wish I could have helped you to win your game, but maybe I did... Your Friend, Coach Patterson."*

At a reunion in 2008, Miss Debbe spoke to Coach P about her younger brother, Mike, now a top executive with a huge corporation over in Ireland. It was Marshall Patterson who turned Mike Jones' life around during a turbulent time in his life by giving him the opportunity to wrestle for FCHS. After the family moved to Germany, Mike Jones continued his wrestling and eventually made the "All Europe" team—no small feat.

"I told Coach P about my brother's success in wrestling and that Mike gave him the credit. I still remember Coach P smiling with pride," Debbe (Jones) Gifford noted.

So, what was it like to grow up as a Military Brat?

Debbe provided a glimpse into the experience—including the emotions and culture shock—by writing this personal essay:

It's the fall of 1970, I'm a sophomore at Dodge City High School in Kansas, and I'm enjoying life with my best friends in the whole world! My father then returns from his second tour in Vietnam and gets orders for Fort Campbell, Kentucky. So, being the outspoken teenager, I stand my ground and proclaim to my parents: "I will never leave my friends. I'm staying here with my grandparents. You will need to move without me!"

A month later, our family—including me—arrives at Fort Campbell, Kentucky, and I immediately suffer another "earth-shattering" blow—the high school. With a student body of about 200, the small school is located on post and consists entirely of Military Brats. It's a big difference from my old high school in Kansas with 900 civilian students. Once again, I stand my ground, refusing to go to school. My parents play along with my tantrum and tell me, "OK, but you'll have chores to do every day while we're at work." About a week or two later, tired of housework and lonely for friends, I give up and go to school.

On my first day at Fort Campbell High School, I enter a classroom and take a seat when I hear: "Hi Y'all! How Y'all doing?" I look around the classroom thinking, "Who is she talking to?" Then it hits me. She's talking to me! And, that's when I met Mary Riddle, who became one of my first and very best friends at Fort Campbell High School. The ice was broken, and I recall everyone I met that day was easy to get to know and accepting of the new girl in school.

Of course, friendliness is among the many admirable traits of a Brat. OK. I get to know everyone, and I'm not the new girl anymore. What's this? There's another new girl in school? Enter Vicky Coleman, who becomes The Third Musketeer. Mary, Vicky and I are inseparable! Later on, The

Three Musketeers decide to go out for cheerleading and become part of the 1971-1972 squad. Up until the time we graduate in 1973, we participate in many other activities at the high school—activities I might not have had the chance to do at a larger school.

At FCHS, the faculty is "top notch." Some of them will become mentors to me and help shape my life. Many of these teachers are not that much older than us, so they have the ability to relate to their students and inspire them to do their very best.

Finally, graduation is here—June 1973. The day is "bittersweet." We are excited to move on to the next chapter of life, but sad to know we will scatter all over the world the next day after our dads get their orders for their next duty station.

I do my best to stay in touch with friends, writing letters in the early years after high school. But life has a way of taking over, and the letters become fewer and fewer.

Fast forward to 2005. The Internet and social media are thriving, and now it becomes easier—especially for Military Brats—to locate long-lost high school friends and organize reunions. Out of the blue, Vicky Coleman locates me, and we pick up as if it was yesterday. In reality, we have not spoken for 31 years! Although reluctant, Vicky convinces me to attend a FCHS reunion that year, and we have a blast reconnecting with fellow alumni! The Three Musketeers are now back together. With that reunion, a tradition is born. The attendees, who now view each other as "family," vow to meet every two years to keep Falcon Pride and the Falcon Nation alive and well.

Dennis Fendler, another former Falcon, also lived a life shaped by the Military Brat experience. A 1972 graduate of Fort Campbell High School, Fendler later attended Murray State University in Murray, Kentucky, before embarking on a career of more than 30 years as a pressman in the newspaper industry. He now lives in Nashville, Tennessee, where he is a professional photographer.

Fendler's military family—which included three younger sisters, Judi, Bridget and Joanie—traveled the world for years, making cherished and lasting memories. In addition to being stationed at a variety of stateside Army posts, the Fendlers lived in Germany and even Vietnam. "I learned how to swim after my father tossed me into the South China Sea," Dennis Fendler quipped.

Dennis' father, Donn Fendler, served as a military adviser to the South Vietnamese Army when the family lived in Na Trangh and eventually Saigon (now known as Ho Chi Mihn City in unified Vietnam) from 1959 through 1962.

As an aside, Donn Fendler—who retired as an Army colonel—earlier in life had been a national celebrity, when, as a 12-year-old boy, he got lost on Maine's Mount Katahdin in July 1939 and survived nine days without food before finding his way out of the wilderness. After his rescue, President Franklin D. Roosevelt presented him with the Army & Navy Legion of Valor's annual medal for Youth Hero of 1939. The dramatic incident was chronicled, at the time, in *Life* magazine and was the subject of at least one book. Colonel Fendler—who turned 88 in July 2015—lost his wife, Ree, in January 2009. For years, he has returned to Maine every fall to visit schools and tell his tale of survival to children.

Donn Fendler, a young Army officer, enjoys a day at the beach with his children and their playmates during his tour of duty as an adviser to the South Vietnamese Army in the early 1960s. His son, Dennis Fendler, a 1972 graduate of FCHS, learned to swim after his Dad tossed him into the South China Sea. (Courtesy of Dennis Fendler)

The Fendler home, near the end of their tour, was located close to the Presidential Palace in Saigon. At the time, Vietnam was a divided country, and it was a very dangerous time in South Vietnam, which was marked by daily violence and instability. Dennis Fendler said there were at least two failed coup attempts to overthrow the government of President Ngo Dinh Diem, who eventually was assassinated in November 1963. Like many Americans who were there at the time, the Fendlers were directly in the line of fire and combat operations. Bullets were flying everywhere, and planes were strafing the palace.

"I came home from school after one of the coups and found my mother hiding under the stairway, holding my baby sister Joanie," Dennis Fendler recalled. "Spent 50-caliber machine gun bullets were scattered all over the driveway."

As the violence worsened, the Fendlers and other American dependents eventually left South Vietnam and returned to the United States.

Mr. Fendler—echoing his friend and classmate, Debbe (Jones) Gifford— said the most difficult part of the Military Brat experience was moving and starting a new life someplace else. The Fendler family was stationed at Fort Leavenworth, Kansas, prior to their move to Fort Campbell in the early 1970s. The move crushed Dennis, who was in high school at the time, and left him with what he described as a "million-pound chip" on his shoulder. Just as he was finding his way in Kansas, he had to pull up roots and face the unknown in Kentucky.

But, like most Military Brats, Dennis Fendler adjusted to the situation and got into the swing of things at his new high school, even reuniting and later graduating with a former schoolmate from his days at Fort Bragg, North Carolina—Mike Wootan. (Mr. Wootan passed away in December 2000.)

Reuniting with old friends often was the upside of the Military Brat lifestyle.

As 10-year-old boys in elementary school, Fendler and Wootan watched on television the unfolding events of the assassination of President John F.

Kennedy. "At Fort Campbell, Mike really looked the same, just a little older," Fendler recalled.

Dennis Fendler said his experiences as a Military Brat definitely helped him in school and in later life. "The Vietnam experience came in handy at Fort Campbell High School when I debated the Vietnam War from our government's point of view and was successful...I had ammunition from both sides of the experience...One of my favorite teachers, Ed Davis, told me how impressed he was at how I handled the debate with the knowledge I had accumulated from the early years."

At FCHS, Fendler said he kept a low profile other than playing basketball for Coach Roy Medlock. Although, he had minimal contact with Coach P, the "Father of the Falcons" still managed to make a big impression on him.

"Coach P once asked me—while I was in the gym alone, working out by doing some gymnastic routines—how he had missed getting me out for wrestling," Dennis Fendler noted, with a laugh. The personal attention from Marshall Patterson boosted his confidence and changed his attitude for the better, he said.

"Coach P was, in my mind, a great man and an excellent judge of all that is good in a human being," Fendler said.

Many of Mr. Fendler's former classmates, by the way, view him as a shining example of something good and special that often results from high school reunions.

In October 2010, Dennis Fendler—who, at the time, was living in Arizona—attended a FCHS reunion. At the event, he struck up a conversation with Susie Chambers, who had graduated the year after him in 1973.

"I barely knew her in high school," he recalled. "We had a study hall together, and I remember talking to her once when she was sitting behind me."

The two hit it off and began a romance that eventually united a couple of Military Brats with so much in common. Dennis and Susie have been together since that initial spark at the 2010 reunion.

While most Military Brats at Fort Campbell moved often and rarely stayed anywhere longer than two or three years, there were exceptions like Preston Owens, and the four Hellums brothers, who now are in business together in Alabama, where they are successful poultry farmers.

They were the Falcon longtimers. With their uncharacteristic stability, the Owens and Hellums families certainly benefited the most from the powerful influence and stern hand of FCHS Coach Marshall Patterson.

When yours truly—young Robert Dollar—lived on the Fort Campbell Army post, Preston Owens and Mike Hellums were friends that I hung out with nearly every day of every week until our graduation from FCHS in 1975.

Preston's father, Sergeant First Class Jesse Edward Owens was stationed at Fort Campbell from 1963 through his retirement in 1975, with the exception of a one-year tour in Vietnam during the late 1960s. Sergeant Owens and his wife, Mary, raised eight children in Stryker Village—four of whom, including Preston, graduated from Fort Campbell High School.

Amazingly, Preston—just like John Bianchini of the Class of 1965—attended Fort Campbell schools from start to finish.

Preston Owens and two of his brothers—Jesse Frederick Owens (known as "Freddy") and Tony Owens—played several sports at FCHS for Coach P and followed their father into the military.

A member of the Class of 1970, Freddy Owens—the eldest—graduated from West Point and spent 20 years as an Army officer before retiring as a major in 1996. Preston Owens, an industrial engineer now living in Pennsylvania, spent six years on active duty in the Navy and another 18 in the Reserve, before ending his military service in 2000. Tony Owens (Class of 1976), after a career in the Air Force, also retired and, at last report, was working a civilian job at Fort Campbell.

Preston's father—who served 24 years in the Army, and later worked for the Army, Air Force Exchange Service on post—succumbed to cancer and died in Clarksville in October 2000 at the age of 69.

Rick, Mike, Ben and Steve Hellums were the sons of Q.T. Hellums—a chief warrant officer—and his wife, Betty Hellums. The family—including a daughter, Penny—lived in the Werner Park housing area on the Fort Campbell Army post for about a decade.

All four of the Hellums boys, during their high school years, played football for Coach P and wrestled for him. Their little sister, Penny (Hellums) Roney, who was in elementary school in those days, probably is best remembered for cheering on her brothers during wrestling matches as an honorary mat maid. Little Penny, an Ole Miss graduate ("Hotty Toddy") is now married, with children of her own, and works for the Alabama Department of Public Health.

Rick Hellums, the oldest of the brothers, graduated from Fort Campbell High School in 1971 and a few years later married Connie Gafford, who, at the time, was the girls' physical education teacher at FCHS.

Mike Hellums met the author of this book for the first time in November 1969 at Fort Campbell Junior High School. Living just a street over from him in Werner Park for five years, Mike and I played "catch" together in the back yard, worked a morning newspaper route, and in high school, rode to and back from classes every day in my old blue Mustang. After graduation, Mike, too, followed in his father's footsteps and joined the military, serving his country in the Navy for several years.

Ben Hellums, who was one of Coach P's wrestling stars, graduated from FCHS in 1977. He later married his high school sweetheart and classmate, Anna (Ashworth) Hellums.

Steve Hellums ended his days at Fort Campbell as the last Hellums brother to be coached and mentored by Marshall Patterson. A member of the high school's first-ever freshman football team, Steve also played on the 1976 and 1978 FCHS state championship football teams. He graduated with the Class of 1979.

In a nutshell, there was a Hellums brother somewhere out on the football field or flopping around on the wrestling mat for at least 10 years of Marshall Patterson's 32-year coaching career at Fort Campbell High School.

During the 1971 football season—after Rick Hellums had graduated, and Ben and Steve Hellums were still too young to compete in high school sports—Mike Hellums stepped up to the plate to keep alive the family tradition of representing the Blue-and-Grey colors of FCHS. He and two other freshmen at the junior high school—Ron Alvarez and John Gomez—served as equipment managers that year for Coach P and the Falcon football team.

While taking care of the team, Mike became a Falcon football player in training, watching and learning from some of the stars on the 1971 football squad. Gilbert Scott, a starting halfback and safety, was one of the headline-makers of that era. Back in those days, Mr. Scott was a long-haired, sweet-talking senior who apparently was very popular with the ladies. So, he had a reputation as a heartbreaker, too,

As one of the unforgettable characters in the Class of 1972, Gilbert Scott certainly had his fans—on and off the football field. The football managers—who heard their share of stories in the locker room—worshipped the senior running back for his status as a "Romeo" with the lovely girls of Fort Campbell High School. The Falcon halfback must have made quite an impression on young Mike Hellums. Just two years after serving as a football manager, a confident and longer-haired Mike Hellums joined the FCHS football team as a player and when he hit the field he was wearing jersey No. 24—Gilbert Scott's old number. And, if my memory is correct, Mike was well on his way to becoming a lady-killer—and a great football player for Coach P's 1973 and 1974 Falcon teams.

Of course, Gilbert Scott made quite an impact on the football field, too. And, as one of "Marshall's Boys," Mr. Scott always had a deep respect for Fort Campbell High School's legendary football coach. "Coach Patterson was a fine man, and a good coach," he recalled. "He lived for coaching."

Coach P—who wore his hair short, sometimes near a buzz cut—and long-haired Gilbert Scott often butted heads during the football season. Not surprisingly, the spats always centered on the length of Gilbert's HAIR. There were many FCHS athletes over the years who argued that the length of their hair had nothing to do with their ability to play football. But, few things—and, certainly not haircuts—were negotiable with Coach P when it came to team rules, discipline, and the well-groomed appearance of his players.

Therefore, it was an exercise in futility to try and convince a coach, who rubbed his head when in deep thought, that shoulder-length hair was the secret formula for putting good football players on the field.

All joking aside, Gilbert Scott was, and remains to this day, an all-around nice guy. Married and living near Nashville, he still wears his hair long, just like in the Seventies.

Let's return to the subject of the Hellums family for a few memories that reinforce the strong bond between them and my family during the Fort Campbell years. Q.T. and Betty Hellums were among my parents' closest friends, and they enjoyed socializing together on weekends—going out on the town or to FCHS ball games. On one occasion—a Saturday night in September 1973—they drove to Nashville for a night of music at the Grand Ole Opry. Tammy Wynette, Roy Acuff and Grandpa Jones were among the entertainers on the program that night. Stringbean was there, too. It turned out to be one of his last performances on the Grand Ole Opry stage. Weeks later, Stringbean (David Akeman) tragically was shot to death, the victim of a home robbery that went awry and also claimed the life of his wife.

While Q.T. Hellums and my Dad were stationed at Fort Campbell, they had to deploy once for a tour of duty in Vietnam and left the fort around the same time—August 1971. Both families were allowed to remain in post quarters while they were off fighting the war. As a Military Brat, this was my second experience of Dad going off to war, and him telling me to look after my Mom and sisters as the "Man of the House." I'm sure my pal, Mike Hellums, got the same speech from his father. Of course, Mike had three brothers to help him take care of his mother and little sister, and big brother Rick probably was the one put in charge since he was the eldest.

Just weeks after our fathers left for Vietnam, the new school year got under way. Mike and I were 14 years old and attending our final year at Fort Campbell Junior High School—as ninth graders. At the time, in addition to serving as a manager for the football team, Mike also was helping me with my morning newspaper route in Werner Park.
Allow me to remind the readers of this book that the author and his friends were very naive and inexperienced in the ways of the world—especially when it came to teenage girls—back in those long-ago days of our youth. The mere thought of our unsophistication brings back the memory of a funny incident that, when it occurred, certainly wasn't the finest moment for two Military Brats with fathers fighting an unpopular war thousands of miles away on the other side of the world. In telling the story, I'm not leaving out names—only because Mike Hellums and the author of this book, Rob Dollar, were as innocent as newborn babes and never ever lost their senses of humor about their infamous brush with the long arm of the law.

It was the middle of October 1971—less than two months after Dad had left for Vietnam. Sister Adele, who was about to turn 14, was hosting a Saturday night slumber party on her birthday. Of course, every teenage girl in the ninth grade was going to be there—and the teenage boys knew it. Back in those days, there was a curfew for kids on post, and the military police patrolled all of the housing areas, strictly enforcing it. On the night of my sister's party, Mike Hellums invited me to camp out in his back yard in a small pup tent. The story should have ended there—with us waking up the next morning and delivering our newspapers. But, instead of turning in for the night and getting some shut-eye, two wide-awake campers decided instead to take a leisurely walk through Werner Park—in the middle of the night, after curfew.

It's probably easy to guess what happened next…Yep. Mike and I, while crossing a street, spotted an approaching MP car. And the two MPs in it, doing their duty, spotted us at the same time…With blue lights flashing, the car sped toward us and one of the MPs—over a loud speaker—ordered us to stop and get down on the ground….Knowing we were out after curfew, and acting like typical teenagers, the command was ignored and we took off—Mike running in one direction, and me in the other…To our surprise, the two MPs jumped out of their car and began chasing Mike and me like we had just robbed a bank. After running clear to the other side of Werner Park, I spotted a shadowy figure that I thought was probably Mike looking for me. Instead, it was the MP that had been chasing me—the one who was fat and out of shape. By this point in time, I wasn't as scared as when the great chase had started, and I was tired anyway. I also reasoned that I couldn't possibly be in too much trouble. After all, it was only a curfew violation. So, I walked over to the MP and asked him if there was a problem. "You're in big trouble, buddy," the fat lawman yelled at me. Then, he grabbed my arm and led me away, back to the squad car where his partner was waiting for him—empty-handed. As I would learn later, Mike Hellums had made a clean getaway by hiding underneath a parked car on the street. My MP puffed out his chest. "I got mine," he said, with a smug smile. Of course, I tried to explain to the two MPs that my friend—who I would not name—and I were not desperadoes, but only campers who were out for a stroll that night, talking about teenage girls and the other mysteries of life.

After getting my name and address, the MPs drove me back to my house to check out my story. As we pulled into the driveway, with headlights shining brightly, the two lawmen burst out into loud laugher. There, huddled under the carport, taking shelter behind my Dad's parked Buick sedan, was half of the male population of Fort Campbell Junior High School…Well, I guess that's probably an exaggeration. Around 15 teenage boys were hanging out under the carport. They had teenage girls on their minds that night and had hoped to hook up at the big slumber party in Werner Park. Mike Hellums, who had escaped during the earlier police chase, was there, too. He had hoped to link up with me at my house, but sure hadn't planned on me getting caught and bringing the police.

The slumber party crashers were sent home, after a good tongue-lashing about breaking curfew, but the two fleeing teens got the royal police treatment that night. They hauled Mike Hellums and me to the police station, where Criminal Investigation Division (CID) agents interrogated us about every crime that had ever been committed in Werner Park. I don't remember any rubber hoses or waterboarding, but there were plenty of bright, hot lights and flying accusations during that nightmare of a night. After what seemed like an eternity, our interrogators finally gave us the benefit of the doubt and accepted the truth that we weren't vandals or Peeping Toms: We were just two dumb teenage boys, who ran from the police, because we had broken curfew. With vindication, Betty Hellums and my Mom took us home, but not before burning our ears with the familiar lecture that the military holds soldiers accountable for the actions of family members.

Three freshmen (from left)—John Gomez, Ron Alvarez, and Mike Hellums—served as the equipment managers for the 1971 FCHS football team. In later years, Alvarez and Hellums played for Coach Marshall Patterson. (Courtesy of Fort Campbell High School)

Remember now, when this incident occurred, Q.T. Hellums and my father were fighting the war in Vietnam. I'm not even sure whether our mothers ever reported the incident to them when they returned to Fort Campbell the following spring. Believe me, Mike Hellums and I have always been grateful for that silver lining in the story. War is Hell, but Hell would have been the preferable place to be, instead of home, if Mr. Hellums and my Dad had been on post the night their teenage sons ran afoul of the law in Werner Park.

The Dollar family moved out of Werner Park in June 1974, when my parents—preparing for retirement—bought a modest, four-bedroom house in Hopkinsville, Kentucky. The Hellums family would continue to live in Werner Park for another five years.

Not long after Q.T. Hellums' youngest son, Steve, graduated from Fort Campbell High School in June 1979, the patriarch of the Hellums clan retired from the Army, and the family moved from Fort Campbell to his native Mississippi.

Q.T. Hellums thought the world of Marshall Patterson and trusted the coach when it came to looking out for his four sons.

Now living in Oneonta, Alabama, Mike Hellums—married, with grown children—said Marshall Patterson absolutely could do no wrong in the eyes of his father. "He always had my Dad's support," Mike recalled. "Coach P could have run any of us to death, and my Dad probably would have said, 'I guess it was his time.'"

In July 1981, Q.T. Hellums died of lung cancer linked to his exposure to Agent Orange while serving in Vietnam. He was 48 years old. Betty Hellums passed away, at the age of 74, after a car accident in Alabama in May 2008.

When the life of Q.T. Hellums was celebrated, and he was laid to his final rest, Marshall Patterson was there at the funeral to support the Hellums family.

Coach P and his wife drove about 300 miles to Bruce, Mississippi—a five-hour trip one way—to pay their final respects to the father of four of his boys. "He said we had to go," Rebecca Patterson recalled. "He said he had to be there for the boys."

Marshall Patterson's kindness and concern simply overwhelmed the Hellums family, according to Mike Hellums.

"It meant the world to us when he showed up."

Dr. Leon Sitter, superintendent of the Fort Campbell school system, presents the author – Rob Dollar – with his high school diploma during graduation ceremonies at the Army post in June 1975. There were 122 seniors in the Class of 1975. (Courtesy of Rose Dollar)

CHAPTER 9: YOUNG AND STUPID

The memory is seared into my brain, like it happened only yesterday and not decades ago in the waning days of my impressionable teenage years. It was a Wednesday, and the date was April 30, 1975. The world, on pins and needles, watched the gripping television images of the last American helicopter lifting off from the roof of the U.S. Embassy in Saigon.

Tens of thousands of South Vietnamese who had helped the United States in a war for freedom were left behind with The Fall of Saigon, abandoned and destined for death sentences or re-education camps. For the most powerful country on the face of the Earth, it was a disgraceful exit from the mother of all quagmires and marked the official end of the long and controversial Vietnam War.

Half-way around the world—actually about 9,000 miles away—at Fort Campbell, Kentucky, Saigon's fall to the Communists was a crushing blow for many of the soldiers of the 101st Airborne Division, which had been the last Army division to leave Vietnam just two years earlier.

The division, during eight years of combat operations, suffered almost 20,000 soldiers killed or wounded in action in Vietnam, more than twice as many as the 9,328 casualties it suffered in World War II. The Screaming Eagles from the 101st also won 17 Medals of Honor for bravery in combat in Southeast Asia.

It was a day to remember, for sure, but not one characterized by pride. However, nearly every other emotion imaginable was reflected on the faces of Fort Campbell soldiers—surprise, humiliation, sadness, anger, contempt, disgust, guilt, shame, and distress.

Vietnam had long divided the country, with many people opposing the war on moral grounds or for foreign policy objectives that were perceived to be flawed. But for professional soldiers like those at Fort Campbell, there was no choice other than to salute and do their duty for their country. When the war finally ended with a whimper, and not a victory for freedom, it had to feel like the end of the world for the men in uniform who had made such great sacrifices over the years. Remember, they watched friends die in bloody battle after bloody battle. They returned to "The World," not to a hometown parade but to angry protesters spitting on them. They endured years of mental anguish that only those who had served in Vietnam could, or would, ever be able to understand. The Fall of Saigon, just five weeks before Graduation Day, was a low point for career soldiers like my Dad and the fathers of the sons and daughters who were part of Fort Campbell High School's Class of 1975.

Of course, it would be decades later, and only after a few blockbuster Hollywood movies, before most Americans—including the Military Brats who went to school at Fort Campbell—would learn about "The Battle of Hamburger Hill" and gain a clearer understanding of the Vietnam War. The epic battle took place between May 10 and May 20 of 1969 in the Thua Thien Province of South Vietnam. It was the last major battle of the Vietnam War and was primarily fought by the "Iron Rakkasans" of the 3rd Battalion of the 187th Infantry Regiment, 101st Airborne Division. U.S. losses during the 10-day battle totaled 72 killed in action and 372 wounded.

The battalion commander who directed the bloody ground assault to take Hamburger Hill was Lieutenant Colonel Weldon F. "Tiger" Honeycutt, who later would retire from the Army as a brigadier general in the summer of 1977 at Fort Campbell where he was the 101st's assistant division commander for operations

Honeycutt's daughter, Diane Elizabeth Honeycutt, was among the Military Brats in my graduating class at Fort Campbell High School. Our class—the 13th in the history of the school, with 122 members—received diplomas from Principal Bill Perry and Superintendent Dr. Leon Sitter during a two-hour ceremony on Friday, June 6, 1975. As the Senior Class president, it was my honor to welcome the audience—which included my parents, and most certainly, The Honeycutts—that packed into the hot, high school gymnasium on that memorable evening so long ago.

As an aside—at the time my sister Adele and I graduated from high school—Dad was attending the U.S. Quartermaster School at Fort Lee, Virginia, preparing for a one-year deployment to Iran and an assignment to serve as a technical adviser to the Iranian Imperial Army. His classmates at the school included two or three Iranian army officers. My father took a weekend leave to attend our graduation ceremony at Fort Campbell High School. Back in those days, The Shah (Mohammad Reza Pahlavi) was still in charge of Iran, and the United States considered the country in the Middle East as a friend and ally. Months later, after Dad was in Iran, I arrived as a freshman on the campus of Western Kentucky University in Bowling Green, Kentucky. Almost immediately, I got a glimpse of what the future had in store for Iran—a full four years before the Islamic Revolution of 1979. Iranian students on campus, after learning that my father was helping train The Shah's military, directed their anger over the political situation in the country on their new American friend— ME. As a result, I instantly became a favorite target of the Iranians, who made it their mission to harass and lecture me. Their message was crystal clear, and they never wavered in their hatred of The Shah: "The Shah is a bad man, Robert Dollar. Tell your father to come home." Like that actually was ever an option….Believe me, there's a lesson here: No one except a Military Brat would ever have to deal with mental terrorism as part of their college experience. A few years later, not long before Ayatollah Khomeini overthrew The Shah, an Iranian army officer—who was attending a military school at Fort Knox, Kentucky—drove to Hoptown on a quiet Sunday to visit with my father. They had worked together during Dad's deployment to Iran. The Dollar family and their Iranian guest enjoyed a pleasant afternoon, topped off by a stimulating discussion of world affairs at the dinner table. It's a good thing, I suppose, that those crazy Iranian students never found out I was collaborating with their enemy.

My father served two tours of duty in Vietnam during his military career and rarely, if ever, shared his war experiences with the family. It was almost an off-limits subject in the Dollar house. The same was true, I suspect, for many of my classmates. That's not to say, though, that there weren't some very lively discussions about the war. After all, it was the burning issue of the day. The late 1960s and early 1970s were very turbulent times in this country, fueled by many cultural changes. Remember, with the Vietnam War at the epicenter, Americans were also struggling with Nixon and Watergate, radical bombings, riots, an energy crisis, and the chill of the Cold War.

Unfortunately for me, Dad often fought the Vietnam War on the homefront by relentlessly venting against long-haired protesters marching in the streets. His anger and frustration, not surprisingly, sometimes made me the favorite target during family disagreements—actually shouting matches—over haircuts, attitude, and the proper way to dress out in public.

It was a bad haircut—forced on me by Dad and apparently done at the hands of a drunken barber—that caused me to miss school on the final day of my eighth-grade year. The back story for the hair-lowering incident, when I look back on it, is slightly amusing. I was supposed to receive an award for "Perfect Attendance" at a school assembly on Thursday, June 3, 1971—the day after I got the bad haircut. Of course, after the assault on my head, there was no way I was going back to school looking like a Hare Krishna. Good thing it was the end of the school year. Gary Stewart, who, at the time, was an eighth-grade teacher at Fort Campbell Junior High School, probably wondered what had happened to that good kid who never missed school. Now, decades later, he knows the rest of the story. Like I said, it's funny now. But I sure wasn't laughing back then, especially when I looked in the mirror and saw what that criminal barber had done to me.

In Dad's defense, it's quite possible he may have been worried and motivated to take action by a couple of incidents that had occurred earlier in the school year. Remember this was 1971, when marijuana use was at an all-time high, and President Nixon had declared a "War on Drugs." My father—his nickname around our house was "The General"—was hard-core military, all the way, and he probably was more conservative than Barry Goldwater. Although Dad had a good sense of humor, it sure wasn't funny to him when I went to a party dressed like a hippie and later hung out for a few hours with one of the country's most famous Vietnam War protesters. But, trust me: It wasn't as bad as it sounds.

The party actually was on Halloween, and my hippie attire was only a costume. But, I'll have to confess I really liked those pink shades. As for that meeting with Country Joe McDonald a few months later, it was strictly a chance encounter. The musician and activist showed up to protest the Vietnam War across from Fort Campbell's Gate 3, in the area now known as Patriots Park. Country Joe, minus The Fish, led a small group of demonstrators in singing "The Fish Cheer." Two of my junior high school classmates—James Lumblo and Dale Nicosia—and I rode our bicycles over to the protest to check it out. It was a big deal, after all. It's likely my father found out I was singing songs with Country Joe after watching a television newscast of the protest later that evening after supper. He never said anything about it to me, but I'm convinced he spotted his boy—on the television screen—lurking around in the background, mingling with those long-haired, anti-war demonstrators.

By the way, it was at that Halloween party that I received my first kiss while playing Spin-The-Bottle. Katie Whitehouse, who was a classmate of mine from junior high through high school graduation, was the lucky girl. Cute Katie always was friendly and full of fun—the kind of girl who leaves a lasting impression. I still have memories of Katie and some of her lovely friends playing football—touch and tackle—with our junior high gang at that old football field near her home in Turner Loop. I lost contact with Katie Whitehouse after our high school graduation, but I don't think she would mind me spilling the beans about that first kiss long ago. After all, she deserves the credit—if any is due—for turning me into a pretty good kisser.

Let's return to the spring of 1975, and the new world that was waiting in the wings for the graduating class of Fort Campbell High School. Make no mistake about it, there were many profound thoughts racing through the heads of my classmates and I with the approach of our day of reckoning. But, Vietnam no longer was at the top of the list. The draft had ended two years earlier, and with Saigon falling to Communist forces, the final chapter of the Vietnam War officially had been written and now was in the history books.

Ironically, nearly a month after The Fall of Saigon and only two weeks before Graduation Day, there actually was a celebration at Fort Campbell to reward and commemorate the 101st Airborne Division's role in the Vietnam War. On Thursday, May 22, 1975, the first-ever (and last) Army rock concert was held at Fryar Stadium. Joe Cocker, Pure Prairie League and Chaka Khan were among the headliners at the concert, which made national news because it erupted into a near riot, with massive fist fights and other crimes breaking out in the crowd of more than 10,000 soldiers and civilians. There were drug overdoses, too.

It's been said anyone who can remember the Sixties wasn't there. Although quite a few of my "hippie" classmates made the scene and attended the rock concert at Fryar Stadium—the huge stage was placed on Coach P's perfect football field—the author clearly was not there that day to witness history in the making. I know, for a fact, only because I still remember—more than 40 years later—the public relations disaster that the incident created for the Army. And, if I'm able to remember anything about the concert, I couldn't possibly have been there. There was no Trini Lopez, either. If he had been a part of the entertainment package, the crowd certainly would have been much larger. I've often joked that, the fact Trini wasn't there playing his guitar, probably was the only reason that Marshall Patterson skipped the concert.

I remember the birds, too. They embarrassed the Army the same year. For those who don't remember, the rock concert fiasco occurred just three months after another public relations disaster at Fort Campbell. That one involved millions of blackbirds that were creating health and aviation hazards at the Army post. The blackbird problem in Hopkinsville, Kentucky, and Fort Campbell gained national attention in the mid-1970s when Army and local health battled animal rights groups in federal court for permission to use Tergitol to exterminate the birds roosting in the area

Although permission finally was obtained—and, the Army actually sprayed Tergitol on February 19, 1975—most of the birds survived because the weather was not cold enough to kill them. Score one for our fine-feathered friends.

But, enough about rock concerts and birds...The most important thing about 1975 for this former Falcon and his classmates was Graduation Day. Tossing our caps into the air, Fort Campbell's newly-graduated seniors— some probably still recovering from the rock concert—scattered like the wind to the four corners of the Earth after our early June graduation, anxious as ever to change the world.

Mentored by Coach P and many other great educators at FCHS, the Class of 1975 certainly was prepared to get into "The Game of Life." Of course, as everyone would find out sooner or later, it's no easy task to make a good tackle at the start of the game—with little practice or playing time.

The 17- and 18-year-old sons and daughters of soldiers that ventured out into the world in June 1975—just like Falcon seniors of earlier years and the many Falcon seniors to follow in the years to come—thought they knew everything there was to know about anything of importance to anyone anywhere on the planet.

Translation for those scratching their heads: *We know it all, and by the way, we're going to live forever.* Now, think about it. Hasn't that been the mindset of all teenagers since the beginning of time? And, by the way, it will never change.

But, the truth—for those who can handle it, and it always becomes easier to accept with every passing birthday—is that the 17- and 18-year-olds in this world know absolutely nothing about life. Teenagers—in two words—are basically young and stupid, but just don't know it yet. Military Brats are no exception. Being prepared to play the game is different from playing it—and playing it well. It takes a lifetime of experiences—good and bad—before any player gains enough wisdom to know the difference, and can run with it.

And so it was, with high school diploma in hand and not knowing they were young and stupid, the graduating seniors of Fort Campbell's Class of 1975 ventured out into the world, going their separate ways. Some went right to work, some joined the military, and some enrolled in college. (Back in my day, the snooty crowd even teased classmates about another fork in the road: *If you can't go to college, you can always go to Austin Peay.*)

As many of us learned to appreciate in later years, Coach P—with plenty of help from his highly-respected colleagues at FCHS—would always be the glue that held together the special memories and friendships of the Military Brats of the Falcon Nation.

Don't forget now—the mid-1970s were the days before the Internet and social media played such an important role in our lives. So expectations were fairly low on the possibility of ever reuniting with Falcon classmates in the future. Because FCHS was on an Army post, with a transient military population, the chances back then were slim to none for successfully organizing a high school reunion that is so common to civilian communities. Those who sought out old classmates lived a nightmare of frustration and heartache. It really took an extraordinary event for the post-high school sons and daughters of soldiers to return to the area in those early years after their graduation. And more times than not, the event that brought them home was not a happy one.

For the Class of 1975, there was at least one such occasion—the funeral of Charles Cunningham, a football player who was one of "Marshall's Boys." Charles—Coach P called him "Charlie"—was the previously-mentioned classmate who had planned to join the Navy with his best friend, Mike Hellums, but apparently changed his mind at the last minute.

Less than two years after our high school graduation—on Friday, February 4, 1977—Charles Cunningham died from injuries sustained in a late-night traffic accident on Kentucky 911 in Oak Grove, Kentucky, not very far from Charlie's Steak House. The fatal wreck occurred just six months after Mark Sabin—a FCHS student known to me and many of my 1975 classmates, although he was four years younger—was killed in a motorcycle wreck near Gate 2 on the Army post.

At the time of the Cunningham tragedy, I was living in Hopkinsville, Kentucky, and finishing up my studies at Hopkinsville Community College, after transferring there from Western Kentucky University. Later that same year, I moved to Richmond, Kentucky, where I attended Eastern Kentucky University for three years and earned bachelor's degrees in police administration and journalism.

Services for Charles Cunningham were held at a funeral home in downtown Clarksville, Tennessee. The chapel was packed with many familiar faces from high school. Teachers and classmates came to grieve and pay their final respects. And, of course, Coach P and his three assistant football coaches—Coach Mills, Coach Bell, and Coach Cobb—were there, supporting the Cunningham family.

For me, and I'm sure many of my former classmates, the heartbreak was mind-numbing, shocking and totally unexpected. Charlie's death served as an early reality check. Remember, everyone in the Class of 1975 was supposed to live forever. He had signed my senior yearbook with a message of hope and optimisim—haunting to this day—that expressed that very sentiment. *"It's been great knowing you these last four years. We've had some great times and they're not going to stop anytime soon. Now that we've graduated, we're stepping into a new world. But hopefully, we'll both make it."*

This was the first funeral for me. And, it also was the first time I had had an up-close and personal encounter with the cruel hand of death, even though I still had haunting memories of the 1972 football season when teammate Dan Tant's little brother drowned while playing in a flooded drainage ditch in Stryker Village, near the high school on post.

I will never forget the unbearable grief of the Cunningham family, the kind words spoken to me by Charlie's father—who had been an active member in the FCHS Booster Club—and the strength and steadiness of Army parents like Q.T. and Betty Hellums. The Hellums and Cunningham families were especially close because of the strong, brother-like bond between the Hellums' second-oldest son, Mike, and Charles Cunningham.

Apparently, unable to get leave from the Navy, Mike Hellums could not attend the funeral. But Q.T. Hellums and other family members were there for the Cunninghams, in his place. A "soldier's soldier," who was no stranger to death and tragedy, Mr. Hellums—with his firm hand on my shoulder—helped me get through a most difficult day that included the "viewing" of a dearly departed friend and football teammate.

Other somber gatherings, shaped by the dark side of life, were in the cards for the Fort Campbell community in the years to come. The shocking death of Ced Perry occurred just four years later while I was working as a reporter for *The Morehead News* in Morehead, Kentucky, following my final year of college at Eastern Kentucky University.

But, on the whole, it would be more than 20 years after the Charles Cunningham funeral before some of the familiar Falcon faces of my youth began to find their way back into my life on a regular basis.

Of course, in the meantime, there were some exceptions. Preston Owens, in the days since high school, had become a friend for life. Over the years, he often would visit me in Hopkinsville whenever he came home to Clarksville to see his folks. Many new memories in our friendship also were made during shared vacations out West, driving the Pacific Coast Highway in California and searching for Mark Twain in the wilds of Nevada. One of the sweetest memories of our enduring friendship took place in Virginia City, Nevada, on a magnificent day in August 2000, punctuated by a glorious sunset. Sitting in a hot, stinking, hole-in-the-wall bar—with hundreds of brassieres hanging from the ceiling, apparently donated by happy female patrons—two extremely lucky sons of soldiers enjoyed the music of our youth, drank a few beers and watched the parade of life in the Wild Wild West.

Every now and then over the years, I also bumped into old classmates still living in the Clarksville area—like brothers Allen Hayes (Class of 1976) and Gary Hayes (Class of 1975), while they were attending Austin Peay State University or Ron Alvarez (Class of 1975), who was busy building houses and his construction business. Two of the three (Allen Hayes and Ron Alvarez) played football for Marshall Patterson. Gary Hayes, a tennis player, was mentored by Rocky Cobb. Not surprisingly, Coach P—always looking out for his boys—helped Allen Hayes get a job at the bus station on post so the former Falcon lineman could pay his bills while going to college.

The author also recalls an occasion when he danced the night away with Cheri Horan-byard and Ed Horan at the old 1191 Nightclub on Fort Campbell Boulevard in Clarksville, a year or so after high school graduation. Of course, I was dancing with Cheri—not her brother, Ed. On that particular night, my sister Adele and I were only doing our father a favor by entertaining two wild and crazy guys that had worked with him as government contractors over in Iran and were visiting our family while vacationing in the States. Their names escape me, but one was from Ireland and the other from Scotland. They didn't dance much, but they sure liked to drink—and not milk. The favor for Dad turned into a bar-hopping "all-nighter," and it just so happened the next day marked the beginning of a new semester at Hopkinsville Community College. So, of course, I had to crawl to my classes in misery early that morning, a feat only possible for the young and really stupid. It was a good thing I fit the description so well.

On other occasions after high school there were times when a former Falcon might come to town to visit friends and relatives, resulting in a short walk down Memory Lane. In the early 1980s, Lance Morrison (Class of 1973)—a teammate of mine on Coach P's 1972 football team, who at the time was living in New York—surprised me when he walked into the newsroom of *The Leaf-Chronicle* in Clarksville where I was working as a reporter. He joked he was looking for Walter Cronkite, but would settle for me if I had the time to spare him. Our visit that day was short, but sweet, and included many stories about Coach P and the days at FCHS.

Not long after the Lance Morrison rendezvous, there was another unexpected walk down Memory Lane for me. One weekday night, while minding my own business at my Clarksville apartment, I got a mysterious telephone call. Some people might even call it disturbing. "Joe, we're down here waiting for you," teased a familiar voice from the past. It was JD Baker, the pint-sized hell-raiser two years behind me in high school. He demanded that I report immediately to "The Library"—not the library with the books, but the drinking establishment near the Austin Peay State University campus. Knowing JD like I knew JD, I could have figured out the destination without his instructions. When I arrived at the The Brary, I heard the infectious, loud laugh of Chuck Powell (Class of 1973) and then quickly spotted him holding court with a table full of smiling ex-Falcons. Now, thinking back, I'm fairly confident it was Chuck Powell who was responsible for pegging me with my high school nickname. A Falcon football great as a bruising fullback, Chuck apparently was the first person to recognize my uncanny resemblance to my football hero during high school—Joe Namath of the New York Jets. Namath was known to the world back in those days as "Broadway Joe." The first time Mr. Powell saw me—a skinny, hunch-backed sophomore, with a big nose and shaggy hair—throw a football 50 yards down the field, his jaw dropped to the ground. The Big Guy was amazed, or at least he pretended to be amazed. He immediately began calling me "Joe Willie," which then morphed into "Broadway Joe," and finally "Joe" for the purpose of small talk.

The details of that night so long ago at The Braryare fuzzy now—forgive me for I must have had way too much to drink—but JD Baker (Class of 1977), his big brother,Ken Baker (Class of 1974), and Ray Soyk (Class of 1976) definitely were part of the pleased-as-punch group enjoying that mini-reunion. Tim Childress (Class of 1977)—it was No. 34 who caught one of the only TWO career touchdown passes ever credited to bench-riding Robert "Broadway Joe" Dollar—may have been there, too. But, if he wasn't, he should have been since it was one of his favorite watering holes, and it would have given me another opportunity to retell that amazing story about the perfect touchdown pass. Tim's younger sister, Debbie, who worked at the bar for a few years while going to college at APSU, probably had heard the story hundreds of times. After all, I was known as a regular at The Brary, where I continued making passes—at the ladies, and not with a football. I'm guessing Debbie Childress heard the tale again that night, probably with a string of other stories about Coach P and high school.

In the early- to mid-1980s, there were several attempts to organize FCHS reunions. But, the very few reunionsthat actually got off the ground—including a multi-class event held at the old Fort Campbell Officers' Club near Cole Park in 1988, with the theme, "Through The Years"—more often than not attracted sparse crowds. The celebration on post, for example, pulled together only 10 of the 122 graduates from the Class of 1975—Tanna Darby, Adele (Dollar) Oates, Debbie Steinhorst, Joanie Fendler, Cheri Horan-byard, Mike Childress, Alan Garcia, Hal Block, Perry Elder, and Glenn Patrick. Locating classmates scattered around the world apparently was just too difficult a task to overcome—until Al Gore, or whoever it was, invented The Internet. Now, I wasn't lost in those days. I just wasn't ready to take that walk down Memory Lane that soon after high school graduation. So, I couldn't have been dragged to a reunion.

The invention of the World Wide Web in 1989 and its subsequent availability years later to the public, at large, definitely was the game-changer for FCHS reunions, opening the doors for the successful events so common these days.

So, who deserves the credit for getting the ball rolling? My vote would have to go to Hale Strasser, a 1991 graduate of Fort Campbell High School. It was Mr. Strasser, an Information Technology professional now living in Iowa, who, in 1997, designed and set up a Fort Campbell High School Forum out there in cyberspace. For years, Hale Strasser served as the administrator for the popular web site, which had multiple threads and other features that enabled FCHS graduates from the 1960s, 1970s, 1980s, and 1990s to post messages and photographs. The new technology made all the difference in the world, with word about the FCHS forum site spreading like wildfire throughout the Falcon Nation.

As a result, Fort Campbell High School took the bull by the horns and for the first time ever in July 1998 organized a multi-class reunion on post that attracted hundreds of former Falcons from across the country. Graduates from 1963 through 1998 attended the reunion. Hale Strasser served on the reunion steering committee, and with his efforts, the event attracted the largest turnout ever for FCHS alumni through that point in time. With encouragement from Hale and high school officials, the author of this book—then a newspaperman in the area—helped out with the publicity efforts for the reunion. My direct involvement persuaded me to attend the big event, which included tours of the old high school and junior high and a banquet/dance at the Top 5 Club. It was my first high school reunion—23 years after leaving FCHS. Although my era at FCHS was underrepresented in terms of turnout—Preston Owens, Rene Ramirez, and David Blackwell were the only faces familiar to me—the event afforded me the opportunity to reunite with teachers I hadn't seen in more than 20 years. Coach P probably made an appearance at the reunion—even though he was busy with the start-up of the football season—but I don't remember seeing or talking to him. Before leaving the fort, I couldn't pass up the opportunity to drop by a place that will forever be special to me: The duplex on the Tennessee side of the Army post that my family, The Dollars, called home for nearly five years—*1335-B Werner Park*. The homecoming was the icing on the cake, and it was captured in a photograph taken by old friend Preston Owens.

Later in 1998, FCHS graduates from the Class of 1974 and Class of 1975—prompted by the success of the summer reunion—reunited for a three-day weekend in early October in Nashville, Tennessee. My old college roommate, Ken Baker, organized the gathering, which was held in a hotel off Elm Hill Pike, near the Nashville airport. The reunion included a reception and hospitality suite at the hotel, golf at Fort Campbell, a dinner at Nashville's 101st Airborne Restaurant, and a cookout and pickup basketball game at the Nashville-area home of Davida (Flippo) Boltz (Class of 1974). At least one FCHS teacher made an appearance at the reunion—Nancy Hicks, who, as it turns out, was quite a favorite with this particular crowd of former Falcons. For a guy who had never been hip on reunions, there was no way I was going to miss out on this fabulous get-together from the get-go—even though it was right on the heels of the summer reunion. I guess I had finally caught the reunion fever. So, after avoiding reunions for more than 20 years, yours truly now had managed to put two under his belt within a three-month period.

The Nashville reunion arguably was one for the record books. The attendees—Eric Shemwell, Bob Eddy, Bruce Yuhas, Earl Linton, Buzz Sanders, Lisa Jones, Steve Cardenas, Debra Soyk, Rhonda Hill, Ken Baker, Mike Coston, Mike Gentry, Ed Overcash, Karen Cooley, Davida (Flippo) Boltz, Debbie (Russell) Rager, Sabrina (McBrayer) Alls, and Laurie Perry from the Class of 1974; Mike Rose, Debbie Cardenas, Ron Alvarez, and the author, Rob Dollar, from the Class of 1975; and Vickie (Flippo) Bouse from the Class of 1976—painted the town of Nashville red. Several Honkey Tonks were visited, where too many adult beverages were enjoyed and probably too many lies swapped. Without going into too many details that might get some people into too much trouble, the sight of old, cigar-smoking classmates baring their souls and sharing their lives—including stories of tattoos in all the wrong places—almost moved me to tears. It was quite touching—maybe even inspiring for a group of Military Brats who would always consider themselves "Falcons Forever."

As an aside, Mike Hudgin, a popular member of the Class of 1974, was there at the Nashville reunion—but only in spirit. Remembered by his classmates as a prankster and all-around nice guy, he chose a career in the military after graduating from high school and later Austin Peay State University. On March 2, 1992, Army Captain Mike Hudgin died in his sleep of an apparent heart-related ailment while attending an Army school in Oklahoma. His death came about two weeks before his 36th birthday. A Gulf War veteran, Mike Hudgin was someone who made the people around him enjoy and appreciate life. The guy was a real cut-up—pure and simple. He couldn't act serious if he was serious about it. There was plenty of cutting up during the 1973 football season when Mike Hudgin, Preston Owens and the author were sidelined with knee injuries. No football for this trio, but we kept the rest of the team pretty loose. After high school, in the late 1970s, Mike briefly dated my sister, Adele, and immediately got on my father's bad side for routinely bringing her home late after their dates. On one of those dates in May 1978, an early-evening tornado actually hit Hoptown and damaged a few neighborhoods near our house. No one, at the time, knew where Mike and Adele were, or if they had been hurt, until they returned home—LATE that night, not knowing anything about a tornado. So, with my family, Mike Hudgin always will be remembered by the nickname that my father tagged him with: "MIDNIGHT." The story behind his nickname still makes me smile whenever I think of him.

Nearly 13 years after the Music City reunion, those great memories turned bittersweet forever with word of the premature death of classmate and reunion host Davida (Flippo) Boltz. A retired Army nurse and captain, Davida died on July 24, 2011, after a 12-year battle with Lupus. She was 55 years old.

Hale Strasser kept the Fort Campbell forum site active, serving as its administrator, for more than 10 years. He finally shut it down after everyone and their brother started communicating through social media—particularly on Facebook. It wasn't long after that that several group pages for FCHS alumni suddenly appeared on Facebook, and as a result, it's been almost like a picnic nowadays to organize a reunion or track down a long-lost classmate.

Rob Dollar, an older and wiser alumnus of Fort Campbell High School, visits his old home in Werner Park while on the Army post for a multi-class reunion that took place in early July 1998. (Photo by Preston Owens)

One of the most pleasant surprises of reconnecting with old classmates has been the discovery that love may indeed conquer all…Many romances that started at Fort Campbell High School eventually led to marriages that are still going strong these many decades later. Those that come to mind include: Stan and Barbara (Scharn) Nelson, Stan and Ruth (Miller) Jackson, Don and Patti (Gillen) Hutchinson, Ronnie and Debbie (Monaghan) Chapman, Dale and Debbie (Teague) Kesterman, Steve and Joanne (Nagrod) Bryant, Chuck and Vicky (Cox) Powell, and Ben and Anna (Ashworth) Hellums.

Now for another keen observation: When it comes to reunions, there's something that always seems to happen at these celebrations, and it never fails to amuse me. Not to be judgmental, but have you ever noticed that memories are fuzzy, at best, at most high school reunions? Many classmates can't remember much of anything that happened back in the

212

day, particularly if the deeds were bad or embarrassing. The forgetfulness might be a case of convenient amnesia or maybe just a symptom of old age, I suppose. Nevertheless, at every reunion I've attended over the years, there have been few, if any classmates, with memories like elephants. Nobody ever remembers doing anything stupid back in high school like some of the stupid things taking place nowadays in the classrooms across this country. I guess, when it comes to raising our kids and grandkids, there's only one comeback that matters: "Do as we say, not as we did."

But the memory lapses often are so surreal. No recollections of such youthful indiscretions as…Streaking…Hanky-Panky…Under-age drinking…Driving drunk…Smoking cigarettes…Toking on marijuana (but certainly not inhaling)…Two-timing a boyfriend or girlfriend…Dirty dancing…Dressing defiantly…Acting like a bully, smart-ass or fool…Rebelling against authority….Cheating in the classroom…Shading the truth…Locker room talk ("Jo Jo's Garage could not have pulled me off of her.")

Nothing ever happened at Fort Campbell High School, right? BULLCRAP. Let's not fool ourselves. Some of those aforementioned sins of reckless youth—and perhaps conduct much worse—occurred at FCHS, too. Take my word for it. I was there walking the halls, and I wasn't blind and deaf. Dumb? Maybe, but it didn't take me long to wise up—especially once I figured out the reason a few athletes were handing their "pee cups" to teammates to fill for them during pre-season physicals at the hospital. Although I was much tamer than many of my classmates when it came to bad conduct, I certainly was no babe in the woods, either. During my senior year, I was an angry and confused young man, lashing out at the world. I blamed Coach P for not letting me play football. I didn't understand, at the time, he was only teaching me "The Game of Life." Robert Dollar was—in the words of Forrest Gump—*"Stupid is as Stupid does."* Sometimes, I shudder at the thought of some of the stupid things I did back in my high school days. *There but for the grace of God go I…*

Let me offer up two stories that will give readers a hint of my nagging guilt. But please know that neither tale of juvenile misconduct comesclose

213

to hitting the top of the Stupid Gauge that measured my stupidity as a high schooler.

The cool thing to do when I attended FCHS was to meet up at the Teen Club and then head out—sometimes in one car or in a caravan—for a road trip to scare up a good time at the Bell Witch property in Adams, Tennessee. In the early 1970s, the trip was about 35 miles one way—traveling to the end of Tiny Town Road, taking a left and eventually hitting U.S. 41 in Trenton, Kentucky, and then heading south through Guthrie, Kentucky, before rolling back into Tennessee and the city limits of Adams.

Of course, the first stop on every trip was the convenience store to pick up some beer. On one of those party nights, the author was driving his sporty Mustang through downtown Guthrie, returning to Fort Campbell, when one of his three passengers tossed a beer bottle out the window. The incident occurred in front of the police station, and the bottle actually bounced and hit a police car occupied by two police officers. Within minutes, there were blue lights behind me, and I pulled my car over to the side of the road. Because I'm such a good guy, my accomplices in this dastardly crime shall remain nameless. But, four Military Brats believed, for sure, they were going to be spending the night in jail. Thank God the police officer in charge gave the "Fort Campbell boys" a break since no one was intoxicated and the only contraband in the car was an 8-pack of Miller Ponies. Our only punishment that nightmare of a night was a stern lecture about the dangers of tossing items from a moving car. Officer Friendly confiscated the beer, too.

Many years later—when I was older, less stupid, and working as a reporter for the *Kentucky New Era* in Hopkinsville—the same nice lawman from my troubled past decided to run for sheriff of Todd County. He came to the newspaper offices to make his formal announcement, and as fate would have it, I was the reporter assigned to interview him. He didn't remember me, and I decided not to remind him of the incident that occurred when I was young and stupid. I didn't want to embarrass him or myself. But, the entire time I was interviewing him, I had a big grin on my face. And, for the first time in years, I was thirsty and had a hankering for a Miller Pony. Needless to say, the lawman received a great front-page story in the newspaper on his candidacy for sheriff—courtesy of a thankful, and smarter, Military Brat. By the way, he won his race for sheriff.

Not long after the Close Encounter of the Jail Kind in Guthrie, those same Fort Campbell boys returned to their wild and wicked ways—cruising for babes and drinking beer. The young and stupid, after all, always are slow at learning their lesson. On a cold winter night, after an uneventful road trip to nowhere, a buddy—he was a football teammate who had had way too much to drink since he wasn't driving—revealed to me for the very first time what he wanted to do with his life after he escaped the bad influences of high school. I think he might have been talking about me. Anyway, after calling it a night, the gang ended up in Drennan Park at a home where the parents were away for the weekend. As I helped my smashed friend inside the house, he suddenly became belligerent and started shouting: "Joe, I'm gonna be a preacher." The rant was repeated over and over, just like a broken record. It got to the point of being ridiculous. While trying to lead my friend over to a couch to sit—or lie—down, he suddenly shoved me, and I went crashing through a sliding clothes closet near the front door. While in the closet—on my butt—the wannabe-preacher told me he was sorry and briefly began sobbing. Gaining his composure, he then added a demand to his religious rant: "Joe, I'm hungry. I want some chili." Not wanting to argue with our big buddy, a can of chili was rustled up and heated on the kitchen stove. Finally, the chili was done, and a large bowl of it was placed on the dining room table for him. By this time, the big guy had found a football helmet in the house and was wearing it. For close to 30 minutes, the Fort Campbell boys watched their inebriated—but content—buddy eat his chili while wearing the football helmet. It was quite a sight to see. Because I was such a bad influence on him, I'm not going to give up his name. Although, my former football teammate achieved great success in later life and rose to the top of his profession, he never became a preacher as far as I know. But, I believe he still loves chili.

DULL never was a word used to describe Military Brats, in my experience as the son of a soldier. Like most red-blooded teenagers in this great country, FCHS students were curious, sometimes bewildered, and most certainly ready for new adventures while trying to find their way in life.

Coach P and the staff at the high school knew—in most cases—what was going on, and worked hard to keep students on the straight and narrow path. But their efforts weren't always successful.

So, sure…Bad decisions sometimes were made back in the day. But, those errors in judgment often resulted in valuable lessons being learned that proved helpful in navigating that long and winding road through life. In my humble opinion, no one should be embarrassed and forced to beg for forgiveness for once upon a time being young and stupid and doing stupid things like every other teenager who's ever walked the Earth. It's a huge step to accept responsibility for mistakes and vow not to repeat them. Learning from those mistakes is part of "growing up" and becoming a responsible and productive member of society. Believe me, there's no greater measure of success for anyone in this life. Forget the money, power or prestige. They mean nothing in the long run, if someone stays stupid—forever.

After high school and college, the author of this book spent 24 years as an award-winning reporter and senior editor at six different newspapers in three states. My journalism career ended in 2003, and it was followed by high-level administrative/communications jobs in city and federal government, and a stretch in the private sector as a staffing supervisor. These days I like to call myself an independent journalist and author. For most of my life, I've lived in Hopkinsville—just up the road from Fort Campbell, where a high school football coach inspired me to do some good and make a difference in this world. The same great man—Marshall Patterson—also taught me the valuable skill of dealing with adversity. And believe me, I've already had more than my fair share of obstacles to overcome in this life so far. I've lost jobs, been the victim of politics and lawsuits, and even had the late Saddam Hussein fire a few scud missiles in my direction. Still, I'm probably a lot more fortunate than many of my old classmates out there.

It was always my job as a newspaperman to chase the truth, wherever it led me. Tell it like it is, and let the chips fall where they may…Therefore, it's not in me, and never has been, to rewrite history so that it's convenient and favorable to my point of view. I'm more than willing to take my lumps. At the same time, I'm not out to embarrass any of my former classmates or teachers about the past. Therefore, no one should lose any sleep about what they've read so far, or will read, in the pages of this book. It's all good—sealed with a pledge that the most extraordinary caution was exercised in the sharing of those special memories of people and events at Fort Campbell High School more than four decades ago. Thanks to Marshall Patterson and other great educators at FCHS, the Military Brats of the Falcon Nation—minus a few bad apples that are in every barrel—turned out to be some outstanding citizens of this great country. That's my opinion, anyway.

For the most part, and with few exceptions, "What happened at Fort Campbell High School stays at Fort Campbell High School." The same standard has been applied to the reports on the FCHS reunions that have taken place over the years. But, as readers already know, mention is made—as it should be—of the FIREBALL THERAPY at these events. Hopefully, no one is offended by this time-honored tradition of remembering dearly departed classmates—with a toast or two or three...It's always been my view that the world would be a much better place if everyone in it celebrated their cherished friendships from the best years of their lives—often and well.

With that thought in mind, keep those fireballs coming this way.

Two students walk down a hall at Fort Campbell High School just a few weeks before graduation for the Class of 1975. Thanks to Coach Marshall Patterson and a few top-notch faculty at the high school, sons and daughters of soldiers were prepared well for "The Game of Life." (Courtesy of Fort Campbell High School)

From left, Preston Owens, Robert "Broadway Joe" Dollar, and Jeff Jacobs sit with their Falcon teammates for a pep rally at Fort Campbell High School during the 1973 football season. The football team posted a 5-4 record that season. (Courtesy of Fort Campbell High School)

CHAPTER 10: 'BROADWAY JOE'

Every Military Brat has a great story to tell, and in most cases, it's about a life that has been challenging, unpredictable, and an adventure from beginning to end. And, when put on the spot, most would insist in a heartbeat they wouldn't have to think twice about living the same extraordinary life again.

Yours truly—"Broadway Joe," as I was once known at Fort Campbell High School—is among those grateful sons and daughters of soldiers who had the opportunity to see the world, and all that's in it, from this most special of views.

It's time now to navigate to the part of the book where the author bares his soul about life as a Military Brat, and how it was he came to meet and befriend one of the greatest high school football coaches in America— Marshall Patterson.

Although I've already shared some of those memories, particularly from the junior high and high school days at Fort Campbell, I want to go back to the very beginning—when it all started—so that everyone can see the complete picture of the Military Brat experience.

The purpose of telling my story is to help readers understand the enormous challenge involved in teaching and coaching Military Brats, who are known for sometimes living difficult and complicated lives. It certainly was no easy task to counsel the children of active-duty personnel and took a special kind of person to get the job done.

So, multiply my story thousands and thousands of times, and everyone should have a pretty good idea about the high mountain climbed by Coach P in his 35 years with the Fort Campbell school system.

Every Military Brat, I'm quite sure, will find my story—The World According to Rob Dollar—familiar since it probably parallels their own experiences as the son or daughter of a soldier. (Note to readers: The author went by his given name of "Robert" from birth through high school, when he picked up the additional nickname of "Joe," which was short for "Broadway Joe." In college and later life, friends and family began calling him "Rob" Dollar and a few other names that aren't printable.)

Here's my Military Brat story, and, believe me, it's no fairy tale:
Once upon a time, the author of this book was known as a proud Military Brat. The life I lived as the son of a career Army officer could not have been sweeter, and I would not trade those years for anything in the world.

I grew up in the old America. It was the era before political correctness, dysfunctional government, destructive greed, and the ridiculousness of social media. No computers, no smart phones, and no stupid Tweets. In the days of my childhood, students carried their books—without a backpack. Teachers used a paddle to maintain order and discipline in the classroom—and parents always backed them up, sometimes even doubling the corporal punishment at home. Back then, schools in this country never had to lock their doors to protect students from crazy people with guns. Out in public, people were much more civil and not so mean-spirited. And, no one ever was asked to take off their shoes at the airport before getting on an airplane.

As a Military Brat, from birth through high school, I lived in many faraway lands and saw some of the wonders of the world that most people will never see in their lifetime and only read about in books. My experiences and adventures over the years—unique to the military life—made me who I am today, and shaped my perspective about the world and the people in it.

Rose and Floyd Dollar pose with their first child – future newspaper reporter and author, Robert "Rob" Dollar – in their home at Fort Sheridan, Illinois, in early 1957. (Courtesy of Rose Dollar)

My father, Floyd Amos Dollar, and my mother, Rose (Savant) Dollar, were born when Herbert Hoover was in the White House. Dad was from Georgia, and Mom was from Wisconsin. They met at Fort Sheridan, Illinois (near Chicago), in the early 1950s. At the time, Dad—who served in Occupied Japan and during the Korean War—had been in the Army for less than a decade after enlisting at the age of 17, and Mom, just a few years out of high school, was working at the Post Exchange (PX). After they married in their early twenties, The Stork made a delivery on November 16, 1956, to a nearby hospital at the Great Lakes Naval Station. Another Military Brat had arrived in the world. It was me. At the time of my birth, Dwight Eisenhower was president. Because he was an old Army general, I immediately liked Ike. My parents liked him, too, but not enough to give me his name. Instead, they named me after my late great-uncle, Robert Stanley Dollar, of Fitzgerald, Georgia. Uncle Robert, who was a sailor in the Navy, had been killed by the Japanese—or maybe sharks—14 years earlier in World War II when his ship was sunk off Guadalcanal in the South Pacific.

Floyd Dollar spends some time with his 3-year-old son, Robert, whlle the Dollar family was stationed in Berlin, Germany, in the late 1950s. (Courtesy of Rose Dollar)

Eleven months after my birth, my sister, Adele, arrived in the world. At the time, Mom and I were living with her parents in Hurley, Wisconsin, while Dad was off serving his country. Four months earlier, in June 1957, my father—after attending a school to become a military policeman—had reported to post-war Germany for his new assignment. It was a year later—in the summer of 1958—before he returned to the States for a 30-day furlough. While on leave, Dad took care of the red tape and paperwork for his family to join him overseas. Before returning to Germany, he drove our family to Columbus, Georgia, to stay with his folks—my grandfather, Ralph Dollar, and step-grandmother, Mary Dollar—until the Army could arrange transportation for the move to Germany.

It was a wait of four or five months, but the call finally came in November 1958. For whatever reason, there was no TWA jetliner in our future. Instead, the Army put the Dollar family into the back of a military transport plane that left nearby Fort Benning in the middle of the night, headed for Berlin, Germany. It was the first time Mom had ever flown in an airplane, and of course, the same was true for 2-year-old Robert Dollar and his 1-year-old sister, Adele Dollar

"I was 26 years old, pregnant, and had two small children with me," recalled my mother, Rose Dollar, who celebrated her 83rd in Hopkinsville, Kentucky, in November 2015. "We were the only ones in the passenger area of the plane…The crew was so nice, and they took good care of us. When we left, it was the week before Christmas…I was so scared, but we got there safe and sound."

Yours truly—amazingly, a veteran of seven decades of air travel—has absolutely no memory of that first experience in the wild, blue yonder, flying off to Germany to meet up with Dad. But, I'm certain as can be that no one asked the Dollar family to take off their shoes when we climbed aboard that bird in December 1958.

A quick history lesson: When World War II ended in 1945, defeated Germany was divided into Soviet, American, British and French zones of occupation. The city of Berlin, though technically part of the Soviet zone, was also split, with the Soviets taking the eastern part of the city. West

Berlin, although surrounded by East Berlin and Communist East Germany, functioned as a free city and political enclave between 1949 and the reunification of Germany in 1990. It was located about 100 miles east of the East/West German border and was accessible by land from West Germany only by a narrow rail and highway corridor.

For the record, our family joined my father in Germany about three months after another young GI by the name of Elvis Presley reported for duty at an Army post in Bad Nauheim. And, only the week after our arrival, Bob Hope showed up in West Berlin to entertain the 3,500 American soldiers serving there. According to a story in the *Chicago Sunday Tribune*, the great entertainer joked during his Saturday, December 27, 1958, Christmas show that West Berlin "was a PX surrounded by Reds." Unfortunately, the Dollar family—due to an exhausted mother-to-be, with two energetic toddlers, adjusting to "living on the economy" while waiting for government quarters—missed out on the Bob Hope show. "I remember hearing about it, but we didn't go," Rose Dollar said. It's too bad I missed the show. Because, if I had seen Mr. Hope as a toddler in Germany, I could have thanked him for the memories, in person, just more than 30 years later, when—as a newspaper reporter—I interviewed him at a charity event in Nashville, Tennessee. The world is small, and strange, indeed.

Living in divided Berlin—about 13½ years after the end of Adolph Hitler and World War II—was no picnic. The city had nearly been destroyed during the war, and its reconstruction still was years away from completion. Dad, as an MP, provided security on trains running from the West, through East Germany and into the free sector of Berlin. He was away from home a lot, leaving my Mom to take care of the family business. In May 1959—about five months after our family's arrival in Berlin—my sister, Linda, was born at the post hospital. Although an American, because her birth took place in Germany, she also became an automatic German citizen. Sister Dede—born in January 1961 after Dad had been reassigned to Frankfurt in Central Germany—became the second member of the family to gain the privilege of dual citizenship. My mother, during her many years as a military wife, was a stay-at-home-mom, so she was always there for her kids—often times having to fill the roles of mother and father. The Dollar family was rich because of the simple things in life—not for having a lot of stuff and two or three cars in the garage. Mom, in fact, never even learned to drive.

Not surprisingly, I remember little to nothing about our family's great adventure in Germany since I was only a small child in those days. But, amazingly, the oldest memory I have of my childhood involves an incident that occurred less than six months after arriving in divided and dangerous Berlin. The memory has always been quite vivid in my mind, probably because the experience was so traumatic. Not long after sister Linda was born in May 1959, the author and sister Adele—only toddlers—wandered away from home. The panic created by our disappearance—even though the Dollar kids were missing for less than an hour —nearly created an international incident. Of course, the initial fears were that Adele and I might have been kidnapped and driven into East Germany—never to be seen again while growing up as good Communists. At the time of the incident, I was almost 3 years old. I remember—like it was yesterday—that Adele and I were outside, playing in a sandbox, when Mom went into the house to check on baby Linda, who was sleeping in her crib. "I was only gone for a few minutes, and when I came back outside, the kids were gone," Rose Dollar said, recalling the incident. Yours truly remembers climbing out of the sandbox and walking up the road hand-in-hand with Adele, until she went one way and I headed in another direction. Of course, when Mom came out of the house and saw that her two kids were gone, she called the MPs and they immediately started looking for us. Before long, they located Adele, just around the block, not far from our house. While a neighbor looked after Adele and baby Linda, Mom and the MPs went searching for me. A hunch led them to the Post Exchange (PX). The store, just up the street from the Dollar residence, apparently was still trying to sell its Easter candy. Just as they arrived and parked the MP car, little Robert Dollar walked out of the PX carrying a large CHOCOLATE BUNNY. I remember Mom yelling at me, and the MPs taking me and her home—without my loot. The chocolate bunny was returned to the PX. In the years to come, as I grew older, I would turn the focus of my attention from chocolate bunnies to Playboy bunnies. But that's another story. Later that night, when my MP father got home from riding security on the Berlin trains, I'm quite sure the disappearing act was high on the family list for discussion and behavior modification. The spanking that Dad gave me for that early run-in with the long arm of the law is a bad memory I've managed to conveniently suppress over the years.

Other than wandering off and nearly giving my Mom a stroke, nothing else exciting happened during the Dollar family's three-year tour in Germany. I was too young for school, travel and love. I never saw Elvis or wrote on the Berlin Wall. In fact, there was no Berlin Wall when our family lived in Hitler's capital city. The wall was not even put up until August 1961—five months after our family returned to the States. Our last year in Germany was spent in Frankfurt, a major financial hub where Germany's major autobahns and railways intersect. When it was time to leave Germany, the Dollar family returned to the States—together, and on a commercial jetliner.

Sometime in April 1961, my father reported for duty at Fort Rucker, Alabama, and our family lived there through the end of December 1962. Upon our arrival, John F. Kennedy had just become the new president of the United States. Sweet Home Alabama, in those days, was anything but sweet although the Dollar kids were much too young to realize it. Alabama, in the Deep South, was among states that enforced segregation through "Jim Crow" laws. The Army and its on-post facilities were integrated, but the races were separated outside the gates of Fort Rucker. Sister Adele and I—although 11 months apart, with me having a late birthday—started kindergarten together on post in August 1962, about the same time Marshall Patterson launched the Fort Campbell High School football program with an integrated team up in Kentucky. Paul "Bear" Bryant, that very autumn, was in his fifth year as the football coach at the University of Alabama, and his starting quarterback was Joe Namath—the same fellow, who, in later years, would become the football hero of a backup quarterback at FCHS by the name of Robert "Broadway Joe" Dollar. Like the time spent in Germany, I don't remember much about those early years in Alabama. But, I've always had a rather vivid memory of an older girl in the neighborhood – a "cougar" in training – playing "Doctor" with me, and a few other playmates reporting the incident to my mother. By the way, 5-year-old Robert Dollar was the patient of the 7-year-old girl, who apparently had big dreams of practicing medicine. The infamous tallywacker-tickling incident occurred around the same time as the Cuban Missile Crisis. Although I don't remember those 13 terrifying

226

days in October 1962, I'm sure my Dad was on edge. After all, Fort Rucker was within the range of nuclear destruction, and the American invasion of Cuba that was under discussion at the time would likely have involved him and other soldiers from Army posts in the South.

FORT RUCKER ELEMENTARY SCHOOL,
Fort Rucker, Alabama
1963-64

At left is the official 1963-1964 school year photograph of the author's first-grade class at Fort Rucker, Alabama. Only schools on military posts were integrated at the time in the Jim Crow South. The author is at the center desk, wearing glasses. (Courtesy of Rose Dollar)

In January 1963—just as George Wallace became governor in Alabama and declared, *"Segregation now, segregation tomorrow, segregation forever"*—Dad began a one-year tour of duty in Korea, while our family waited for his return to the States at my grandmother's house in Hurley. My mother's older brother, Peter Savant, was out of the Army and back in town. So, "Uncle Peter" helped take care of the Dollar family. Frigid, snowy Northern Wisconsin was not anything like sunny Alabama. The climate, culture, and way of life were as different as night and day. In Alabama—"The Heart of Dixie"—30 percent of the population was black during the early 1960s. There were very few—if any—blacks living in Northern Wisconsin back in those days. In Hurley, where the population was well under 2,000, I don't ever recall seeing a black resident anywhere in town. Hurley and neighboring Ironwood, Michigan—12 miles from Lake Superior—were settled by white immigrants during the mid-1880s. They came from Sweden, Germany, England, Italy, Poland and Finland to work in the iron ore mines and lumber industry. It was not unusual, at all, to go anywhere in the Hurley-Ironwood community and still hear residents—particularly the older ones like Grandma Savant, who was born in Italy—speaking in their native tongues. Talk about culture shock. But, it was just part of the Military Brat experience. So is irony. It was a

Hurley native—the FBI's Joseph Sullivan—who led the investigation of the highly-publicized murders of three civil rights workers in Mississippi in 1964. The case was the subject of a hit 1988 movie—*Mississippi Burning.*

Sister Adele and I completed kindergarten in the Hurley School District in late May, and later in the fall of 1963, started first grade at South Side Elementary School—in the very same building, where Mom had attended classes back in the 1930s. Sisters Linda and Dede were still years away from going to school, but they kept Mom busy at home. There are only two things I remember about that year—1963—in the Great North: The tons of snow from January through April, which resulted in snow banks on the streets that hid the houses, and watching the television coverage of JFK's assassination in late November. Both life events apparently made an impression on my young mind.

When Dad returned from Korea in January 1964, the Army sent him—and our family—back to Fort Rucker. The Army post—located less than an hour's drive from the Florida state line, and about two hours from Columbus, Georgia, where my father's parents lived—would be our home until the summer of 1965. Not much had changed in Alabama, where George Wallace still was making headlines in the governor's mansion, and the state remained at Ground Zero for the Civil Rights Movement. The Selma-to-Montgomery March and "Bloody Sunday"—when police attacked 600 civil rights marchers, protesting for voting rights, on the Edmund Pettus Bridge—occurred in March 1965, just four months before the Dollar family left the state and country. Just like our first tour at Fort Rucker, whenever soldiers and their families ventured off post and into the nearby civilian communities, it was a black-and-white world when it came to businesses, restaurants, public facilities, and transportation. In a most ironic situation—only appreciated decades later after the author had grown up and learned his history—I finished the first grade at Fort Rucker Elementary School, in an integrated class on a federal installation in segregated Alabama. Hard as it is to believe, considering what was happening in Alabama in the 1960s, there were two black students in my class, and the teacher was a young black woman named Arrie L. Nolan. I still have the photograph of Mrs. Nolan's 1963-1964 first-grade class: It shows me sitting directly across—desk to desk—from one of those black classmates. While at Fort Rucker that second time around, I started playing Little League baseball, and sister Adele and I made our First Communion. I also recall—in living color—watching the 1964 World Series between the New York Yankees and the St. Louis Cardinals, with my father, on our brand-new console color television. Color television was a big thing in the black-and-white world of the mid-1960s.

Two military policemen are at the center of another jarring memory from the Alabama days. No, they weren't coming after me this time, like in Germany. I remember watching them pull up and park their car in the neighborhood, before walking into the woods just down the street from my house. After a few minutes, the MPs returned to their car with a GIANT rattlesnake—dead, I assumed—slung over their shoulders. It took both of them to carry the snake because it was so huge. My eyes bugged out of my head. Not surprisingly, 8-year-old Robert Dollar stopped playing in those Alabama woods. No more berry-picking for me.

Not long after the snake scare, Dad received orders for another overseas assignment. The Army was sending the Dollar family to Vicenza, Italy. Mom—who spoke fluent Italian because her parents had immigrated to the United States from Italy in the early 1900s—was happy with the destination and the fact the family could accompany Dad on his tour of duty. Not caring much for Germany, she sure didn't want to go back there. Now, Italy was another story. It definitely had its perks for a young Army wife with parents who came from the old country. Mom actually had Italian cousins in Asiago, a small town not far from Vicenza, near the foothills of the Swiss Alps. In July 1965, the Dollar family boarded a TWA jetliner in New York City and headed for sunny Italy for Dad's three-year assignment as a supply sergeant. He was assigned to the 5th Battalion of the 30th Field Artillery at Camp Ederle, which was the U.S. Army Garrison in Vicenza under the umbrella of the Southern European Task Force (SETAF). Not long after our arrival, the Dollar family moved into government quarters in a huge housing area a few miles from the Army camp. It was called "Villaggio Della Pace," which—in Italian— means "Village of Peace." Camp Ederle and Villaggio were linked by a free, around-the-clock shuttle bus service. Each large building in the Villaggio housing area accommodated four military families. The Dollar family's address was 223A Villaggio Della Pace. The unfenced vineyards of an Italian grape grower were directly behind our quarters, and nearby were two huge swimming pools, a tennis court, and a basketball court that provided recreational opportunities for Villaggio residents. Vicenza was as beautiful as a post card. Located 25 miles west of Venice and just south of the Swiss Alps, it was widely recognized as one of the most scenic Army posts in the world. There was unrestricted access to Villaggio, and Italian families lived on every side of the American housing area. Everyone was friendly, and some military families even employed the locals—like my family, who had two lovely Italian maids, "Rita" and "Rosina." They showed up at our house on their bicycles a few times each week to help out my Mom with her housework.

The Dollar family lived in Vicenza from July 1965 through July 1968. Sister Adele and I completed third- fourth- and fifth grades at Vicenza American Elementary School, and, as Catholics, made our Confirmation. Sisters Linda and Dede began their school days while our family was in Italy. Back in the mid-1960s, Vicenza's school system for elementary, middle and high school students was located in a single complex on Camp Ederle near the library, movie theater, and Post Exchange (PX). One of the most famous graduates of Vicenza American High School—she graduated and left Italy about three years before I started walking the halls of the school building—later became a famous Hollywood actress. At Vicenza American High School, the student was homecoming queen and a cheerleader for the Cougars. Her name was Sharon Tate, and she starred in the 1967 cult movie classic, *Valley of the Dolls*. Of course, she's probably more famous for being murdered by Charles Manson's drug-crazed "family" out in Los Angeles in August 1968. About a decade after the notorious murder case, while I was a student at Eastern Kentucky University in Richmond, Kentucky, I helped escort the man who prosecuted Charles Manson—Vincent Bugliosi—to a lecture hall on campus. He gave a fascinating talk that day about Charles Manson, who had been born in Kentucky. But, during my encounter with Mr. Bugliosi, the small talk was about tennis, not Sharon Tate the Military Brat. There was another Close Encounter of the Famous Kind during the Dollar family's three years in Italy. At one point in my Dad's assignment in Vicenza, Lieutenant Colonel Peter Abruzzese was his boss and the commanding officer of the battalion responsible for the Army's Sergeant Artillery Guided Missile System. Dad and Peter Abruzzese became lifelong friends, even after the colonel retired from the Army in 1970 and went to work on Capitol Hill. For about three years, from 1971 to 1974, Colonel Abruzzese and his family lived in Alexandria, Virginia, outside Washington, D.C. Their next door-neighbor, at the time, was a man who came out of nowhere to become America's vice president and then president—in less than two years, after the collapse of Richard Nixon's presidency. Peter Abruzzese's friend and neighbor was Gerald Ford, and Ford's daughter, Susan, actually baby-sat for the colonel's family on a regular basis.

The Dollar family—with the kids now much older—took full advantage of living in Italy. Most, if not all, of the major tourist attractions in Northern Italy were visited on family vacations or school field trips—like The Leaning Tower of Pisa, Milan, Venice and Verona. The great art treasures in Florence and Padua were admired, in person, on numerous occasions. And, of course, our family visited—and hosted—my Mom's Italian cousins from Asiago many times. A few of our Italian relatives spoke broken English, but Mom, with her fluent Italian, helped everyone hurdle the language barrier. The patriarch of the Italian family, then in his early sixties, had lived through World War II and enjoyed toasting his hero, Benito Mussolini, at family dinners. My Dad just smiled politely, and drank his wine. World War II had been over for 20 years when our family arrived in Vicenza. But there were still many reminders of the terrible war that was fought on the European continent. Once, I remember a student bringing a Nazi helmet—with a bullet hole in it—to class for Show-and-Tell Day. He had found it in a creek, near his housing area. The World War II souvenir was quite a hit.

In school, tetherball was the big rage, and everybody played it to gain status on the playground. Before I got good at the game and won some respect—as the new kid on the block—I was picked on frequently by some of my classmates. Once, I was sucker-punched in the stomach by two bullies during recess. In later years, when I moved to Fort Campbell, Kentucky, I ran into the little thug who had instigated that schoolyard fight in Italy. He had become a nice guy. It was just another experience of the Military Brat life—reuniting with friends and foes at the next Army post.

Robert Dollar (far left, second row) stands with his Little League baseball team teammates in Vicenza, Italy, in the summer of 1967. In the background is Vicenza American High School. (Courtesy of Rose Dollar)

"We are The Braves. The Mighty, Mighty Braves. Everywhere we go, people want to know. Who we are. So we tell them. We are The Braves. The Mighty, Mighty Braves....."

During three summers in Italy, the author—then 9, 10 and 11—played Little League baseball for the Giants, Braves and Pirates, and fondly recalls the bus trips to nearby Verona to play some of the Little League teams in that Italian city known worldwide for the tale of Romeo and Juliet. There was a season of Little League football in Italy, too. Like many of our friends, the Dollar kids also made it to the movies on post every Saturday after our Catechism classes. In my free time, I collected baseball cards, read the newspaper, and bought and traded comic books.

Everyone was into comic books, I think, because there was no American television to watch. Those were the days, of course, before satellites and cable television. Therefore, the only voices heard on The Boob Tube in Villaggio Della Pace were speaking Italian—and not English. Watching Westerns—with Italian-speaking cowboys and Indians—were a hoot, at first, but soon got old and ridiculous. No television for kids who grew up with TV was a rather cruel torture, but I still managed to make the best out of the sad situation. Military Brats, after all, learn to adapt and overcome any obstacle.

Those three years in Italy were filled with many happy days, but the images of two haunting experiences have outlasted many of the warm memories. In my fourth-grade year, sometime in late 1966 or early 1967, a popular classmate disappeared from class. He was there one day, and then he was gone forever. Finally, there was an explanation for his absence—his father, an Air Force pilot, had been killed in a plane crash during a training accident. The sudden death of a father at war, or on duty performing a dangerous job, always was the worst fear for the son or daughter of a serviceman. But it was a fear every Military Brat had to live with every day. Not long after that tragedy, there was more heartbreak at the American School in Vicenza. On June 5, 1968, near the end of my fifth-grade year, I returned to class from recess around 10 in the morning and discovered my teacher, Gayle Fischer, listening to the radio and crying her eyes out. She had just heard the news bulletin that Robert F. Kennedy had been assassinated during a presidential campaign event in Los Angeles. Kennedy's death came less than two months after the slaying of Martin Luther King Jr. in Memphis. The military community in Vicenza—soldiers and their families alike—shook their heads in disbelief. What was going on back in the United States?

In the summer of 1968, sometime around the middle of July, the Dollar family climbed aboard a TWA jetliner in Milan, Italy, and headed for The Big Apple and America. The biggest excitement on the return trip to the States was during a stopover in Paris, where little sister Dede, who was 7, got sick in the lobby of the airport. It could have been another international incident, but a drink of 7Up saved the day. After Dad completed his tour in Italy, the Army selected him for promotion to warrant officer. He also had orders to go to Vietnam once he finished a military school and completed the requirements for his commission. The war in Vietnam was at its peak in 1968, and this would be my father's first tour of duty in the Southeast Asian country. So, once again, the Dollar family headed for Grandma Savant's house in Hurley—after a quick trip to visit Dad's folks in Georgia—to spend another year waiting and worrying while Dad was at war, serving his country.

The Dollar kids—now 12, 11, 8, and 7—were worldly and wise, and as a result, the extended stay at Grandma Savant's house this time was much different than past visits. During the earlier days, "The Lady with The Stick" would terrorize the Savant house whenever my siblings and I got loud or unruly. Grandma Savant blamed this spiteful woman—never seen, but reported to live just around the corner—for the loud pounding noises heard every time mischief broke out in the house. Apparently, the stick lady didn't like noise. Years earlier, just before the family left for Italy, I had stumbled upon the truth about "The Lady with The Stick." After hearing the pounding noises, instead of running and finding a place to hide, I went down into the basement and caught Grandma Savant pounding on the ceiling with a large stick. Grandma Savant ended her clandestine trips to the basement after getting busted that day by the grandson she liked to call—in her thick Italian accent—"Roberto." Not coincidentally, "The Lady with The Stick" also stopped making her visits to the Savant house. So, for the 15 months the Dollar family spent in Hurley in 1968 and 1969, there were no pounding noises in the big, white house on Second Avenue. Just peace and quiet.

As the "Man of the House," what I remember most about that stay in Wisconsin in the late 1960s was the fear that something would happen to my father overseas. It seemed like every night, while watching television, the news about the Vietnam War was bad and getting worse. Hundreds of soldiers were being killed or wounded every week. In those days, it was not so easy to keep in touch with loved ones. Overseas telephone calls were rare, so people communicated by writing and receiving letters. Because Vietnam was on the other side of the world, and at war, sometimes it would be weeks or even up to a month before the family heard from my father. There was nothing that could be done except to worry—and pray. During this period of time, my siblings and I were enrolled in the Hurley School District and walked a few miles into town every day—even in rain and blizzards—to attend classes. Just like in the earlier days, there still were no minorities in the Hurley school system. The Dollar kids—temporary residents while their father served in Vietnam—also were just about the only students who had not remained classmates year after year since kindergarten. Sister Adele and I completed our sixth-grade year at South Side, and then entered the seventh grade at J.E. Murphy High School in September 1969. It was another unique experience—students from seventh through 12th grade under the same roof. But, the school was a shorter walk, only a block or two behind my Grandma Savant's house. It's not easy being an outsider in any community. Thank God our classmates in Hurley, who had grown up together, accepted the here-today, gone-tomorrow Dollar kids and made going to school there fairly pleasant. As a seventh-grade student in Hurley, I attended my first dance—and actually danced, with GIRLS. I also received the only "C" I ever got in my life—in shop. That was another jarring experience. But I guess I'm lucky I didn't saw off my arm.

It was during the Hurley days in the Swinging Sixties, while on the verge of becoming a teenager, that I also discovered the fine articles in *Playboy* magazine. At the time, I still hadn't had that talk with Dad about "The Birds & The Bees"—not that he could have told me anything I didn't already know, or thought I knew. The memory of man—astronaut Neil Armstrong—taking his first steps on the moon on July 20, 1969, also sticks out in my mind. At the time of the history-making event, the Dollar family was on a Greyhound bus on the way to Detroit, Michigan, to visit my Mom's two sisters and their families.

Sometime in November 1969, Dad, sun-tanned and looking fit, returned from Vietnam. There was no parade or back-slapping from anyone in town. But, it was a happy day for Mom and her kids. And, it also was time to move—AGAIN. Dad already had gotten the word from the Army that Fort Campbell would be his next stop. The tired, reserved warrior relaxed for a week or so before the family left Wisconsin in our early-1960s Rambler station wagon, traveling to Kentucky in the middle of a blizzard. After a day of driving through Wisconsin and Illinois, and a night at a hotel, the Dollar family crossed the state line into Kentucky. A few hours later, just before reaching Fort Campbell, Dad stopped for gas in a small town about 13 miles north of the Army post. The service station was in downtown Hopkinsville. No one knew it then, but one day, the Dollar family would call this Kentucky community HOME.

When the Dollar family passed through the main gate at Fort Campbell around Thanksgiving 1969, the major tenant—the 101st Airborne Division—was still deployed to Vietnam, fighting the war. With the unit's absence, the Army was using the post as a training center for new Army recruits—a mission it performed through April 1972. On a historic note, the All-Volunteer Army—along with the opening up of opportunities to women in the military—was less than five years down the road from becoming reality. For about a week, while waiting to move into our quarters in Werner Park, our family stayed at the fort's guest houses— located, at the time, in a row of World War II-era, white, wood-framed buildings, off of present-day Bastogne Avenue, not too far from Stryker Village.

Sister Adele and I still had our seventh-grade year to complete and enrolled at Fort Campbell Junior High School. At the time, the school was for seventh-, eighth- and ninth-grade students. The new high school—for grades 10-12—on South Carolina Avenue had only opened the year before our arrival at Fort Campbell. Younger sisters Linda and Dede only had a skip and a hop to make it from our new home at 1335-B Werner Park to Jackson Elementary School—about 100 yards up Mississippi Avenue.

As a student at Fort Campbell Junior High School for three years, I was very lucky to have some really outstanding teachers like Sarah Patsy Unfried, Walker McCutcheon and Gary Stewart. Of course, I also have to mention Houston Mills—the gym teacher and assistant high school football coach, who died in 1987. After all, Coach Mills was the guy who made me learn to climb a rope and square dance, and he even introduced my tired and skinny legs to the torture of "The Tree" and "The Twig."

Already, in the pages of this book, I've introduced readers to some of the running buddies—like Preston Owens, Mark Brown and Mike Hellums— who were a big part of my junior high years. And, I've openly shared a few embarrassing memories from the era—including the adventures of "The Spy Club," the bad haircut that ruined a perfect attendance record, hanging out with Country Joe McDonald, and my first kiss. So, there's really no need to go over some of the same ground.

At least one other incident is deserving of a quick mention only because it shows that Military Brats—though smart and disciplined—are not always angels. Sometimes they get into trouble, and sometimes trouble can find them. Sarah Patsy Unfried—bless her soul—learned that lesson the hard way. In the spring of 1971, Mrs. Unfried and the other eight-grade teachers organized a daylong field trip to her husband's large farm in South Christian County. Up to 100 students went on the trip to learn about farming operations and a farm family's way of life. Of course, as is always the case, a few bad apples spoiled the learning opportunity. Misbehaving students managed to damage some very expensive farm equipment during the visit, and some young couples in love even got caught fooling around in the haylofts. The field trip came to an abrupt halt, with buses immediately recalled to the farm to return students to school. It was there in the principal's office, where a handful of Military Brats—including the son of a full-bird colonel—were taught there are always consequences for bad behavior. The instructor of that lesson—it may have been Mrs. Unfried—reinforced the talking points by swinging a large, wooden paddle that left the bottoms of the problem students unbelievably sore for the rest of that beautiful spring day. Maybe even for the rest of the week. Poor Mrs. Unfried…The field trip was a good idea that just didn't work out. I'm not positive, but I'm pretty sure the incident ended the field trips to the Unfried family farm.

Sarah Patsy Unfried, who eventually retired after a long teaching career with the Fort Campbell school system, passed away in January 2010. She was 65 years old. God bless her soul for caring about the sons and daughters of soldiers.

Walker McCutcheon and Gary Stewart, like Mrs. Unfried, were exceptional teachers in the classroom who connected with their students. Each of them was the kind of teacher that no student ever forgets. They had great personalities and made learning something that always was fun and challenging. Mr. McCutcheon—who I've always remembered for being such a dapper dresser and huge Elvis fan—is happily retired these days. He and his wife spend a lot of time in Memphis, Tennessee, looking for Elvis and listening to The Blues. As for Gary Stewart—known today as Dr. Gary Stewart—he went to work as a professor at Austin Peay State University in Clarksville, following his retirement from the Fort Campbell school system.

During my junior high school days, I delivered newspapers every morning before going off to school. Eventually, newspapers followed me into the classroom when I began writing for the school newspaper—*The Jr. HIdrogen Bomb*—as the assistant sports editor during my eighth-grade year. For the life of me, I've never been able to remember a single thing I wrote for that paper, which essentially was a gossip sheet. Nevertheless, I guess the experience certainly was another early clue about my calling in life.

It was while I was an eighth-grader at Fort Campbell Junior High School that I first crossed paths with Marshall Patterson, the football coach at the high school. Every year, Patterson and his assistant coaches put football prospects through "Spring Football" practice to evaluate the team's strengths and weaknesses and prepare for the upcoming season. Junior high and high school students who wanted to play varsity football in the fall were invited to attend the three-week tryouts to showcase their talents. Spring football stretched from the end of February through the middle of March, and ended with the traditional Blue-White scrimmage game. Looking back, I must have been out of my mind at the time for thinking I was ready to play high school football—physically or mentally. In late February 1971—six months before I was to start my ninth-grade year at the junior high school—I was a tall, skinny kid, who might have weighed 120 pounds, soaking wet. I wasn't fast, and I wasn't strong. And, as I'd soon find out, whenever I got hit by kids much bigger than me, it HURT and was no fun, at all. I don't think Coach P or any of the other coaches said two words to me the entire spring; I kind of got lost in the crowd. Nevertheless, I stuck with the program, finished the three weeks of practice and managed to get into the scrimmage game, I think, for a few plays as the running back that didn't get the ball. For some reason— maybe because it wasn't a very pleasant experience for me—I don't recall much about those three weeks of Spring Football other than the first day of practice, and another day when it rained and drills were held inside the gym. What I remember about the first practice was the new guys—many, like me, nervous junior high school students—lining up for our equipment and getting harassed by Ron and Gene Southers. The two brothers, who were a few months from graduation, had been star football players and wrestlers during their careers at FCHS, and they were having a great time that day scaring the daylights out of the "boys" going out for football. Many of those young football prospects quit the team in the weeks that followed after deciding the game wasn't their cup of tea. Sometimes the coaches helped them make that decision. The day it rained cats and dogs—my second memory—is a good example. The rookies believed, because of the bad weather, that it would be an easy day of practice inside the gym, maybe doing some running and lifting weights. The veterans on the football team, aware of Marshall Patterson's coaching practices, knew better. And, with that secret knowledge, they smiled suspiciously. They knew what was coming: "HAMBURGER DRILLS." There were football players in that gym about to get POUNDED like hamburger meat. The dreaded practice session involved players in full gear, divided into two lines, and going one-on-one during full-contact drills on wrestling mats. The echoes from the ferocious hits inside the gym made the practice very loud and intimidating, and it really got vicious when the luck of the draw paired up mismatched opponents—like little me and the biggest guy on the football team. Of course, I got creamed, but taking it like a man—even though I was terrified enough to nearly crap in my pants—earned me some respect and got me through that practice from hell. I've never forgotten it, and the big guy—it may have been Steve Scott or Ron Taylor—who picked up my crumbled body from the mat, concerned enough to offer an apology for hitting me so hard: "Are you OK, little fella?"

There was no Robert Dollar on the 1971 FCHS football team. I passed on the opportunity to be a part of the team when players reported that summer for the start of the football season, knowing I was nowhere near ready to try and play varsity football. Only three freshmen were on the 1971 team—Lee Provow, Darrell Harrison and Steve Lasker. And, as previously noted, three other freshmen—Mike Hellums, John Gomez, and Ron Alvarez—were equipment managers for the team.

When Spring Football rolled around again in late February 1972, I was ready to give it another shot. I knew what to expect, and I had an idea about what I wanted to do on the team—play quarterback. Friends, who knew I could throw the pigskin, encouraged me to try out for quarterback. So, when it came time to pick a position and join that group for tryouts on the first day of practice, I trotted over to where the quarterbacks were working out. Two of them were upperclassmen and starters from the 1971 team—Eric DeLeon and Wes Barnett—and the third, track star Roger Richardson, was a sophomore-to-be, just like me. Marshall Patterson, after spotting me with the quarterbacks, wandered over and asked me—the only guy in the group he didn't know—if I was lost. Apparently, he failed to recognize me as the little guy who nearly was killed a year earlier during the "Hamburger Drills" in the high school gym. Looking Coach P in the eyes, and with a little bit of cockiness, I let him know then and there that I was not lost: "I'm a quarterback," I told him. He grinned, rubbed his head and then said, "OK. Let's see what you've got." The QBs already had begun throwing passes to players trying out for wide receiver, so I was more than ready for my turn. Calling a post route, I heaved a perfect spiral that sailed more than 50 yards through the air and into the hands of the receiver, who caught the ball without breaking stride. The pass play was quite sensational, and everyone around let out a cheer. Coach P, who was watching the action with one of his assistant coaches, raised his eyebrows and chuckled. Walking off, shaking his head, he only had a few words for me: "Stay with the quarterbacks, son." With those words, "Broadway Joe" had arrived on the scene of Falcon Football, anxious to make his mark on the 1972 FCHS football season. It wasn't long after my baptism under fire that Chuck Powell tagged me with that football nickname that would stick with me for life. Before long, even Coach P began calling me, "JOE."

I played football—or more accurately, *tried* to play the game—at FCHS during the 1972, 1973 and 1974 seasons. The only glory I found on the football field was leading pre-game warm-up exercises as one of the Falcon quarterbacks and team leaders. My entire career as a field general, except for a dozen or so plays, was spent on the sidelines—riding the bench. As a junior, in 1973, I injured my right knee in practice before the second game of the year and was out for the entire season. Looking back, I like to joke that my high school football career strangely paralleled Richard Nixon's second term in the White House: It began with high hopes and ended in humiliation and disappointment. Of course, I wasn't a crook or a Republican—just a young, stupid kid who got confused about things and made some bad decisions. In all fairness, Coach P and his assistant coaches tried their best to make a football player out of me. But, the only real talent I had was the ability to throw a football, which wasn't much of an asset on a run-oriented team that rarely ran a pass play.

Now, before continuing with a few high and low points of my three years at Fort Campbell High School, I want to refresh the fuzzy memories of some of my classmates out there. The author was not the only person with a nickname back in the day. Coach P—already known to his wife and childhood friends as "Buddy"—also had a colorful nickname at FCHS. Remember? Many football players and other athletes—in my days at FCHS, anyway—secretly referred to the legendary football coach as "Socket Eyes" or "Old Socket Eyes." I don't remember who came up with the nickname, and that's really not that important. Now, the nickname— I've always wondered whether Coach P knew about it—was certainly not a sign of disrespect. Usually it was a reaction to Coach P doing his job and putting his foot in someone's butt. No one ever wanted to disappoint Marshall Patterson or make him angry, and the nickname reflected the intimidating look that appeared on Coach P's face whenever he was rubbed the wrong way. Everyone loved and respected Marshall Patterson, but there were many days when he wasn't very popular. Most of the time, the anger or resentment directed his way had something to do with the disciplining of a player or the team. Think about it. For a group of football players who occasionally were run up and down the field until their tongues hung out, "Socket Eyes" just didn't seem so unreasonable of a nickname for the coach cracking the whip and blowing the whistle.

Military Brats are not always angels. Therefore, Coach P and the rest of the faculty often had their hands full, maintaining discipline and order in the classroom and on the athletic field. They meant business, too. All students were expected to toe the line when it came to following rules and behaving in a respectful manner. It was unacceptable for athletes to skip school and perform poorly in the classroom. Training rules—like no smoking, and no drinking alcohol—were strictly enforced, and punishment meted out, as soon as school officials got wind of the violation. More times than not, parents helped correct the bad behavior by supporting the decisions of teachers and coaches.—without question. The case of the Falcon "streaker" is a good example. It involved a free spirit who played football with me on the 1973 and 1974 teams, back in the days when the high school was located off of South Carolina Avenue, not far from Gate 4. Before jumping into the shower after football practice one afternoon, the player—a Falcon running back who shall remain anonymous so he can maintain his dignity—was dared to run buck naked from the gym dressing room to the trees near Gate 4, and back. He accepted the dare and bolted out the door, wearing nothing but a smile and his sneakers. After completing the 400-yard dash—at break-neck speed—the nude runner discovered that the door to the dressing room had been locked. So, he started banging on the door, only to have Coach P open it and see him standing there naked. Teammates—especially the instigators of the prank—couldn't stop laughing. But there was no chuckling from Coach P, who didn't find "streaking" particularly funny, even though, at the time, it was a fad sweeping the nation. The same was true for Principal Bill Perry and the football player's father—a high-ranking Army officer. As a result of the incident, the player was suspended from school for a few days. When he returned to school, and football practice, Coach P got the second crack at him—punishing the show-off with an after-practice workout from hell. Even the player's father got into the act, sending his son back to school with a new look—a buzz haircut. The lesson: *If you don't mind showing your ass to everyone, then you shouldn't have a problem showing the world your bald head.*

During my three years at Fort Campbell High School, I participated in numerous activities such as Key Club, National Honor Society, Fellowship of Christian Athletes, and Student Council. Legendary teacher Elinor "Mama" Martin even tried her best to teach me and several sophomore classmates—including Patty Chikalla, Lance Hoffman, Jeff Jacobs, and sister Adele—French as a foreign language. But, I got lost in the learning experience, which to me was like something out of The Twilight Zone. (Pardon my French if I mention here that Patti Chikalla's late father—Colonel Gerald G. "Chick" Chikalla, who had more medals than Audie Murphy—played football at West Point in the early 1950s for an offensive line coach who would become one of Marshall Patterson's coaching heroes—a guy named Vince Lombardi.) In my junior year, I ran for Student Council president and narrowly lost the election, not to my worst enemy but to my best friend—Preston Owens.

My final year at FCHS was nothing to brag about, when it came to football and my relationship with Coach P. Early in the season, it became painfully clear to me that I would not be the team's starting quarterback for the 1974 season. Although I didn't like it, I had to accept the fact that someone better suited to the running game was going to start at QB. My role on the team would be that of a backup signal-caller who had to be ready to save the day—if called on, for whatever reason. While I had reluctantly accepted my fate, for the good of the team, the same was not true for my father. Dad was a great athlete in his day, and it just tore him up that I was riding the bench instead of getting into the game. He believed I was wasting my time, if I wasn't going to get to play. The situation created such a conflict at home that I decided I had to do something to make it go away. And so it was—in mid-September, just before the fourth game of the season—that I marched into Coach P's office one afternoon and announced that I was leaving the team for family reasons. Coach P—sitting at his desk—hardly looked up. My visit was anything but a surprise. I'm sure he believed he could talk me into remaining on the team just like the many other players that showed up at his office every football season wanting to throw in the towel. At some point, he saw that I was serious and his demeanor changed from calmness to agitation as I nervously attempted to explain—and justify—my decision. Now, the last thing in the world I wanted to do was to disappoint Coach P. But, I also didn't want to continue to embarrass my father by not getting any playing time. Dad and Coach P were the two authority figures in my life, so I was really between a rock and a hard place. In hindsight, I guess I could have done a better job of explaining my dilemma to Coach P. But, our conversation was short and to the point, maybe because I was afraid he would talk me out of leaving the team and the turmoil would continue at home. Anyway, after handing him my football equipment, I left his office, with him trailing after me, letting me know in no uncertain terms that I was making a big mistake. Maybe so, but my father sure was happy with the decision when he learned of it. Of course, I knew full well at the time that I was the person who would have to live with the choice I had made for the rest of my life.

Later that same week, when FCHS played Castle Heights Military Academy on the road in Lebanon, Tennessee, my father decided he wanted to go to the Friday night game to watch the team lose without their best non-playing QB. It was a miserable rainy night, but the two of us—along with Mark Brown and his father—made the 150-mile round-trip to sit in the bleachers with the rest of the wet FCHS fans and watch the Falcons easily win the game, 26-7. The fact the team could still win games without me riding the bench wasn't even the worse part of the night. After I had left the team, another senior, Scott Dennis—who played on defense and the specialty teams—inherited my game jersey (No. 12). Of course, at this stage of the football season, the preprinted programs sold at the games still listed Robert Dollar as No. 12 on the Fort Campbell roster. Anybody with half a brain should be able to figure out what happened that rainy night in Lebanon. It turned out to be a sensational night on the football field for Fort Campbell's Robert Dollar, who was making tackle after tackle. Every time the announcer called out my name instead of Scott Dennis' name, I wanted to crawl into a hole. For me, it was total humiliation. Dad, on the other hand, got a good laugh out of his son being recognized as the MVP of the game. With me off of the football team, my father was a happy—and far less tortured—man. And, at this point in my life, that's what counted the most for this son of a soldier.

Despite quitting the football team, I never got the traditional "Quitter's Treatment" from my former teammates, who, I think, understood my predicament. During the remainder of my senior year, I also never had any problems with Coach P. He was one of the Senior Class sponsors, so—as class president—I often worked with him on school projects. He was always cordial, helpful and a true gentleman in dealing with me. But, our relationship was never the same after I left the football team. There seemed to be a distance between us. I even detected what I perceived as a subconscious brush-off whenever I spoke to him at school. Maybe it was my imagination, but I'm pretty sure Coach P started calling me "Robert" much more often than "Joe" once my football-playing days at FCHS were history.

Like most of my classmates, my days as a Military Brat, for all practical purposes, ended with my high school graduation. From there, it was off to college for five years before I embarked on my life's calling as a newspaperman, independent journalist and author.

Dad retired from the Army as a Chief Warrant Officer 3 in late March 1978, ending a 30-year career. Upon his retirement, the Army awarded him the prestigious Legion of Merit. My Mom received a Certificate of Appreciation from the Department of the Army that thanked her for "her own unselfish, faithful, and devoted service" during Dad's career in the Army. The commendation—signed by General Bernard W. Rogers, then the Army's chief of staff—applauded Mom's supportive role as a loyal Army wife: "Her unfailing support and understanding helped to make possible her husband's lasting contribution to the nation." Dad lost his passion for life after he left the Army. In the mid-1980s, my parents' marriage ended, and my father moved to Georgia. He died in early June 1995, just a few weeks before Father's Day. As a tribute, I wrote a column on his legacy that was published on June 17, 1995, in Hopkinsville's daily newspaper—the *Kentucky New Era*—with the headline, "Proud son salutes late father's life of achievement."

Here are the heartfelt words of that column—reprinted in its entirety with the permission of the *Kentucky New Era*—that easily could have been written by just about any son or daughter of a soldier:

Father's Day will be bittersweet for me this year.

For the first time in my life, I won't be able to let my father know just how important he is to me. I won't be able to hug him or laugh with him or even ask him for advice I'd probably ignore.

You see, my father died earlier this month just about the time I started thinking about that Father's Day card I never got the chance to buy. My sisters and I buried him June 6 in his hometown of Fitzgerald, Georgia, where he spent the last few years of a remarkable life.

Let me tell you about Floyd Amos Dollar, a man any son would be proud to have as a father. Dad enlisted in the Army in 1948 as a 17-year-old high school dropout. Hard work helped him to rise through the ranks and retire 30 years later as a chief warrant officer. He was a highly decorated veteran of the Korean War and served two tours of duty in Vietnam with the 101st Airborne Division (Air Assault).

After leaving the Army, Dad found success again as a food services administrator and businessman. Like many career military men, civilian life was a big adjustment for my father. I can still hear his most frequent— not to mention funniest—complaint: "Nobody's in charge out here!"

Throughout his life, Dad loved people and had a wonderful sense of humor. He was an outstanding cook, taught himself how to play the guitar and even returned to school and completed two years of college classes. My father lived life to the fullest and left his loved ones with many great memories.

At his funeral, several of his friends comforted me with the same words: 'Your Daddy was quite a character.' That's something I won't argue. Dad would be the first to admit he was far from perfect. No one is who walks this Earth. He had his faults and weaknesses. In the end, he fell victim to demons that tormented him and then took his life at the age of 63.

Our relationship over the years had its ups and downs, like every father and son. But we loved and respected each other up to the day of his death.

Dad was buried with full military honors at the foot of his grandmother's grave. He wanted his final resting place to be near his beloved grandmother, who raised him after his mother died while he was still a young boy. It was the only request he ever made of me.

Before he was laid to rest, a member of the military honor guard presented me with the American flag that draped his coffin. It was—and I'm sure always will be—one of the proudest moments of my life.

Dad made many sacrifices for that flag. For him, it represented everything good about a country where it was possible for a poor boy from the dirt fields of Georgia to make something out of his life.

I'll always cherish Dad's flag. And when I look at it, hopefully on every Father's Day for the rest of my life, I'll remember all the good that he did in this world.

My Dad, who survived two wars, died way before his time. He missed the opportunity to watch his two grandchildren—Jake Oatts and Jill Oatts, the children of daughter Adele (Dollar) Oatts—grow into fine young adults. And, he never got the chance to meet his great-grandson—Jill's wonder child, Dominic White.

Come to find out, the same—or very similar—sad stories played out for the fathers of many classmates at FCHS. Far too many of these old soldiers—with their supportive military wives—had looked forward to living a long, good life during their retirement years. Unfortunately, it was not in the cards.

Agent Orange—linked to service in the Vietnam War—was responsible for a lot of the premature deaths. According to government officials, about 2.8 million U.S. servicemen — out of 7.4 million who served in Vietnam between 1962 and 1971—were exposed to Agent Orange, one of several potent defoliants deployed by the military to destroy the Vietnamese jungle and, along with it, the hiding places of the enemy.

Only in recent years—thanks to reunions and social media—has the terrible toll taken on the Falcon Nation by Agent Orange become so painfully clear.

Vicky (Craig) Coleman, a 1973 FCHS graduate, lost the father who lovingly called her "Cupcake" as a child to lung cancer caused by his exposure to Agent Orange. A Green Beret who served three tours of duty in Vietnam, he died in 1989 at the age of 57. Vicky's stepfather, a Marine major, also was a victim of Agent Orange. He died in 2011 at the age of 78 from prostate cancer.

Tanna (Darby) Nichols, who graduated with the Class of 1975, reported that her father was 77 years old when he died in 2013. He had suffered for years from type 2 diabetes that the Army eventually blamed on his Agent Orange exposure as a pilot in Vietnam.

Norm Miller, who played on the 1976 state championship football team, lost his father at the age of 72 in 2009. His death from leukemia also was linked to Agent Orange.

At least three other Agent Orange-related deaths of fathers of FCHS Military Brats have been documented already in the earlier chapters of this book: The Mahaffey sisters lost their father at the age of 52 in 1986; the Hellums brothers lost their father at the age of 48 in 1981; and Debbie (Jones) Gifford lost her father at the age of 72 in 2005.

There were many other premature deaths—not involving Agent Orange—of old and gallant soldiers from the Fort Campbell community over the years. Two FCHS classmates—brothers Jeff and Steve Mollohan—lost their father in Vietnam as young kids, and their stepfather in the 1985 Gander air tragedy as adults. Life, for sure, isn't always fair.

But in the end, it always helps for Military Brats to believe—in their hearts, anyway—the words of one of America's most famous generals, Douglas MacArthur: *"Old soldiers never die; they just fade away."*

CHAPTER 11: FORGIVE AND FORGET

Fort Campbell High School may have been more than 30 years in the rear-view mirror, but this old and much wiser former quarterback still had some unfinished business to resolve there with the great football coach who had taught him how to play "The Game of Life."

My Act of Contrition, long overdue, would take place in October 2006 in the unlikeliest of places—the upstairs party room of a smoky bar in downtown Clarksville, Tennessee. It was in that bar, where I made my peace with Marshall Patterson.

For "Broadway Joe"—the author of this book—The Road to Redemption had begun almost a decade earlier with a mysterious e-mail that showed up out of the blue one day on my relatively new, first-ever home computer.

With the subject line, ANOTHER OLD FRIEND, the Sunday, June 14, 1998, e-mail read: *"My man Dollar! This is another blast from your past. We played lots of tennis together at Cole Park and drove around in that blue Mustang. Guess who?"*

The sender's e-mail address was not familiar to me. But, I knew right away the cryptic message was from the girl I had taken to my high school Junior-Senior Prom back in the spring of 1975—the former Miss Julie Mahaffey. Yes, the same beautiful girl who later dated Coach P's son—Stephen Patterson.

More than two decades after leaving high school, Julie—now Julie (Mahaffey) Augeri—was serving in a command post with the Army Reserve out in Arizona. Married to an active-duty Army officer, Julie and her husband, Rich—they met in the early 1980s at Officer Candidate School (OCS) at Fort Benning, Georgia—were the proud parents of two children.

Over the years, I had lost touch with the Mahaffey sisters, just like most of my other high school classmates. Julie and Selene attended FCHS in the mid-1970s when I was there, while Melissa, the youngest, was in junior high. The oldest of the girls, Lorrie, was the one I knew the least, only because she had graduated from high school in Virginia. But, life is strange. As it turned out, ironically, Lorrie Mahaffey was the only Mahaffey girl that stayed on my radar screen—only because she became a national celebrity and television star. A singer and actress, she met *Happy Days* television actor Anson Williams while working as a singer on a variety show in Nashville, Tennessee. The next thing I knew she had a recurring role on *Happy Days* and later starred in another television series, *Who's Watching the Kids?* Lorrie and Anson Williams got married in California, and I read about the beautiful mountain-top wedding in the January 2, 1979, issue of *The Star*. The tabloid story on the nuptials included a photograph of the bride, groom, and the entire Mahaffey family—including my missing classmates. Unfortunately, like many Hollywood marriages, things just didn't work out for Anson and Lorrie. Thankfully, the lovely lady found true happiness years later in a new marriage with her true soul mate in life.

Miss Julie and I reconnected at a time when the Internet was only a few years old, and everybody and their brother was using it to try and locate old friends. While reading *Stars & Stripes*—the newspaper that serves the American military community—earlier that year, she came across a story about the July 1998 multi-class reunion at Fort Campbell High School. After further research, she located a newspaper column I had written to promote the reunion. The column led her straight to me. Julie was unable to attend the July 1998 reunion, and she also missed the reunion in Nashville three months later.

However, she made it clear to me she was quite adamant in her desire to reunite with our old high school crowd at least once—before the sands of time had run out. But, of course, time waits for no man or woman, and life got busy and crazy for many people—particularly soldiers and journalists—after the September 2001 terrorist attacks on America. During those early years of two wars and too much fear, there was little talk of a Fort Campbell High School reunion. Plans were put on hold. Contact with Julie was rare. Her military responsibilities got ramped up a few notches, after all, and I was running a daily newspaper, even doing some reporting from Kosovo and the Kuwait-Iraq border.

In the years that followed our cyberspace reunion, Julie and her family—as a result of a new military assignment—moved from Arizona to Huntington Beach, California. It was there in that seaside city in Orange County that she literally ran into Tina (Nitch) Figarsky, a 1977 FCHS classmate. As it turned out, the two former Falcons had been living just around the corner from each other for more than a year and didn't know it. Taken as a sign from God, Julie and Tina, unbeknownst to me, almost immediately began laying the groundwork for a reunion of the 1975, 1976, and 1977 classes at Fort Campbell High School.

Sometime in early 2006, Colonel Julie (Mahaffey) Augeri contacted me unexpectedly to help her and Tina (Nitch) Figarsky make the reunion a reality for that coming October. By this time, Julie's family was living in Virginia, while she was on active duty as the commander of the 3300th Strategic Intelligence Group at Bolling Air Force Base in Washington, D.C. Still in Hopkinsville, Kentucky, I had left the newspaper business and now was working in city government, serving as the executive assistant to the Mayor of Hopkinsville. My boss and close friend—Rich "Da Mayor" Liebe—was a retired police detective who had served in the Army at Fort Campbell during the mid- to late-1970s.

Thanks to Hale Strasser's Fort Campbell High School Forum web site out in cyberspace, the Reunion Committee—Julie, Tina, and me, soon to be joined by Mark Brown, our old classmate living in Connecticut—already had the perfect vehicle to organize and promote the reunion. The forum also provided an opportunity for the reunion organizers to have some fun while trying to coax reluctant classmates into committing to the event. The daily banter between old classmates was nothing short of hilarious. It helped build the excitement for the reunion, which was scheduled for Friday, October 13, 2006, through Sunday, October 15, 2006.

Tina (Nitch) Figarsky, a 1977 FCHS graduate, holds a birthday cake while fellow Falcon alumni help Coach Marshall Patterson celebrate his 72nd birthday at Fort Campbell's Fryar Stadium in October 2006. The birthday surprise took place during a reunion of the 1975, 1976, and 1977 FCHS classes. (Courtesy of FCHS alumni)

In the early spring, Miss Tina flew out from California to visit family in the area, and while she was in town, she and I took care of the arrangements for the reunion. The Riverview Inn, in downtown Clarksville, was booked to provide the lodging for guests and serve as the meeting point for reunion activities. As for the banquet and dance, it would take place in a large party room at The Front Page Deli, a short walking distance from the hotel. Contracts were signed for a caterer and disc jockey. Everything was set for the big party—except the guests.

Like the great military planner she was at the peak of her Army career, Colonel Julie took the bull by the horns and pulled out all of the stops to get as many of our 1975 to 1977 classmates to the reunion as humanly possible. She worked the telephones, e-mailed friends of friends and joined the rest of the committee with almost daily jabs at each other on the FCHS Forum web site.

The author of this book worked some magic, too, with his contacts in the media and local communities. Advance articles and week-of-the-reunion stories ran in the local newspapers—some based on interviews with Miss Julie.The mayors of Hopkinsville and Clarksville (Rich Liebe and Don Trotter), meanwhile, prepared proclamations for the reunion, and scheduled appearances to meet with the FCHS graduates coming to the area.

Classmates began rolling into town and checking into The Riverview Inn the night before the official start of the three-day reunion, and it became evident quite early that the turnout was going to be huge.

Because of a last-minute family issue, Mark Brown had to cancel his plans to come to Clarksville. Nevertheless, his co-organizers and co-conspirators—Julie, Tina and yours truly—were there at the hotel to meet and greet about 100 former classmates from the mid-1970s. The message on the reunion T-shirts reassured our guests: "What Happens at Fort Campbell…Stays at Fort Campbell."

The list of attendees for the 2006 reunion was impressive. It included: David Storie, Chip Thomas, Eugene Pawlik, Lou Menetrey, Rick Larson, Jeanne (Kruwell) Key, Diana (Camp) James, Janice (Brown) Tucker, Kelly Brown, Rick Burns, Preston Owens, David Blackwell, Glenn Patrick, Pam (Schmoker) Sutton, Lynn (Greaux) Addison, Ben Hellums, Anna (Ashworth) Hellums, Melody (Walpole) Walls, Roger Richardson, Charlie Richardson, Cheryl Brainerd, Mike Perry, Allen Hayes, Keith Odister, Mickie Grigsby, Pam (Hicks) Brisendine, Michael Lambert, Mimi Jones, Stacey (Horner) Reed, Frank Balkus, Mike Samouce, and Ron Alvarez

The reunion kicked off the late afternoon of Friday the 13th—which just so happened to be Marshall Patterson's 72nd birthday. After a "Happy Hour," alumni boarded buses to go to the new high school on Fort Campbell for a pre-game "Tailgate Dinner." Upon arriving at the school, near Drennan Park, alumni saw a familiar face waiting for them—Lee Lange. Now, Mr. Lange was my favorite teacher at FCHS, and the only one who always called me "Broadway." In high school, he even wrote a "Letter of Recommendation" that was so good it got me accepted into the University of Notre Dame. Unfortunately, "The Fighting Irish" had to do without "Broadway Joe" since finances changed my college plans and sent me off to Western Kentucky University. A Wisconsin native, Mr. Lange served in the Army at Fort Campbell and then left the service to earn his college degree at Austin Peay State University in Clarksville. He completed his student teaching at FCHS during my sophomore year and later was hired to teach biology.

Greeting the reunion group at the front doors of the high school, Mr. Lange had not changed a bit, and he remembered just about everyone there even though three decades had passed and retirement was just around the corner for him. Unlike most of my classmates, I had already reconnected with Lee Lange since the high school years, running into him on one occasion in the early 1980s at a Clarksville restaurant. It was just before he started coaching the boys' and girls' cross-country teams at Fort Campbell High School—and winning multiple state championships in the sport. Coach Lange was so good at coaching that he apparently became the first FCHS coach to get inducted into a Hall of Fame. In 1989, the Kentucky Track & Cross-Country Coaches Association selected Lee Lange for induction into its Coaches Hall of Fame.

Old "Broadway" gave Lee Lange a firm handshake and big hug on that beautiful fall day in 2006. It would be the last time I would ever see this fine man. Not long after his retirement—on October 24, 2010—Lee Lange died of cancer at his Clarksville home at the age of 63. Always giving, he donated his body to medical research and his family donated a 20-year-old Norwegian Spruce—taken from the front yard of the Lange home—to serve as Tennessee's official Christmas tree at the state capital in December of that year.

Now, let's get back to the 2006 reunion. After dinner and a tour of the new high school—which included a look at our old class portraits—alumni trekked off to Fryar Stadium and the homecoming football game. There, at the stadium, former Falcons started scanning the crowd for Marshall Patterson, who had coached his last football game back in 2000. Coach P, since his retirement, had become a permanent fixture at home FCHS football games. He was in his usual place that night, high up in the stands, just below the Press Box. The alumni group—including me—made a beeline to our beloved coach, where handshakes and old memories were swapped until game time. The highlight of the night—in addition to a Falcon football win—was Tina (Nitch) Figarsky presenting Coach P with a birthday cake and alumni singing *"Happy Birthday"* to him. The gesture of love and respect from the sons and daughters of soldiers left a big smile on Marshall Patterson's face. He may even have shared a chuckle that memorable night.

On Saturday morning—after a Colonel Mahaffey-led "Fun Run" that was run by very few, only because too many former Falcons had too much fun running around the night before—alumni enjoyed breakfast with several FCHS teachers. Then, the buses were boarded again and the group returned to Fort Campbell for a tour of their old haunts at the Army post. Stops were made at the old high school, now known as Mahaffey Middle School, the Teen Club, and the numerous housing areas. Time definitely had not stood still at Fort Campbell, as evidenced by new construction just about everywhere. The post now had the world's largest military Post Exchange (PX) and even an airfield that could land the Space Shuttle. After the tour of the post ended, the busses dropped everyone off at the hotel. The afternoon was wide open for adult beverages and the swapping of even more outrageous lies. Some former Falcons used the free time for sight-seeing trips in the area. As for Colonel Mahaffey and me, there was a grudge tennis match on tap that afternoon at nearby Austin Peay State University. A full-blown tennis tournament might have been played on the campus that day instead of just a single match if only more of the standouts from the old FCHS Tennis Team—like Debbie Cardenas, Selene Mahaffey, Jim Stanton, Perry Elder, Gary Hayes and Ted Cushman—had showed up for the reunion. But, as it turned out, there were too many no-shows. Now, for Miss Julie, tennis had long ago become an important part of her life since it was an activity that helped her maintain her standing as a physically-fit Army officer. As for me, I hadn't picked up a tennis racket in more than 20 years. In fact, there were even days—many of them—when I was allergic to exercise. But the colonel had challenged her old prom date, and I could not deny her the opportunity to humiliate me. Not surprisingly, our tennis match turned out quite ugly for me—once the King of Tennis at Fort Campbell High School. Just like a woman, Miss Julie changed her mind, and decided at the very last minute that she wanted to play doubles instead of facing me in a singles match. And, of course, she already had a "ringer" in mind for a partner—David Storie, a former Falcon football player who also happened to be an excellent tennis player. Colonel Mahaffey and Mr. Storie—who once played on the FCHS tennis team, but unlike me, never gave up the sport—shellacked me and Tina (Nitch) Figarsky in the doubles match. By the time the torture had ended, I was winded, limping and looked like I hadn't played tennis in 20 years. Colonel Mahaffey, on the other hand, was *HOOAH*. She was smiling and content, even looking forward to more exercise on the dance floor later that night.

Back at the hotel, I headed for my room—in the vicinity of the Hospitality Suite—to get some rest. Before I got there, I bumped into another of "Marshall's Boys" coming down the hallway. It was my old friend Mike Perry, a member of the Class of 1976. Even though Mike had remained in the area after high school, working his farm in rural Montgomery County, he was reclusive and rarely, if ever, made it to reunions. On this particular occasion, old football teammates had formed a posse and went out to his farm to bring him to the hotel for a few hours. When he saw me, he yelled out, "Hey Joe…It's me…The Phantom…Remember?" Hearing those words, I had to smile at my old pal during our encounter in the hallway. "I haven't forgotten," I responded, with a half chuckle. It was old "Broadway" who had nicknamed Mr. Perry "The Phantom" because he had a knack for disappearing at the most inconvenient of times. He never seemed to be at the place, where he was supposed to be. When I unsuccessfully ran for Student Council president in the spring of 1974, Mike Perry—as the Big Man on Campus (BMOC)—was supposed to introduce me at the school assembly prior to the election. When my turn came to speak, "The Phantom" was nowhere to be found…He had struck again. But that was just Mike Perry, a Military Brat who—from high school to later life—carved his own path in the world as a maverick.

The main event of the 2006 FCHS Reunion occurred Saturday evening just up the street from the hotel at The Front Page Deli. Because the ballroom at the hotel already had been booked for a wedding, the dinner/dance—with the theme, "Forever Young"—was held in the upstairs party room of the popular restaurant/pub on Franklin Street. It was an easy walk of two to four minutes.

Marshall Patterson and a small group of FCHS teachers—Frank Davis, Mary Davis, Roy Medlock, Nancy Hicks, Patsy Pendleton, and Mike Moffitt—showed up as the special guests for the evening of fun put together by Colonel Mahaffey and Tina (Nitch) Figarsky.

Of course, Julie and Tina roped me—the mayoral assistant—into serving as the master of ceremonies for a program that included a slide show, photo opportunities and prizes. Poor girls…They had no way of knowing how dangerous it was to put a microphone in my hands. As the guy in charge for the evening, I surprised the members of the Reunion Committee with certificates—signed by Governor Ernie Fletcher—that made each of them an Honorary Kentucky Colonel. History teacher Nancy Hicks' husband—Montgomery County Circuit Court Judge Ross Hicks— pretended to be impressed that I had the Kentucky governor's ear when it came to political appointments. But, the good judge already had one of those useless certificates on his office wall. So, he knew better than anyone that a "nobody" usually becomes a Kentucky Colonel by knowing somebody who's really a "nobody" just like them—but just really good at sucking up to career politicians. It's the American political system.

As the night of celebrating and dancing neared an end, I noticed Coach P standing alone in a corner, looking out of his element in one of Clarksville's favorite night spots for the party crowd. The irony of the situation hit me, even if no one else noticed. Here was our legendary football coach—the master of discipline—in a rowdy place where many of his former players were drinking alcohol and even smoking cigarettes or cigars. Heck, I got nervous just being in the same room with the coach, again feeling like that high school kid so afraid of getting caught for violating training rules.

Now, I had been looking forward to an opportunity on this night to talk to Coach P and set the record straight. Since leaving high school, I had only seen him a few times, in my role as a newspaper reporter. For me, there was still some unfinished business with him from the high school days. I had quit the football team in my senior year, and let him down. The incident had always been one of the few regrets in my life. Maybe, just like someone who goes to a priest to confess their sins and ask for forgiveness, I was hoping Marshall Patterson would grant me a full pardon for being young and stupid in high school. Regardless, I wanted to make sure Coach P knew that I appreciated the time and energy he put into me as a high school student and athlete. I wanted him to know that most of the good things that had happened to me in "The Game of Life" were the result of lessons he had taught me and my football teammates.

Sheepishly, I walked over to my old football coach and shook his hand. Small talk was exchanged, particularly about the tremendous success achieved by so many of the old football players at the reunion.

Looking around the party room, Coach P let me know he was really proud of his boys— boys he had helped turn into men. David Storie was a dentist. Preston Owens was an industrial engineer. David Blackwell was a college professor on his way to becoming a dean at a prestigious university. Rick Larson was a high school principal and former football coach. Allen Hayes was an Information Technology professional at a major health clinic. Ben Hellums was a poultry farmer. Roger Richardson was a restaurant executive. And then, there was Charlie Richardson— maybe standing the proudest among "Marshall's Boys" that memorable night.

If there was a classmate whose journey through life had surprised the Falcon Nation, it most certainly was Charlie Richardson. He just may have been the most shining example of Marshall Patterson's unique ability to transform the lives of distressed young people.

Coach P, during his career as head football coach at FCHS, was blessed with the gift to determine rather quickly the best way to motivate each of the players on his team. Not every athlete, after all, responded the same way to discipline and authority. He knew when to use words, and he knew when someone might benefit more from what could be called a gentle push in the right direction.

Charlie Richardson's older brother, Roger Richardson, was a star athlete for four years for the Falcons in three sports—football, wrestling and track. He was a natural and very coachable. Because Charlie Richardson always seemed to be in Roger's shadow, he apparently had a hard time finding his way in school. He was more of a challenge for Marshall Patterson, who nonetheless worked that much harder to turn him into a good student and athlete.

Remembered by classmates for his "bad boy" reputation, Charlie Richardson lived on the edge as a free spirit in high school, spending much of his time raising hell with best friend Ray DeJesus. The two were inseparable. After leaving high school, Ray DeJesus served in the Marines for 12 years before he died of a self-inflicted gunshot wound at his home in Hopkinsville in late September 1989. He was 31 years old at the time of his death.

Charlie Richardson, at some point after he left FCHS, found his calling in life and became a career police officer for a large city on the East Coast.

At this joyous reunion, surrounded by old classmates who were now responsible adults, I finally mustered up the courage to make my peace with Marshall Patterson. "Coach, I want you to know that I really appreciate everything you did for me back in high school. You and these other great teachers are responsible for the people here tonight making something out of their lives."

Coach P smiled. "Thanks, Joe. But, you know, we always had the greatest kids in the world to work with at Fort Campbell High School. We're proud of every one of you."

When Marshall Patterson called me "Joe," it was music to my ears. It was like the entire world had been lifted off of my shoulders. I knew right then—standing in the presence of greatness, feeling the love—that Coach P had never stopped believing in me. "Broadway Joe" was forever a Falcon, and one of "Marshall's Boys."

Those words shared that night were the last I ever had with Marshall Patterson. Not long after the 2006 reunion, Coach P began having minor problems with his memory. No one thought much about it, and there were no other health-related symptoms that suggested something was wrong.

Then one day, Coach P and his wife drove to Nashville, Tennessee, to check out an antique store. As a young man, Marshall Patterson had lived in Nashville and knew the city like the back of his hand.

When it was time to leave the city, Rebecca Patterson noticed that they were driving around in circles. Finally, Coach P pulled over to the side of the road.

"Cissie, I can't remember how to get home," he told her.

"The Long Goodbye"—Alzheimer's disease—had begun.

Marshall Patterson (third form the right) poses with other FCHS teacher favorites at the 2006 reunion of the classes of 1975, 1976, and 1977. With him(from left) are Nancy Hicks, Roy Medlock, Mary Davis, Frank Davis, Patsy Pendleton, and Mike Moffitt. (Photo by Rob Dollar)

CHAPTER 12: THE FINAL WHISTLE

Marshall Patterson's wonderful life ended most fittingly on a football Sunday in America, with God Almighty blowing the referee's whistle to call him home.

The legendary football coach of the Fort Campbell High School Falcons, who had suffered from Alzheimer's disease for several years, died peacefully in the late afternoon hours of January 19, 2014, at his home in Clarksville, Tennessee.

For many alumni of the Falcon Nation, especially the football lovers, this day was supposed to be about fun and excitement—not sadness—since the National Football League playoffs were on television and the Super Bowl was only two weeks away. (The Seattle Seahawks and Denver Broncos subsequently won their championship games and advanced to meet on February 2, 2014, in the Super Bowl, which was won by Seattle, 43-8.)

But, no one knew, when the sun rose that day, that the end was so near for the "Father of The Falcons."

On the last day of his life, Coach Marshall Patterson was surrounded by his loving wife, Rebecca Patterson, and his three adult children—Stephen Patterson, Marsha (Patterson) Anderson, and Dr. Jeanann (Patterson) Pardue. The family, after being told his body was slowly shutting down, held what would become a deathbed vigil on that Sunday. They laughed and cried, while sharing beautiful memories, and reportedly even watched a video that celebrated Coach P's successes, on and off the field, over nearly four decades of playing "The Game of Life." With his doctor daughter taking charge of his care, Coach P lived his final day on this Earth the same way he had lived every other day—setting the perfect example when it came to giving unconditional love and respect to those in his life.

Just before Coach P took his last breath, Jeanann called for her mother and siblings to gather at his side. "He looked up and smiled at us," Rebecca Patterson said. A faint laugh may have shadowed the sudden smile. The family interpreted the reaction as a Heavenly gift that restored what the dreadful Alzheimer's disease had stolen from Coach P in the final years of his life—his dignity.....There was no reason to believe anything different: Marshall Patterson, at the very end, recognized the family that loved him so dearly, and he remembered the many sons and daughters of soldiers that he so brilliantly mentored in "The Game of Life." And then, the great football coach closed his eyes and was gone.

Early Sunday evening, after leaving Gateway Medical Center in Clarksville, Rebecca Patterson made a few telephone calls to let friends and some of "Marshall's Boys" know of her husband's death. Two old Falcon quarterbacks—Sam Green and Rob Dollar—were among those she called to express the family's appreciation for not forgetting their old coach and mentor.

Before the end of the night, the word of Coach P's death had already begun to spread throughout the Falcon Nation, thanks to social media. Family, friends and the Fort Campbell community—in the days that followed—mourned Marshall Patterson's passing along with colleagues in the Kentucky and Tennessee sports worlds and thousands of sons and daughters of soldiers around the world.

There were many tributes to Coach P in the print and broadcast media, but one of the better ones that truly captured the man and summed up his wonderful life was published two days after his death in the *Kentucky New Era*, the daily newspaper in Hopkinsville, Kentucky.

Trent Singer, then the newspaper's assistant sports editor, wrote the article, which carried the headline, "Remembering A Legend." Mr. Singer interviewed several of "Marshall's Boys" for his story, including the author of this book. (Note to readers: At the time of Marshall Patterson's death, Josh McKillip was just a year away from being named the head football coach at FCHS. Shawn Berner—a Patterson successor— already had resigned the head coach's job the previous January to spend more time with his family.)

Here is the story that appeared in the *Kentucky New Era* on Tuesday, January 21, 2014, about the death of Marshall Patterson—reprinted in its entirety with the permission of the newspaper:

Legendary status is only awarded to a distinct handful of individuals, and among those is Marshall Patterson.

After battling a long illness, the 79-year-old Patterson died Sunday evening at Gateway Medical Center in Clarksville, but it's his storied legacy that has shaped and sustained the Fort Campbell community.

Patterson's accomplishments at Fort Campbell are unparalleled. He became the school's first football coach in 1962 and held the role for 32 straight seasons, winning two Class 1-A state titles (1976, 1978) and one Class 2-A state title (1979). During his tenure, he amassed a 227-120 all-time record, which ranks 24th in state history. He also initiated the school's wrestling program, which claimed a state title in 1971.

"To me and to a lot of his former players, he is Mr. Fort Campbell," said Fort Campbell statistician Donny Caver, who played two seasons in the early 1980s under Patterson. "He loved football, and he loved the players — such a great coach and my favorite coach I ever played for."

Last fall, a number of former players and supporters submitted letters to the Kentucky High School Athletic Association, urging the organization to take action and make Patterson a member of the Dawahares/Kentucky High School Hall of Fame.

The letters revealed stories and fingerprints of a man of great character — a coach, a mentor and a legend.

When Shawn Berner took over the Falcons' football program in 2002, one of the first things on his agenda was seeking advice from Patterson.

"He welcomed me with open arms and shared all kinds of valuable information that I was able to use," Berner said. "He was an instrumental part in giving me advice along the way."

Perhaps it was Patterson's advice that led to Berner's success at Fort Campbell. More importantly, none of it would have been possible without the efforts of Patterson, who literally built the Falcons' football program from the ground up.

"He took a brand new high school and turned it into a perennial powerhouse," said Josh McKillip, who played running back and linebacker under Patterson for four seasons in the early 1990s and now serves as the Falcons' defensive coordinator. "Everybody knew about Fort Campbell. He put multiple people into college."

Darrell Wallace is just one of many great athletes that played under Patterson at Fort Campbell. He competed for the Falcons in the early 1980s before playing at the University of Missouri, where he amassed 2,607 career-rushing yards and was inducted into the school's athletics hall of fame in 1997.

"He was loyal to Fort Campbell," said Rob Dollar, another one of Patterson's former players who was a backup quarterback from 1972-74. "When you think about Fort Campbell football, you always think about Marshall Patterson. He instilled loyalty into his players and the concept of teamwork. ... It was never about 'I' It was always about 'We.'"

The players from those days identified themselves as "Marshall's Boys," a title that unified the Falcons with their well-respected coach.

"He reminded me of (Alabama coach) 'Bear' Bryant," Caver said. "He was low-key in the interviews. ... He'd downplay everything, and then just go out there and kick your butt."

The coach finished his career with a 20-12 mark in the playoffs. Nine of those losses came at the hands of Mayfield.

However, when Fort Campbell made its first playoff appearance in 1976, Patterson ended the season on top and won the Class 1-A state championship.

"He never had a person playing for him freshman to senior year," Caver said of the school's constant shuffling of soldiers, which created adversity for coaches like Patterson. "He didn't know what he'd have for the next year. He could have an entirely different team the next year. ... That's what was amazing about Coach Patterson. He was able to mold these kids into winners and into young men."

The only coach who comes close to matching Patterson's accolades is Berner, who led the Falcons to three Class 2-A state titles (2007-09) before stepping down last year.

"Our philosophies were very similar in terms of wanting to run the football. We ran the football first," Berner said. "The only difference was Coach Patterson ran the football first, second, third and fourth option. That's all he did.

"He knew the wishbone offense very well, and more importantly, his kids knew it very well."

Berner coached two Mr. Football winners and sustained Fort Campbell as a perennial powerhouse. However, Berner's 110 victories come nowhere near Patterson, who is the school's all-time winningest coach.

Despite the vast difference in the two coaches' offensive philosophies, Berner says there are obvious similarities in what they both expected from their players.

"We were very different in ways but very similar in terms of wanting our kids to be very good at certain things and very disciplined any time they were on and off the field," Berner said. "We both had great defense, and I think that's where we have a lot of similarities."

Patterson led Fort Campbell to a runner-up finish in the 1980 Class 2-A title game, was named Kentucky Coach of the Year three times and coached the 1981 team in the Kentucky-Tennessee All-Star game. USA Today ranked his 1982 team No. 17 in the nation.

Outside of football, Patterson also established Fort Campbell's wrestling program in 1964 and served as the team's coach for 17 years. In Patterson's seventh year, the Falcons claimed a state title against "David vs. Goliath" odds.

"We were going up against schools that had over 4,000 people. Fort Campbell had 377 people, as I recall," said Steve Bryant, who was a junior grappler on the 1971 state championship team. "That's extraordinary to go up against schools with 10 times more people and come out on top like we did."

Fort Campbell finished runner-up in Bryant's sophomore season. Like many others under Patterson, Bryant went on to graduate with a four-year (college) degree. He always remembered his old coach.

"I remember he had these very basic wrestling books sitting on the desk in his office," Bryant said. "He just picked up a lot of this stuff from books, and he taught the basics over and over.

"I'm sure his basic military training taught him that if you continue to rehearse the same situations and then switch them up a bit with other basic moves, you can come up with the permutations and combinations of eight basic moves. We did extraordinary supreme physical conditioning. We trained every day."

The absence of a father who is deployed overseas is a challenging time for every student at Fort Campbell.

McKillip recalls leaning on Patterson during his playing days, while his father was deployed for two years.

"My father was gone in some of the most impressionable years of my life," McKillip said. "I very easily could have been out listening to my friends or trying to make decisions on my own. ... At least I had somebody there while my dad was gone that gave me stability."

Patterson provided support for many young students through several major wars, including the Vietnam and Gulf Wars.

"He was an old soul," said Kevin Acevedo, who took part in gymnastics for four years under the tutelage of Patterson. "He believed in giving everyone a chance. He cared. That's what was amazing. ... He'd call you into his office, and he wanted to know what was going on."

Coaches at Fort Campbell must overcome a multitude of obstacles in order to have success. Patterson gave ordinary students a purpose and shaped their lives into a greater framework.

"He was able to take all that doubt and channel it into football and wrestling," Acevedo said. "He made it to where it was more than about the game of football. It was a life thing."

Patterson was also Fort Campbell's athletic director, during which the school claimed 27 state titles under his direction. On top of that, he was a 33-year sponsor for the Fellowship of Christian Athletes at Fort Campbell.

"Anybody who has a stable program for 32 years in that environment is a phenomenal coach," Berner said. "Many people don't understand the challenge that you could go out in June and lose many of your people to a PCS move just because of the nature of the military."

Dollar points to Patterson's physical attributes when defining his mystifying presence.

"He was kind of a big man physically," Dollar said. "He just had a way about him of commanding respect. ... He was a disciplinarian. He was fair, but he meant business."

McKillip echoed similar sentiments and says he's carried many of Patterson's teachings into his own coaching philosophy.
"He had a presence about him that when he spoke, everybody listened," McKillip said. "The thing about him was he was just a man of integrity. ... It was always about doing the right thing and doing everything with integrity."

Beyond coaching, Berner says Patterson left his imprint on every person he met.

"He set a standard there that many people continue to live by," Berner said. "He had a lasting impression on every single player that played for him, along with everyone he came into contact with like myself."

There are countless stories regarding the legendary coach. Caver, who does color commentary for the Falcons' football team on WKDZ, recalls one in particular. Patterson approached him in 1984 and asked if he'd like to take over the duties as the team's statistician.

"I told him I'd give it a shot," Caver said. Thirty years later, he hasn't missed a game.

Two years ago, Dollar was at a class reunion, when he and several others came to a strange discovery.

Somehow, their beloved football coach had been forgotten from the Kentucky High School Hall of Fame.

"I had always assumed that he was in the Hall of Fame," Dollar said. "A couple of us decided we had to do what we could to get him into the Hall of Fame."

People began inquiring about how Patterson was overlooked from the prestigious honor but came to the conclusion that more letters of recommendation were needed.

"Just on his record alone, it speaks for itself," Acevedo said of Patterson's Hall of Fame credentials. "I can't think of any other coach that had a career as long as he did... He's more than deserving."

McKillip says Patterson accomplished more than most coaches and with much less.

"I just think it's a crying shame it hasn't happened," McKillip said. "The thing that no one is talking about is he was dealing with a military installation. He was dealing with a community where he had to start over every single year."

The deadline to submit letters to the KHSAA was last fall. Many of Patterson's former players from all around the country organized through social media and did their part to pay tribute to the legendary coach.

"He deserves to be in the Hall of Fame. I just can't imagine how it happened that he's not in there," Dollar said.

Sam Green, who was Fort Campbell's first starting quarterback, has commissioned a bronze bust be made in Patterson's honor.

"He's a Hall of Famer, no question," Berner said. "He's not only a Hall of Famer in Kentucky. In my opinion, he's a Hall of Famer if there's some sort of national hall of fame."

Several familiar names sent letters of recommendation, including former New Era sports editor Joe Wilson and former president of the Christian County Chamber of Commerce Carter Hendricks, whose letter stated "it only seems fitting that Coach Marshall Patterson should enter heaven as a Hall of Fame Coach and be able to shake the hand of his good friend and recent Hall of Fame inductee, Coach Jim Perrin."

Sadly, the opportunity for Patterson to witness his Hall of Fame induction in person will never happen. But as several of his former players expressed, Patterson was never focused on the material aspects of his legacy.

He had bigger goals in mind.

"He was such a special person," Berner said. "You'll hear that from so many people, especially anybody that played for Coach Patterson. I think it'll sound like a broken record player, but that's what you'll hear."

Marshall Patterson and his wife, Rebecca, pose for a family portrait with their three grown children—(from left) Marsha (Patterson) Anderson, Jeanann (Patterson) Pardue, and Stephen Patterson. The photograph was taken during one of Coach P's final Christmases. (Courtesy of Marshall Patterson family)

CHAPTER 13: COACH'S FUNERAL

When it came to coaching and bringing out the best in his athletes, Marshall Patterson was second to none. Always the consummate professional—calm, cool and collected—he often was at his best when the pressure was greatest or when the game was on the line.

In more than 40 years of coaching, Coach P never lost his cool. But, there was at least one time when his emotions got the best of him for a few minutes—only because he loved his son so much.

It happened during the 1975-1976 wrestling season. Coach P's Falcon wrestlers were hosting the Northwest High School Vikings in a match at the Fort Campbell High School gymnasium. That particular year, Patterson's teenage son, Stephen, was a star wrestler for the Clarksville, Tennessee, high school and was set to wrestle one of his father's top wrestlers in the dual meet.

Rebecca Patterson, who usually supported her husband's sports teams, was there in the gym that blustery winter day, but this time to cheer for her wrestler son. Not surprisingly, when it came time for Stephen Patterson's match, Coach P—who normally sat in a chair at the edge of the wrestling mat while coaching his team—found himself in quite a predicament.

He couldn't root for his son without being disloyal to his FCHS wrestlers. "It was the hardest thing I ever saw Buddy go through," recalled Rebecca

Patterson. "He couldn't stay out there on the mat, so he left the gym and went into the dressing room to wait until Stephen's match was over." Rocky Cobb, Patterson's assistant coach, took charge of the team in his absence. Mrs. Patterson said Stephen Patterson lost that match to the Fort Campbell wrestler. Although she could not remember the victor's name, former Falcon wrestler Norm Miller (Class of 1978) said he was pretty sure it was Ray Soyk (Class of 1976). Soyk, who wrestled 167 pounds, was good enough to go to the state tournament that season, but lost in the early rounds of the competition.

Stephen Patterson, who eventually earned a college wrestling scholarship, was the apple of his father's eye. Rebecca Patterson said her husband and son enjoyed an especially close relationship, and when Stephen Patterson followed in his father's footsteps and became a high school coach after college, there was no prouder father in America.

So, with Marshall Patterson's death on January 19, 2014, it was only fitting that the son of the "Father of The Falcons" would lead the celebration of Coach P's wonderful and meaningful life on this Earth.

Marshall Patterson's funeral was held five days after his death on a sunny, bitter cold Friday at the Chapel of Neal-Tarpley-Parchman Funeral Home on Madison Street in Clarksville. Burial followed in Riverview Cemetery.

Love and reverence—along with a crowd of about 250—filled the small chapel for Patterson's mid-afternoon funeral services. The day before he was laid to rest, hundreds of other friends and colleagues had come to the funeral home to pay their last respects and console family members during a visitation that lasted six hours.

FCHS graduates from just about every era in Coach P's coaching career packed the chapel to bid him farewell. They came from near and far. Early Falcons Stan Nelson and his wife, Barbara (Scharn) Nelson, Class of 1965 graduates, drove up to Clarksville from Alabama. The Blue-and-Grey alumni sat shoulder-to-shoulder with former Northwest High School football players who had been coached by Patterson in the final years of his career.

"Marshall's Boys" came to town, with their heads held high, to honor the man who molded them into men. It was literally a "Who's Who" of the FCHS sports world. The four Hellums brothers—Rick, Mike, Ben and Steve—were there. They had not forgotten Coach P making the trip to Mississippi for their father's funeral back in 1981. Jimmy Thomas, who played football at FCHS and later served as one of Coach P's assistant coaches, was there, too. So was Mike Cassity, a former University of Kentucky football star who became a successful assistant football coach in the college ranks. They were joined by Ronnie Chapman, Mitch Waters, John Bianchini, Danny Betancourt, Rick Larson, and Norm Miller. There's no doubt that several other former Falcon standouts attended the funeral and were somewhere out in the crowd, but just not seen or known to the author of this book.

As most people know, funerals often turn into reunions. And ironically, it's the dearly departed that brings friends and relatives together who may not have seen each other in decades. This was the case for many of those who attended Marshall Patterson's funeral.

As I pulled into the front driveway of the funeral home, the first person I saw was my old junior high and high school classmate, Mike Hellums, who was walking up the sidewalk to the door of the chapel with two of his brothers, Ben and Steve Hellums. They had driven up from their homes in Alabama. My older and grayer friend—still a lean, mean fighting machine like he was in high school, but now sporting a beard—apparently recognized my Mustang and me at the same time, which explained the ear-to-ear grin on his face. I stopped my car on the spot, rolled down the driver's side window and started talking to old Mike Hellums like it had been only yesterday and not nearly 40 years since our last conversation.

After a few minutes of quick conversation, I parked my car and entered the funeral home. Once inside, and after expressing condolences to the Patterson family, "Marshall's Boys" and other alumni of the Falcon Nation—including John Ignacio, Jacqui Oliver, Tina (Barnett) Moberly, and Cheri Horan-byard—gathered in small groups to catch up on each other's lives before the start of the funeral. If he had been alive, Coach P surely would have been smiling while the lies and stories were swapped among his beloved Military Brats. There was plenty to talk about, for sure—decades of living "The Game of Life."

John Ignacio, a champion golfer for FCHS back in the day, enjoyed the pats on the back from former classmates for his once-in-a-lifetime experience of umpiring the Little League World Series in Williamsport, Pennsylvania, just months before the Patterson funeral. Sun-tanned Ronnie Chapman, a state champion wrestler who quarterbacked Coach P's 1970 football team, tolerated the good-natured teasing he got that day from old friends envious of his good life in sunny Florida.

Yours truly—Rob Dollar—had a great story to tell Mike Hellums, and I couldn't wait to tell it. Quite the doozy, I knew he would enjoy it since it put the spotlight on his most famous deed as a Falcon football player. Mr. Hellums will always be remembered among the FCHS faithful for a legendary tackle—it initially was called a "Falcon Lick" but later became known as "The Hellums Lick"— during the 1974 football season.

Fort Campbell was playing its archrival, Trigg County High School, a team that had defeated Coach P's Falcons at least three years in a row. The Wildcats were led by a speedy freshman tailback named Victor Grubbs, who was the younger brother of former All-Stater and Trigg County football legend Selby Grubbs. Coach P's game plan for victory was pretty simple: Stop Victor Grubbs from having a big game. In an effort to drive home the point, every time Victor Grubbs' name was mentioned in practice the week of the game, Falcon coaches expected the entire football team to get angry and yell, "Falcon Lick."

The big game took place on Saturday, September 14, 1974, at Fort Campbell's Fryar Stadium, and it was not a good day for Victor Grubbs. Early in the fourth-quarter, he took a pitch from the Trigg County quarterback on a sweep around the left end. Mike Hellums, a "Hawk" in Coach Rocky Cobbs' defensive backfield, sprinted forward and toward Grubbs and the ball....Both players dropped their heads and shoulders and then collided at full-speed near the line of scrimmage. The thunderous crack of two helmets coming together echoed throughout the stadium, stunning the crowd to silence. If truth be told, the ferocious hit may have been heard across the entire Army post—it was that loud, just like a clap of thunder. Grubbs nearly swallowed his mouth piece after the lick and had to be carried off the field. Mike Hellums managed to slowly pick himself up from the ground, but was clearly dazed. He then stumbled back to the huddle—the *wrong* huddle. The Trigg County players, after realizing Mike was in their huddle, gave him a gentle push toward his own teammates, who, of course, greeted him like a conquering hero. Mike Hellums never got a big head for making the play of the game. But, I'm pretty sure he had a splitting headache the rest of the day.

Coach P was a very happy man that Saturday afternoon in September 1974. FCHS won the game, 28-0. It was the worst beating ever taken by a Joe Jaggers-coached Trigg County football team. I will always remember the bus ride back to the high school gym to shower and dress after the game. Members of the football team took turns yelling the name, "Victor Grubbs," which then was followed by the roaring chant: "Hellums Lick."

As was the usual routine, the football team reviewed the film of the game at the Monday afternoon practice. Coach P, who always ran the movie projector, must have replayed the "Hellums Lick" a few hundred times that day. But, no one got tired of seeing it. As for Mr. Grubbs, he was still hurting a full week after the hit and did not even dress for Trigg County's next game against the Caldwell County Tigers.

Mike Hellums, of course, enjoyed the retelling of the tale and was anxious to hear THE REST OF MY STORY.

The back story involved a Close Encounter of the Family Kind that occurred many years after Mike Hellums' glory on the football field. In 2013, while I was working as a staffing supervisor for an employment agency in Hopkinsville, a young man came into my office, looking for a factory job. There was nothing unusual about that, but what was unusual was his name—Victor Grubbs Jr.

Curious, I asked him if he was related to the famous football-playing Grubbs brothers from Trigg County, and he confessed he was the son of the youngest brother, Victor Grubbs.

Thinking back to the day of the infamous "Hellums Lick," I chuckled and told him I not only had a job for him, but a story about the day one of "Marshall's Boys" cleaned his daddy's clock on the football field. Young Victor smiled as I gave him the play-by-play description of the football game that his father never got to finish.

"My Daddy never told me that story…I'll have to ask him about it," Victor Grubbs Jr. quipped.

After learning I had educated Victor Grubbs' son by giving him a FCHS football history lesson, Mike Hellums jokingly thanked me for helping to preserve his legacy as a Falcon football player.

In addition to old students, an impressive delegation of retired teachers and colleagues from FCHS joined the Patterson family and their many friends at the funeral. The teacher mourners included Rita (Chaney) Cardenas, Patsy Pendleton, Sherrie Pennington, David Kerr, Connie (Gifford) Hellums, Frank Davis, Roy Medlock, Tom Morgan and Rocky Cobb.

W.L. "Willie" Burnett, a retired educator who had been the assistant principal at Fort Campbell High School during the 1970s, was there, too, to offer his condolences to Rebecca Patterson and her children. A native of Trenton, Tennessee, Burnett and Coach P had many things in common, but particularly a love for sports. A star athlete in high school, Burnett was inducted into the Gibson County Hall of Fame in 2007. For 37 years, he also served as a high school football and basketball referee.

Like Marshall Patterson, W. L. Burnett was a history-maker and someone who always led by example. He was the first black football official in the Ohio Valley Conference, where he worked games from 1971 to 1992, and the first black elected to Clarksville City Council. He served 20 years on City Council and was an unsuccessful mayoral candidate.

Shawn Berner, second only to Coach P in career wins as head football coach at FCHS, mingled with former players at the funeral and expressed his appreciation to the Early Falcons for their unwavering loyalty and devotion to the "Father of The Falcons."

There were many more proud Falcons around the country who wanted to attend Coach P's funeral, but were unable to make the trip to Clarksville for various reasons. But each and every one of them—including my new buddy and fellow old quarterback Sam Green, who was subpoenaed to appear in court that day to testify as a witness in an Oklahoma case—were there in spirit.

The funeral services for Coach P were short and sweet. His son, Stephen, who, at the time was living and working in Georgia as a high school football coach, gave a very moving remembrance speech about his father. He talked about their close relationship, the quality time they spent together over the years on fishing trips and even the shared laugher that resulted from a memorable frog-gigging misadventure.

Marshall H. Patterson
1934-2014

In Loving Remembrance

About 250 mourners packed the chapel at Neal-Tarpley-Parchman Funeral Home in Clarksville, Tennessee, on a bitter cold day in late January 2014 to bid farewell to the "Father of The Falcons." (Courtesy of Marshall Patterson family)

Mark Ray, who coached at FCHS in Marshall Patterson's later years, informed mourners about "Patterson's Pearls of Wisdom," which he explained were the guidelines used by Coach P to shape the lives of thousands of students and athletes over the years.

Connie Jackson, a FCHS physical education teacher, shared her special memories of a mentor she described as a "very special man." She spoke in great detail about the Marshall Patterson philosophy for teaching and coaching, and that was to *always* err on the side of the student.

The Reverend Skip Armistead—who, as a youngster, was a student in Coach P's Sunday School class—delivered the eulogy, describing Coach P's remarkable life from birth to the day of his death. The Reverend B.J. Brack assisted Reverend Skip Armistead in the officiating of the funeral services.

The celebration of Coach P's life ended with the singing of the Fort Campbell High School alma mater as his casket was taken from the chapel and put into a Hearst for the funeral procession to Riverview Cemetery, where he was buried.

Mike Cassity, Rocky Cobb, Frank Davis, Todd Hood, Roy Medlock, Tom Morgan, Bryce Smith, and Webb Williams served as the pallbearers. The family designated the late Houston Mills, the late Bill Perry, and Coach P's former football players from Fort Campbell High School and Northwest High School, and former FCHS wresters as honorary pallbearers.

Marshall Patterson retired as the head football coach at FCHS after the 1993 season, but continued to serve as the athletic director through mid-1995. In May 1994, Rocky Cobb, following 28 years as an assistant coach, was hired to succeed Coach P as the top Falcon. After getting the head coach's job, Coach Cobb summed up his feelings to a *Kentucky New Era* sport writer in Hopkinsville, Kentucky, with a memorable tribute to his friend and mentor: *"It's like following Bear Bryant."*

Prior to the start of Coach P's funeral, I went looking for Coach Cobb, who, as previously mentioned, was my tennis coach for three seasons at

FCHS. Someone had to point him out to me because I failed to recognize him when he walked past me in the lobby of the funeral home. It had been about 20 years since I had last seen him. As the head football coach at FCHS, he came to Hopkinsville in the late 1990s to have his photograph made at the *Kentucky New Era* offices for the newspaper's annual high school football section. At the time, I was still working at the daily newspaper as the associate editor. He popped his head into my office, grinned and said, "You've still got *that* long hair." I just smiled and shot back, "I guess I'll always be Stuck in the Seventies."

To make a long story short, when I cornered him at the funeral, Coach Cobb didn't recognize his old quarterback and tennis player, either. I guess I had changed in appearance, too, and no longer was in tip-top physical condition. But, I still had the hair...Of course, it was now gray. I suppose that was the reason Rocky Cobb flashed that big grin at me.

During our short reunion, I thanked Coach Cobb for the influence he had in helping to shape my life, and I'm glad I had the opportunity to do so. Less than two years later—on December 20, 2015—Coach Rocky Cobb died at his home in Clarksville at the age of 73. Rocky Cobb—just like Coach P—fittingly passed away on a football Sunday.

The author was lucky enough to spend a few minutes with Rebecca Patterson on the day of Coach P's funeral. Not minutes after arriving at the funeral home, she walked over to me and took me by the arm. It kind of surprised me because I had never known her very well. In fact, back in high school, I don't remember ever talking to her. Maybe she had heard an earful about me from Coach P. Nevertheless, she knew who I was, and graciously thanked me and the rest of the alumni of the Falcon Nation for our thoughts and prayers as well as the continuing efforts to honor her late husband.

On behalf of the sons and daughters of Fort Campbell soldiers, I thanked Mrs. Patterson and Coach P's three children—Stephen, Marsha and Jeanann—for sharing this great man with the military community over the years.

Standing face-to-face with Stephen Patterson, who looked and sounded so much like his father, I couldn't help but think back to the days when I knew this now grown man as a lanky, blonde-haired junior high student who spent summers working out with his father's football teams. He had sweated, hurt and pushed his body to the physical limits during those preseason conditioning drills....And, just like every good Falcon football player, he bit his lip and put up with his Dad's Trini Lopez music.

The day the Falcon Nation said goodbye to Coach P will long be remembered as the end of a golden era because God most certainly broke the mold when He made Marshall Patterson.

About three weeks after Coach P's death, the Tennessee General Assembly adopted and passed legislation—House Joint Resolution No. 585—that honored the life's accomplishments of the "Father of The Falcons."

Here are the words of that resolution, signed by Governor Bill Haslam in Nashville, Tennessee, on February 10, 2014, and now proudly displayed at the Clarksville home of Rebecca Patterson:

A RESOLUTION to honor the memory of Coach Marshall H. Patterson of Clarksville.

WHEREAS, the members of this General Assembly were greatly saddened to learn of the passing of Coach Marshall H. Patterson; and

WHEREAS, Coach Patterson was an exemplary public servant and consummate educator who worked assiduously to improve the quality of life for his fellow citizens in numerous capacities; and

WHEREAS,. he graduated from Tennessee Polytechnic Institute with a Bachelor of Science in 1957, and attained a Master's in Education from George Peabody College for Teachers in 1959; and

WHEREAS, Coach Marshall H. Patterson served in the U.S. Army at Fort Gordon in Augusta, Georgia, from 1957-1959, was commissioned as a

Second Lieutenant, achieved the rank of First Lieutenant, and after leaving active duty, obtained the rank of Captain in the Army Reserve; and

WHEREAS, Coach Patterson began his coaching career in the Fort Campbell School System in (1960) and shepherded the football program at Fort Campbell High School from its infancy when he started the program in 1962, established the high school as a football power, and created a legion of admirers through thirty-two years of coaching football and wrestling, teaching, and serving as the athletic director at Fort Campbell High School; and

WHEREAS, during his tenure as head football coach at Fort Campbell High School, he put the Falcons football program on the map with three state titles in 1976, 1978, and 1979; and

WHEREAS, he also secured a state title in wrestling in 1971; and

WHEREAS, Coach Patterson led the Falcons to 227 wins in football in his thirty-two years as head coach before he retired in 1993; and

WHEREAS, because of these successes, Coach Marshall H. Patterson was ranked in the State's top ten in coaching wins at the time of his first retirement; and

WHEREAS, Coach Patterson possessed a passion for the game and devotion to the youth of his community; he returned three years after his first retirement to serve as head football coach at Northwest High School, where he guided the Vikings to the playoffs twice before he retired once more in 2001; and

WHEREAS, he was an active and devout member of the New Providence United Methodist Church, which he served faithfully for many years; and

WHEREAS, Coach Marshall H. Patterson enjoyed the loving companionship of his wife of 56 years, Rebecca Roach Patterson, and was the proud father of Stephen Patterson and his wife, Sheila; Jeanann Pardue and her husband, Randy; and Marsha Anderson and her husband, John; proud grandfather of Taylor Patterson, Benjamin Pardue, Philip

Pardue, Tessa Patterson, Mary Marshall Anderson, Stephen Pardue and Jack Anderson; loving brother of Aldene Williams; and dedicated uncle of many nieces and nephews; and

WHEREAS, he was preceded in death by his parents, Marshall Gray Patterson and Grace Holman Patterson Liggett, and his grandson, Christopher Patterson; and

WHEREAS, Coach Patterson was deeply devoted to his family, and he always endeavored to remain true to family values of the highest order and enjoyed the time he spent with them, including fishing with his son and antiquing with his wife; and

WHEREAS, Coach Marshall H. Patterson leaves behind an indelible legacy of integrity and probity in public life, compassion and loyalty in private life, and diligence and dedication in all his chosen endeavors; and

WHEREAS, it is fitting that this General Assembly should pause to remember the bountiful life of this exceptional educator and human being; now, therefore

BE IT RESOLVED BY THE HOUSE OF REPRESENTATIVES OF THE ONE HUNDRED EIGHTH GENERAL ASSEMBLY OF THE STATE OF TENNESSEE, THE SENATE CONCURRING, that we honor the memory of Coach Marshall H. Patterson, reflecting fondly upon his impeccable character and his stalwart commitment to living the examined life with courage and conviction.

BE IT FURTHER RESOLVED, that we express our sympathy and offer our condolences to the family of Coach Marshall H. Patterson.

The resolution was quite an honor for a teacher and football coach from Lewisburg, Tennessee. That kind of special recognition isn't given out every day, and to just anyone, in the Volunteer State. It was special, indeed.

In early December 2014—only a month before the one-year anniversary of Coach P's death—I was surprised to hear from Rebecca Patterson. She sent me a lovely Christmas card and a hand-written note that again expressed her family's appreciation for my continuing efforts to try and get Coach P into the Hall of Fame.

The letter left me teary-eyed, knowing deep down in my heart that no one—but, especially me—could ever do enough to pay back a man who lived a life of always doing for others. Mrs. Patterson's letter included an inspirational story that demonstrated Coach P's enormous love for the sons and daughters of soldiers, even in sickness and right up to the very end.

Here is that letter, dated December 11, 2014:

Dear Rob,

I have let too much time go by without telling you personally how I appreciate all you have done to keep Marshall's memory before us all. All of you who shared school days and football seasons with him will always be an important memory for us all. You young people who shared those days at FCHS brought supreme happiness to his life, and for that I will be forever grateful.

One of the last football memories came in the dark of night, when he was still verbal. He awakened me, asking that I take him to FCHS. "The boys are on the field," he said. "And, they won't know what to do if I'm not there." At length, I convinced him it was yet midnight, and we would go out in the morning.

Of course, when morning came, he had forgotten his wishes. Somewhere, in his wonderful heart, he never forgot I am confident. Thank you for all your support.

Most Sincerely,
Rebecca Patterson & Family (Stephen, Jeanann, Marsha)

Whenever I think about Marshall Patterson's life and legacy, I'm reminded of an observation made long ago by the late Vince Lombardi, the great football coach of the Green Bay Packers. What is it, he was asked, that makes a man great. The football coach answered: *"The measure of who we are is what we do with what we have."*

Marshall Patterson always gave everything he had to his Military Brats, and in doing so, he'll always be the person most deserving of the credit for the great deeds they do in this world.

Rest In Peace, Coach P.

Former FCHS football players (from left) Jerry Weesner, Ray Metts, Greg Markley and Eric Stickles visit the grave of Marshall Patterson in Riverview Cemetery in Clarksville, Tennessee, in October 2014. (Photo by Kim Allen)

CHAPTER 14: THE MOVIE

In life, timing is everything. Just ask Shawn Berner, who became head football coach at Fort Campbell High School in 2002 and later led the Falcons to three straight state football championships and 112 wins over 11 seasons.

Coaching Military Brats at Fort Campbell, Kentucky, Berner made headlines and a name for himself while working miracles at the helm of a powerhouse team affected daily by America's ongoing War on Terror.

An early successor to Marshall Patterson, Coach Berner just happened to be in the right place at the right time the day Hollywood knocked on the door at the Army post, drooling to tell America the story about the football-playing Military Brats of Fort Campbell soldiers.

And really, no one should blame Shawn Berner for answering the knock.

The idea for a movie about Coach Berner and his Fort Campbell Falcons football team sounded like a winner—a sure thing. For most Americans, the 9/11 terrorist attacks still were relatively fresh memories and the country's love affair with its military remained in full bloom at the time of the announcement in early 2015.

The official statement hit the Falcon Nation like a bolt of lightning. The parties involved in the film project finalized their deal, apparently after months of negotiations. The public found out about the movie just a few weeks short of the two-year anniversary of Shawn Berner's resignation as FCHS head football coach.

Variety magazine got the scoop. The weekly entertainment publication disclosed in its February 20, 2015, edition that a movie was in the works about the Fort Campbell High School football team and the coach who led the program for more than a decade while America was at war.

In February 2015, Hollywood producers announced that they planned to make a movie about the football-playing sons of soldiers at Fort Campbell, Kentucky. The script may include the tragic death in 2009 of Falcon player Tim Williams. His jersey was retired and now hangs on the wall at Fort Campbell High School. (Photo by Rob Dollar)

According to *Variety*, the movie—with the working title, *Sons of Soldiers*—planned to focus on Shawn Berner's relationship with his football players and the impact on the team of military parents rotating in and out of war zones in Iraq and Afghanistan.

Variety further reported that the producers had already obtained the life rights of Shawn Berner and were in the process of developing the project and arranging a financing package.

Now, it's crystal clear from those published reports that Shawn Berner never went looking for glory on the Silver Screen. He's a fine man and a great coach, who was just doing his job when a journalist from *Sports Illustrated* showed up one day to profile the Fort Campbell High School football team in a story that placed the program in the national spotlight.

Reporter Andy Staples focused his September 22, 2010, feature story on the uniqueness of Berner's coaching situation. It included gripping accounts of a player losing his father in a helicopter crash in Afghanistan and another player collapsing and dying during preseason training. *Variety* reported that Staples' story—pointed out to one of the movie producers, who was a friend—was credited with being the motivation for the film project.

There's little doubt the magazine story was a riveting account of the ~~Military Brat life~~ on an Army post. Even Vice President Joe Biden read the *Sports Illustrated* story. He was so moved that he made a visit to Fort Campbell High School on Friday, February 11, 2011, to visit with Shawn Berner and the Falcon football team.

The timing of the announcement on the movie, of course, could not have been worse. When the news broke, FCHS alumni were in the middle of a heated campaign to get legendary football coach Marshall Patterson— who, after his retirement, had helped Berner adjust to his new job on the Fort Campbell Army post—inducted into the Dawahares/ Kentucky High School Athletic Association (KHSAA) Hall of Fame.

Not surprisingly, social media exploded after the newsflash on the movie. It was especially upsetting to the Early Falcons of Fort Campbell High School. Not that Shawn Berner was undeserving of a movie about his experiences as the head football coach at Fort Campbell High School…No one disputed his coaching credentials or his character…His record and reputation, from 2002 through 2012, made him more than worthy of recognition.

But, Shawn Berner was not the "Father of The Falcons." Falcon old-timers argued that Hollywood, with the movie project, was lionizing Shawn Berner for doing the same great deeds on and off the football field that Marshall Patterson had done *FIRST*—and for a much longer period of time. It was a hard pill to swallow.

A former FCHS student from the 1970s got to the heart of the matter with a social media post: "What about Coach P?"

A good question, indeed. And a fair one, too.

Many disappointed Early Falcons expressed hope that the movie—at least in some small way—might acknowledge the role of Marshall Patterson in the history of Fort Campbell High School.

Ian DeSilva, who played football for Shawn Berner on the 2007 state championship team, recalled that Coach Berner had enormous respect for Marshall Patterson and often relied on him for help with the team. In a Facebook post on the Fort Campbell High School Alumni Group Page, DeSilva wrote: *"Coach Berner brought in Coach P before our first of the three state titles...He spoke to us and got us fired up. His legacy was anything but forgotten."*

In defense of Shawn Berner, it should be duly noted that forces beyond his control placed him in the most awkward of situations: This fine man was a phenomenal, young football coach at Fort Campbell High School, but destined to forever remain in the shadow of a coaching legend there— through no fault of his own.

And again, Coach Berner was in the right place at the right time. Timing was the bottom line. It was the only thing that mattered, when it came to the movie.

When Marshall Patterson coached and mentored players with fathers deployed to wars—like Vietnam, Grenada, Panama, the Persian Gulf, and Somalia—the mood in America was much different. Patriotism was not at a fever pitch. And, Hollywood sure wasn't interested in a feel-good story about Military Brats, even if one of their fathers was killed in combat.

Shawn Berner's reign at FCHS also benefited greatly from the new technology that has made communication so much easier in the world. It helped enhance, and spread, his legacy. There rarely are any untold stories nowadays. Back in the old days, the sons and daughters of soldiers didn't have computers, smart phones and the Internet to interact on a daily basis with their deployed fathers in faraway places. There was no instant communication. Life moved much slower during Marshall Patterson's days as a teacher and coach.

Now, add the heartbreaking death of a popular player—and later the unexpected loss of a young coach—to a Hollywood movie script, and it's no wonder the moviemakers came running to Shawn Berner after learning the story of the Fort Campbell High School football program.

Consider for a moment the two Falcon tragedies that occurred on Shawn Berner's watch. Tim Williams, a 16-year-old junior offensive lineman collapsed on the field during a preseason workout on July 28, 2009, and died the next day of hypothermia. His Falcon teammates dedicated the 2009 season in his memory, going 15-0 and winning their third straight state championship. Williams' No. 73 jersey subsequently was retired and permanently hung on the wall at the high school. A few years later, in December 2011, one of Shawn Berner's longtime assistant coaches— Tyrone Johnson, who had coached Tim Williams since the seventh grade and was particularly close to him—died suddenly after suffering a severe asthma attack.

Shawn Berner—just like Marshall Patterson, when he was at the helm of the Falcons—was the glue that held the FCHS football team together during the worst of times. So, Hollywood's interest in Berner's story makes sense. Tragedy and perseverance, after all, make for a very successful formula when it comes to selling tickets at the box office.

Coach Berner also must be given his due. There are very few high school coaches in America who have accomplished what Shawn Berner accomplished at Fort Campbell High School in only 11 seasons as the head football coach.

A native of Fort Myers, Florida, Berner joined the FCHS football team as a 26-year-old assistant coach in 2001. He became the Falcons' head coach the following year. Under Berner, Fort Campbell won three straight Kentucky Class AA state titles from 2007 to 2009 and had more than 50 players sign to play football in college. Two of those players—Micah Johnson and Antonio Andrews—were named Kentucky Mr. Football.

In late January 2013—after 11 seasons as head football coach at FCHS, and only one losing season—Shawn Berner resigned his job to spend more time with his family. His overall record with FCHS was 112-31. In addition to his three state championships, Berner was 25-8 in the playoffs, taking seven district titles and four region crowns. He also coached the 2011 Falcons to the Class 3-A semifinals.

Marshall Patterson's overall record as the head football coach at FCHS for 32 seasons was 227-120. His playoff record was 20-12. Patterson-coached teams won three state championships in the late 1970s, and the 1980 squad was runner-up in the Class AA state championship game.

Only Coach Patterson and Coach Berner have career winning records while serving as the head football coach at Fort Campbell High School. Through the 2015 football season, there had been only four other head coaches in the school's history, with all of them having more losses than wins during their coaching stints.

Rocky Cobb, the longtime Patterson assistant coach, succeeded Coach P in 1994 and led the Falcons for seven years, compiling an overall record of 36-43. His 1995 team made it to the state championship semifinals.

Ronnie Bell, another veteran Patterson assistant coach, succeeded Cobb and served as head coach for only the 2001 season before he was replaced by Shawn Berner. Bell's record for his one year at the helm of the FCHS program was 3-7.

In 2013, following Shawn Berner's resignation, Tony Butler—a Berner assistant for three years—was named head coach and led the Falcons for two seasons, finishing with an overall record of 8-15, with one playoff win.

Josh McKillip, another Berner assistant who played football for Coach P at FCHS in the early 1990s, succeeded Butler and coached the Falcons to a 2-9 record in 2015—his first year on the job.

In summary, no true, die-hard Falcon of any era should have bitter feelings about a movie that casts Fort Campbell High School in a positive light. Let's only hope the film—if it indeed becomes a reality—will also acknowledge, in some way, Coach P's contributions to the wonderful FCHS story. But, of course, Hollywood is going to do what Hollywood wants to do. So, no one should act surprised if whatever comes out of La-La Land fails to meet expectations.

Sam Green greets former FCHS Falcons at the 2014 multi-class reunion, while soliciting signatures for a petition on behalf of Coach Marshall Patterson's induction into the Hall of Fame, (Photo by Rob Dollar)

As part of the spirited campaign to recognize Coach P – the "Father of The Falcons" – for his great deeds on and off the field, FCHS alumni commissioned the sculpting of a bronze bust of their beloved coach. The bust was presented to FCHS officials in October 2014, just four months before the Falcon Nation learned of plans for a movie about the football team and a coach who had succeeded Marshall Patterson. (Photo by Sam Green)

At the time this book was in the process of being published, no further information had been released on the *Sons of Soldiers* movie or its scheduled release date. Sometimes it takes years before a film shows up on the screens of movie theaters in America. And, of course, it's not unusual at all for a proposed project—even one with story rights bought, and in hand—to never see the light of day and end up on the scrap pile.

The author believes in his heart that, if there ever is a movie to see, the Falcon Nation will embrace and promote it in the same generous spirit that Marshall Patterson would have done—if he were still alive. Coach P was a gracious man and did not have a selfish bone in his body. He never pursued recognition or personal honors. For the 32 years he was coaching the Falcons, he often joked that he was the greatest football coach in the history of Fort Campbell High School. Then, he would pause, chuckle and add the fact he also happened to be the only head football coach ever employed by the school.

There's absolutely no doubt in my mind that Coach P would have been the first person in line to congratulate Shawn Berner on the movie. After all, the proposed project embodies all that is good and positive at his beloved Fort Campbell High School. I think he might even have quipped—with a twinkle in those blue eyes—that Coach Berner was much younger and better-looking than him, so it only made sense that Hollywood would make his protégé and successor the hero and main character in the FCHS movie.

Then, Coach P, with that mystical look on his face, probably would try to put the subject to rest, maybe even using the same words that worked so well for the movie character Forrest Gump: *"That's all I have to say about that."*

And, that would be the end of it.

For "Marshall's Boys" and the Falcon Nation, when all is said and done, Marshall Patterson's story is, and always will be, larger than the Silver Screen because the "Father of The Falcons" was larger than life.

Every day was his Day in the Sun at Fort Campbell High School.

CHAPTER 15: THE HALL COMES CALLING

Life isn't always fair. But, every once in a blue moon, the voice of reason shows up to right a terrible wrong and deliver that happy ending.

More than six years after he was nominated for the Dawahares/Kentucky High School Athletic Association Hall of Fame, Marshall Patterson—the "Father of The Falcons"—got his CALL TO GLORY.

KHSAA commissioners, perhaps responding to a spirited three-year public relations campaign mounted by Falcon alumni on behalf of the late Fort Campbell High School football coach, finally got it right and selected Coach P for posthumous induction into the Hall of Fame.

The formal announcement on the Class of 2016 inductees—which included Marshall Patterson—came on Sunday, November 22, 2015, during a news conference at the KHSAA offices at 2280 Executive Drive in Lexington, Kentucky.

However, "Marshall's Boys" and the Falcon Nation already had been rejoicing over the news for more than two weeks, only because the cat was let out of the bag. Not surprisingly, the "secret" leaked out—innocently, of course—that Fort Campbell High School's Marshall Patterson was on the list of the new Hall of Fame inductees. The early celebration was on…There simply was no stopping it.

The glorious moment in time for the Patterson family was bittersweet, for sure, since Coach P had not lived long enough to see the day when his peers and the Kentucky sports world recognized him as being among America's best-ever high school coaches.

But, it was what it was....

The actual voting for the new Hall of Fame class was done over a two-week period in early September 2015. After the Selection Committee tallied the votes, KHSAA officials notified inductees and their families of the results in mid- to late-October, so that they could make plans to attend the late November news conference.

Although inductees, families and school officials had been sworn to secrecy on the matter, it was just one of those secrets that could not be kept—certainly not for two to three weeks, not even in a military community like Fort Campbell where everyone was used to keeping big secrets. With confirmation—the first week in November—that Marshall Patterson had been voted into the Hall of Fame, the excitement simply overwhelmed some of Coach P's most devout followers at Fort Campbell High School.

The match had been lit, and it didn't take very long for the news to spread like wildfire. By late Thursday evening, November 5, 2015, Josh McKillip, a former player for Coach P and the head coach of the FCHS football team, had gone public with the big news, sharing his joy with the world on his Facebook page.

His post read: *"Great news for Ft. Campbell football fans. Got word today that Coach Patterson will be inducted into the KHSAA Hall of Fame! The committee finally got it right. Don't know of anyone else I would think is more deserving."*

Shawn Berner, a former head football coach at FCHS from 2002 through 2012, was quick to respond to McKillip's post: *"This is great news. Very well deserved. One of the best ever!"*

NEW ERA SPORTS

Patterson joins Hall of Fame

Coach led Falcons to four state crowns

BY DAVID SNOW
THE EAGLE POST

Marshall Patterson, the first football coach and athletics director at Fort Campbell High School, was named among the 12 inductees of the 2016 Class of the Kentucky High School Athletic Association Hall of Fame.

The announcement was made Sunday in a press conference at the KHSAA offices in Lexington. The 12 members in this year's class will be the 29th inducted into the KHSAA Hall

of Fame and consists of former high school coaches, athletes, officials, administrators and contributors.

The Class of 2016 will be inducted in ceremonies scheduled for Saturday, March 19, at the Lexington Convention Center. The Class of 2016 will also be recognized during the semifinals of the 2016 KHSAA Boys' Sweet 16.

The induction of the 12-member Class of 2016 will bring the total number of honorees in the Hall of Fame to 445.

Patterson built a powerhouse from the ground up at Fort Campbell High School,

transforming the Falcons from a fledgling program when the school began football in 1963 into a three-time state champion. He guided Fort Campbell to its first state championship in 1976, as the Falcons knocked off Bellevue, 22-0, at Commonwealth Stadium to claim the 1A state title.

The 1978 season would mark the first of three straight trips to the state football finals for Fort Campbell, with the Falcons defeating Paintsville, 15-13, for the program's second 1A state championship.

SEE PATTERSON PAGE 82

In late November 2015, the Kentucky High School Athletic Association announced that Marshall Patterson had been voted into the organization's Hall of Fame as a member of the Class of 2016. The announcement made headlines in newspapers throughout Western Kentucky, including the *Kentucky New Era* in Hopkinsville, Kentucky. (Courtesy of *Kentucky New Era*)

By the following morning, a few local media outlets—*The Leaf-Chronicle* newspaper in Clarksville, Tennessee, and radio stations in Hopkinsville, Kentucky, and Cadiz, Kentucky—had picked up the Marshall Patterson story, apparently after getting wind of it from Josh McKillip's Facebook post.

The premature release of the Hall of Fame announcement, I suppose, proves something I figured out several years ago with the explosion of social media: As long as there's a Facebook or Twitter, and at least two people know something about anything, there's no such thing as a secret anymore in this brave, new world. Take that to the bank, my friends.

Marshall Patterson's journey into the Hall of Fame—from nomination through the formal induction banquet—took about 6 ½ years to complete.

Arguably, the efforts of the Falcon Nation—in generating letters and petitions on Coach P's behalf—may have made a difference in the

KHSAA's decision to bestow the prestigious honor on the legendary FCHS football coach in what would have been his final year of eligibility. It was Scott Lowe—a former FCHS assistant football coach and one-time Falcon football player—who originally nominated Coach Patterson for induction into the Hall in September 2009.

In early November 2015, Scott Lowe was in Germany, teaching and coaching, when a KHSAA commissioner informed him that his former coach and mentor had been voted into the Hall of Fame. During that overseas telephone call, the commissioner also told Lowe that the organization—in its long history—had never seen a better organized campaign in support of inducting someone into the Hall of Fame than the one undertaken by FCHS alumni on behalf of Marshall Patterson.

The 17-day wait for the Hall of Fame news conference was like Chinese water torture, but the big day finally arrived for the Falcon faithful to scream to the world that Fort Campbell High School had a Hall of Fame football and wrestling coach. Rebecca Patterson and her three grown children—with their spouses—showed up in Lexington to represent Coach P at the Hall of Fame news conference. Most fittingly, one of "Marshall's Boys"—a resident of Lexington—was there for the big event, too.

That son of a soldier was none other than Dr. David W. Blackwell, the dean of the University of Kentucky's Gatton College of Business and Economics. Dave Blackwell played football for Coach P at FCHS for two years and was an All-Western Kentucky Conference offensive tackle on the 1975 Falcon football team. After learning about the news conference from the author of this book, wild horses could not have kept Dr. Blackwell away from the event. He knew he had to be there to support the Patterson family and pay tribute to his great football coach.

Falcons throughout the world had the opportunity to watch history in the making—in real time—since the Hall of Fame news conference was available via webcast, streamed live on the KHSAA Internet site.

Joe Angolia, the communications director for the KHSAA, served as the master of ceremonies at the news conference. Angolia welcomed the inductees and family members and introduced KHSAA Commissioner

Julian Tackett, who kicked off the event with an overview of the selection process. Tackett's short speech emphasized the exclusivity of the Hall of Fame. He noted that the pool of potential athletes, coaches, officials and contributors eligible for induction into the Hall of Fame was astronomical—something that became quite clear by simply doing the math.

"I want you to think of some numbers here," Tackett said. "There are 74,000 student-athletes EVERY year playing in our state. There are 4,500 officials and 12,000 coaches…There are almost 300 schools."

Tackett continued: "From that group, this small group is selected to be a Hall of Fame representative. That should make you feel very good. It should make you feel very proud and hopefully a little bit humble as you go forward. It's a lot of people that start at the top of that funnel that get down to the bottom that we can recognize."

Associate Commissioner Butch Cope, after Tackett's remarks, introduced the newest members of the Dawahares/KHSAA Hall of Fame. With the 12 inductees from the Class of 2016—representing the 29th induction class for the organization—the Hall of Fame's membership rose to 445, according to Cope.

Cope, in presenting the Class of 2016, called out the name of each inductee during the ceremony and provided a short narrative on his or her Hall of Fame credentials. The honoree—or a family representative in some cases—then was allowed to address the audience. When the time came to honor Marshall Patterson, Stephen Patterson—also known as "Coach P" at Paducah Tilghman High School, where he is a teacher and assistant football coach—rose from his chair and went to the podium to speak from the heart for his late father.

"Thank you. And, on behalf of our father, Marshall Patterson, I would like to thank Julian Tackett and the members of the Selection Committee for the tremendous honor of inducting our father into the Dawahares Hall of Fame," Stephen Patterson said.

"He would be humbled and very appreciative of this pinnacle honor. If our father was here, the first person he would thank would be his wife, Rebecca Patterson. Her support and sacrifice through the years, he would say, were foundational to the success he was able to achieve. Second, to Scott Lowe, Sam Green, and Rob Dollar, who—because of what Coach P meant to them and Fort Campbell High School—spearheaded the efforts to gain support for his induction into the Hall of Fame. And finally, and most importantly, the entire Fort Campbell community—fellow coaches and teachers, students, athletes and parents—without you, this amazing journey would have been impossible.

"Upon announcing his retirement from Fort Campbell High School, my Dad was quoted in the newspaper as saying, 'I value every minute that I have had here. I never had a day that I was not excited about coming to work.'"

The son of the "Father of The Falcons" then ended his speech with a Thumbs-Up salute to his Dad and the Falcon Nation and a two-word cheer: "GO FALCONS!"

Marshall Patterson entered the Hall of Fame with some mighty good company. In fact, the news conference had barely ended before talk began that the 2016 selections might rank as the KHSAA's best-ever, overall induction class.

Inducted into the Hall of Fame, with Marshall Patterson, were:

- Sam Ball (Henderson County High School) – An All-State lineman in 1961 for Henderson County High School in Henderson, Kentucky, Ball later was an All-American at the University of Kentucky. He played for the Baltimore Colts during a five-year career in the National Football League that included two Super Bowl appearances.

- Freddy Ballou (Madison/Model High School) –Ballou rushed for over 5,000 yards and scored 50 touchdowns to lead Madison/Model High School to a 34-4 record while playing for the

Royal Purples in Richmond, Kentucky, from 1959 through 1961. He was an All-America selection in his senior year.

- Dr. James "Pete" Bowles (Contributor) – For 33 years, while he was a primary care physician with Trover Clinic in Madisonville, Kentucky, Dr. Bowles served as the team physician for Madisonville-North Hopkins and established himself as a leader in Western Kentucky in the field of sports medicine.

- Brigette Combs (Whitesburg High School) – During the early- to mid-1980s, Combs led the Whitesburg Yellowjackets to three consecutive appearances in the KHSAA girls' state basketball tournament. During a standout four-year career, she totaled 2,672 points, 1,920 rebounds, and 585 steals. A two-time, First-Team All-State selection, Combs was named Kentucky's Miss Basketball as a senior in 1985.

- Joseph Federspiel (DeSales High School) – Federspiel was a two-way football player at DeSales High School in the mid-1960s, starring as an offensive guard and linebacker for the Colts. He later earned honors playing football for the University of Kentucky and then played 10 years (1972 through 1982) in the National Football League.

- Dominic Fucci (Tates Creek High School) – Fucci was a standout baseball and basketball player at Tates Creek High School in Lexington, Kentucky. As a Commodore, he was named Kentucky's Mr. Basketball in 1975. Later, he starred in basketball and baseball at Auburn University. Fucci also played professional baseball for a few years after being drafted by the Chicago White Sox in the 5th Round of the 1979 Major League Baseball Draft. Later in his life, he coached basketball and baseball at three different highs schools in Kentucky for a total of 29 years.

- Clarence Gaines (Paducah Lincoln High School) – During the 1940s, "Big House" Gaines was a basketball, football and track standout at Lincoln High School in Paducah, Kentucky, where he graduated with salutatorian honors. He later played football at

Morgan State University in Baltimore, Maryland. After graduating from college, Gaines became a successful college football and basketball coach at Winston-Salem State. In 1967, the North Carolina school won the NCAA Division II National Championship in basketball. Fifteen years later, Gaines became the first black coach inducted into the Basketball Hall of Fame. He also was inducted as an inaugural member of the College Basketball Hall of Fame in 2006.

- Bert Greene (Olive Hill High School) – From 1954 through 1959, Greene was a star basketball players for Olive Hill High School, scoring 3,172 points over five seasons to lead the Comets to three appearances in the boys' state basketball tournament. He later played basketball at Morehead State before returning to Olive Hill, where he coached the Comets until his retirement in 1979. Greene served as a basketball official for 10 years after he left coaching.

- Charles Hunter (Ralph Bunche High School) – For two seasons, 1961 and 1962, "Big Game" Hunter starred on the basketball court for Ralph Bunche High School, establishing himself as one of the most prolific scorers in the state. After high school, he attended Oklahoma City University and led the school to four NCAA Tournament appearances. In 1966, the Boston Celtics selected Hunter in the 6th Round of the National Basketball Association Draft.

- Tenesha Blakey-Marshall (Valley High School) – In the 1990s, Blakey-Marshall dominated girls' track in Kentucky. A four-year All-State honoree in track, she won 10 state track and field titles during a standout career at Valley High School, where she also starred on the basketball team. As a senior in 1994, Blakey-Marshall was named Kentucky's Gatorade Female Athlete of the Year. The Kentucky Department of Education also recognized her that year as the state's Outstanding High School Female Athlete.

- G.J. Smith (Hazel Green, Laurel County, South Laurel High School) – Dubbed "The Kentucky Long Rifle," Smith was a star basketball player for Hazel Green High School in 1970 and 1971.

After high school, Smith went on to play at the University of Kentucky, from 1972 through 1975, as part of Adolph Rupp's final recruiting class. He was a member of the Wildcats' NCAA National Runner-Up team in 1975. For 25 years, from 1977 through 2002, Smith coached high school baseball at Laurel County and South Laurel. He had a career record of 662 victories (.767 winning percentage), with 15 district titles, six regional championships and four appearances in the state tournament semifinals.

Four months after the KHSAA announcement, Marshall Patterson and the 11 other inductees were formally honored at the annual Hall of Fame Banquet, which took place on Saturday, March 19, 2016, in the Bluegrass Ballroom at the Lexington Center in conjunction with the boys' state basketball tournament. The honorees also were recognized later that evening in an on-court ceremony during the semifinals game of the basketball tournament.

Ironically, Marshall Patterson was not the only person with strong ties to Marshall County High School in Lewisburg, Tennessee, to get voted into a Hall of Fame in 2015. Just seven months before Coach P got his call from the Dawahares/KHSAA Hall of Fame, Bob Edens was among eight sports figures inducted into the Tennessee Secondary School Athletic Association's Hall of Fame.

Edens spent 20 years as the football coach at Marshall County High School—the same high school where young Marshall "Buddy" Patterson had played football and two other sports in the early 1950s. Edens' overall coaching record at Marshall County High School was 169-79, with one TSSAA state championship in 1984. He retired from coaching in 1999.

If Marshall Patterson had not been inducted into the Hall of Fame, it certainly would not have been the end of the world. Coach P, after all, was a man who never chased personal honors during his life. Rebecca Patterson said her husband, if he had lived to see the honor, probably would have shrugged it off. "I really think he would have been more overjoyed just to see the efforts made on his behalf by his former athletes and students," she noted.

The Falcon Nation, too, would have survived the disappointment of a snub. All through the fight, the attitude—best expressed on a tribute T-shirt designed by Josephe' Williams, one of "Marshall's Boys"—for Falcons, everywhere, had been that Coach P, is and always will be, "Already in My Hall of Fame."

But, as it turned out, Marshall Patterson was not forgotten. The fears were for naught. The Falcon Nation—with no quit in it—rose to the occasion to help win the game for Coach P. The Blue & Grey alumni got their happy ending—a Hall of Fame coach for Fort Campbell High School.

When Stephen Patterson spoke at the KHSAA news conference, he shortened the family's acceptance speech due to time constraints. So, the full speech—written by Coach P's two daughters, Jeanann (Patterson) Pardue and Marsha (Patterson) Anderson— was not heard by the audience at the Hall of Fame news conference or those who watched the webcast of the event.

The author of this book believes the Patterson girls hit it out of the park with words from the heart that perfectly summed up their father's legacy. He would have been so proud of them and his son, Stephen.

Here is the rest of the acceptance speech the Patterson sisters wrote for brother Stephen to deliver on what surely was one of the happiest days of their lives:

To quote one of (Marshall Patterson's) players, "To be a Falcon, you had to be someone. He instilled that pride in us."

For our Dad, it was never about wins and losses. Rather, it was about the vehicle athletics provided to build character and vision in young men and women.

With this in mind, it is fitting to share with you an excerpt from a letter written to him by a parent of one of his senior football players:

Dear Coach Patterson:
I could not let this time go by without thanking you for the positive effect you have had on my son's life.....My son has gladly taken from you advice that he might not have followed so readily had it come from us. You have shown him how to set goals and how to work at achieving those goals. You have helped him learn how to discipline himself to increase his chances of reaching those goals. More importantly...you have been an example to him of how a person can still have high morals in this day when morals are scarce.....He will take the lessons he has learned from you with him always. They are a part of him, as you will always be a part of him and so many other young men that have played for you. I am not signing this letter because I realize that I could be any of hundreds of mothers whose sons will always carry a special place in their hearts for you.
Gratefully,
A Falcon Mom

After retiring, my Dad was asked to come back and speak to the Falcons as they prepared for an upcoming state championship game. These were his words:

"Every player has a role to play and whether you are first team or third team you must be able to look each team member in the eye and say, 'I will not let you down.'"

In his speech to the players, he went on to share (some) favorite quotes: "Life's battles are not always won by the stronger or faster man, but sooner or later the man who wins is the man who thinks he can."... "It's not what you did yesterday that counts but what you are going to do when the whistle blows and the game of champions begins."

All the wins, the state championships, and now certainly the induction into the Hall of Fame are pinnacle moments in a career.

But for Dad, Coach P, his pinnacle moment was every day he got in his 1968 Volkswagen Beetle and drove to Fort Campbell High School to spend another day doing what he loved.

That was his reward—His Hall of Fame.

303

Because Marshall Patterson so loved his job, he was able to change the world for the better every single day he showed up for work at Fort Campbell High School to teach and mentor his Military Brats.

Today, there are thousands of FCHS alumni—now much older and wiser—doing lots of good everywhere in this world. Because of Coach P, they're making a difference every day—winning game after game in "The Game of Life."

Few people leave this Earth with that kind of a legacy.

God broke the mold after he made Marshall Patterson. There just aren't any teachers and coaches like him anymore. And, it's really a crying shame the kids growing up nowadays don't have someone like him as a role model to show them the way through this difficult world.

So long, Coach P. Thanks for believing in your Band of Military Brats. You were, and always will be, THE BEST.

Marshall Patterson's widow, Rebecca Patterson, and his son, Stephen Patterson, accepted his Hall of Fame plaque and medallion at a ceremony in Lexington, Kentucky, on March 19, 2016. With them in this photo are Patterson assistant coach Mark Ray (left) and Josh McKillip, a former FCHS player and current head coach of the Falcon football team. At far left is KHSAA Commissioner Julian Tackett.(Photo by Rob Dollar)

FOR THE RECORD

KENTUCKY

Marshall Patterson,
Fort Campbell High School Falcons
*No. 24 on KHSAA Football Coaching Wins List
(As of December 15, 2015)FCHS photo

Total Wins	Career Record	Seasons	Title Games
227	227-120 (.654)	32 (1962-1993)	3-1

TENNESSEE

Marshall Patterson, Northwest High School Vikings

Total Wins	Career Record	Seasons	Title Games
18	18-43	6 (1995-2000)	0-1

FCHS STATE CHAMPIONSHIP GAMES

Year	Coach	Score	Opponent	Location
1976	Marshall Patterson	22-0	Bellevue	Lexington
1978	Marshall Patterson	15-13	Paintsville	Richmond
1979	Marshall Patterson	26-0	Pikeville	Louisville
2007	Shawn Berner	21-7	Newport Ctr. Catholic	Louisville
2008	Shawn Berner	26-23	Newport Ctr. Catholic	Louisville
2009	Shawn Berner	29-9	DeSales	Bowling Green

*1976 & 1978 football teams played in Class A
 1979, 2007, 2008 & 2009 football teams played in Class AA

AFTERWORD

The writing of this book truly represented a labor of love for the author. As one of "Marshall's Boys," it allowed me the opportunity to revisit the wonderful memories of growing up as a Military Brat, while more importantly paying tribute to one of the most influential people in my life.

That person, of course, was Marshall Patterson—a friend, teacher and mentor to thousands of Military Brats as the legendary football coach at Fort Campbell High School for more than three decades.

It was in the immediate months after his January 2014 death that the idea for this book began to take root and grow. At the time, Coach P was under consideration for induction into the Dawahares/Kentucky High School Athletic Association Hall of Fame. Work on the book began in early 2015, and just as it neared completion, the KHSAA announced that Marshall Patterson had been voted into the Hall of Fame as a member of the Class of 2016. The incredible joy brought about by the announcement became the icing on the cake for this project. It gave the book something that many readers often look for on those final pages—a happy ending.

Coach P lived a wonderful life that certainly was more than deserving of that happy ending. His family—wife, Rebecca Patterson, and children, Stephen Patterson, Jeanann (Patterson) Pardue, and Marsha (Patterson) Anderson—made many sacrifices over the years, so he could fulfill his responsibilities as a teacher, coach, mentor, and role model at Fort Campbell High School. It was their unwavering support and loyalty that made it possible for Coach P to accomplish the body of work that earned him his invitation into the Hall of Fame.

With that thought in mind, make no mistake about it: "Mrs. Coach P" and her kids will always be the unsung heroes in this story about a remarkable man who made a difference in so many lives. As for the role of those two old Falcon quarterbacks (Sam Green and yours truly), they only wanted to honor their old football coach by doing what he taught them to do as field generals: Call the plays, keep the ball moving, and fire up the team.

Not surprisingly, the Military Brats of the Falcon Nation came through in a big way and made enough noise to get Coach P inducted into the Hall of Fame.

Let's thank God for a MISSION ACCOMPLISHED!

Rob Dollar photo

ACKNOWLEDGMENTS

This book, in no way, pretends to represent the complete and definitive account of Marshall Patterson's performance in "The Game of Life." At best, it's only a snapshot of his great deeds as seen through the eyes of some of the Military Brats he coached and mentored at Fort Campbell High School for more than three decades.

In telling this story, the author—who was one of those Military Brats—relied heavily on his own high school memories and the recollections of now older and wiser FCHS alumni from the 1960s, 1970s, 1980s, and 1990s.

Marshall Patterson will always be remembered as a man of few words and many deeds. More often than not, Coach P's acts of kindness on behalf of his students and athletes took place, not under the bright spotlight of publicity, but instead when no one was watching him. He never sought, or wanted, personal recognition for his passion of mentoring and molding the lives of young adults. Therefore, it should come as no surprise to readers that it's quite possible that some of the most extraordinary feats of this great man may be missing from the pages of this book—known only to Coach P and those recipients of his kindheartedness.

The author could not have pursued and completed this book without the assistance and encouragement of many friends and supporters—in the local community and throughout the Falcon Nation.

Sam Green, who was Marshall Patterson's first quarterback, was my inspiration to write the book. For three years, he championed the cause of persuading the Kentucky High School Athletic Association (KHSAA) to recognize the life achievements of his beloved high school football coach. As my right-hand man and task master on this project, Sam—or "QB 1" as I like to call him—provided me with invaluable research assistance and shared his wonderful memories of walking the halls of Fort Campbell High School as an Early Falcon in the 1960s. His great love and respect for Marshall Patterson motivated me to keep going whenever the going got tough. And, believe me, sometimes it got real tough.

Another Falcon friend, Debbie (Jones) Gifford, a former cheerleader and member of Fort Campbell High School's Class of 1973, also deserves a pat on the back for her role in making this book a reality. The author relied heavily on her judgment and feedback. She constantly bounced ideas off of me, and cheered me on, just like she did in her cheerleading days long ago when I was trying to play high school football for Marshall Patterson and the Falcons.

My best friend in the world, and old newspaper colleague, Tim Ghianni, is another person who made major contributions to this book. In addition to sharing his Marshall Patterson stories with me, Tim helped edit my manuscript and made it sing with his world-class writing and editing skills. His support was most appreciated and made a world of difference in the final product.

The author further wishes to express his gratitude to the Fort Campbell Dependent Schools for its cooperation and support in the writing and publication of this book. A special "Thank-You" most certainly is in order for three administrators at Fort Campbell High School—Principal Hugh McKinnon and Co-Athletic Directors Anthony Shingler and Ira Turner. The author sought, and was graciously granted, permission to use—at my discretion—the Falcon mascot artwork as well as any photographs that originally appeared in past Fort Campbell High School yearbooks and publications. This material was most helpful in enhancing the story of Marshall Patterson's unique relationship with the thousands of Military Brats he taught and coached over the years. The kindness and support of the Fort Campbell football community is most appreciated and will never be forgotten.

It also should be noted that manyother of the photographs that appear in this book—as well as on the front and back covers of the dust jacket— were shared with the author by friends and former FCHS students, who also contributed their own personal stories about Coach P and his influence on their lives. Thank you so much to those loyal alumni and supporters of the Falcon Nation for helping me to pay tribute to this great man and coach.

Throughout the years, several area newspapers and their staffs thoroughly covered and reported on the exploits of Marshall Patterson's football and wrestling teams. In writing this book, dozens of sports stories were located and researched for relevant details such as final scores and highlights. As a result, the author wishes to recognize and credit the outstanding work of the *Kentucky New Era* in Hopkinsville, Kentucky, *The Leaf-Chronicle* in Clarksville, Tennessee, *The Eagle Post* in Oak Grove, Kentucky, *The Cadiz Record* in Cadiz, Kentucky, and the *Fort Campbell Courier*—the command information news source for the Army at Fort Campbell, Kentucky. These fine newspapers and other media outlets in the area recorded history in the making, and without their important contributions, the Marshall Patterson story would not be known to future generations.

The *Kentucky New Era* and its top management—Taylor Hayes and Chuck Henderson—are deserving of special recognition and praise for authorizing the author to reprint in this book two articles previously published in the newspaper. Mr. Hayes and Mr. Henderson also allowed me to use a photograph from the 1991 football season that originally appeared on the *Kentucky New Era* sports pages. In acknowledging this kindness, the author wishes to remind readers that the Hopkinsville newspaper—a former employer of mine—has been second to none in support of the Fort Campbell community over the lifetime of the Army post.

In closing, I would be remiss not to mention and thank Rebecca Patterson and her three grown children, Stephen Patterson, Jeanann (Patterson) Pardue, and Marsha (Patterson) Anderson. Coach Patterson loved his family dearly, and they willingly made many sacrifices over the years for the sake of the Falcon Nation.

They are most deserving of our eternal love and owed an enormous debt of gratitude for sharing Coach P with the many thousands of Falcons for life, who are out there doing good in this world.

REFERENCES

A History of Fort Campbell, John O'Brien, The History Press, Charleston, South Carolina, (2014), Source in Chapter 2

"Beautiful Boy (Darling Boy)," Song written by John Lennon (Lyric, *"Life is what happens to you while you're busy making other plans"*), Geffen Records, New York, New York, (1980), Chapter 1

Cadiz Record newspaper, Cadiz, Kentucky, "Coach's Corner" (Mike Wright), September 3, 2014, edition; "One of Bear's Boys: A Tribute to David Sadler" (Joe Kelly Jaggers), March 25, 2009, edition; Web Site, www.cadizrecord.com, Retrieved June 15, 2015, Source in Chapter 6

Chicago Sunday Tribune, Chicago, Illinois, December 28, 1958, edition; http://archives.chicagotribune.com/1958/12/28/page/10/article/west-berlin-is-a-px-surrounded-by-reds-says-hope, Retrieved September 9, 2015, Source in Chapter 10

Dawahares/Kentucky High School Athletic Association Hall of Fame (KHSAA), Lexington, Kentucky, Web Site, http://khsaa.org/special-programs/dawahareskhsaa-hall-of-fame/, Retrieved May 2, 2015, Source in Chapter 5

Forrest Gump, Paramount Pictures, Hollywood, California, (June 1994), Chapter 9, Chapter 14

Fort Campbell Courier newspaper, Fort Campbell, Kentucky, January 6, 2005, edition, (Chapter 2); February 17, 2011, edition, (Chapter 14), Source in Chapter 2, Chapter 14

"Fort Campbell High School Alma Mater," Written by Sharon Elizabeth McCoy, (1962), Chapter 3

Fort Campbell Schools, Web Site, http://www.am.dodea.edu/campbell/, Retrieved April 11, 2015, Source in Chapter 2

"Get Up Offa That Thing," Song written and performed by James Brown, Universal Music Group/Polydor Records, Santa Monica, California, (1976), Chapter 4

Hoosiers, Orion Pictures, Los Angeles, California, (November 1986), Chapter 7

"If I Had a Hammer," Song written by Pete Seeger and Lee Hayes (Performed by Trini Lopez), Warner Music Group/Reprise Records, New York, New York, (1963), Chapter 1

"I Just Wasn't Made for These Times," Song written by Brian Wilson and Tony Asher (Performed by The Beach Boys), Gold Star Studios, Hollywood, California, (1966), Chapter 1

Interviews/Recollections (March 2015-January 2016), Rebecca Patterson, Sam Green, Rose Dollar, Bob Connelly, Stan Nelson, John Bianchini, Norm Miller, Rick Larson, Mike Moats, Debbe (Jones) Gifford, Dennis Fendler, Preston Owens, Sabrina (McBrayer) Alls, Terrance Summerhill, Rebecca (Wissmann) Milliner, Kerri (Smith) Lovelass, Jenny Ahn-Wangoe, Chad Corley, Chip Hutcheson, Scott Burnside, Ray Duckworth, Tim Ghianni, David Ross, Julie (Mahaffey) Augeri, Mark Brown, Hale Strasser, Ray Metts, Chuck Powell, Mike Hellums, Steve Hellums, Gilbert Scott, David Blackwell, Vicky (Craig) Coleman, and Tanna (Darby) Nichols

It's a Wonderful Life, RKO Radio Pictures, New York, New York, (December 1946), Chapter 4

Kentucky High School Athletic Association (KHSAA), Lexington, Kentucky, Web Site, http://khsaa.org/, Track Records & Hall of Fame Inductees, Retrieved May 20, 2015, Source in Chapter 6

Kentucky New Era newspaper, Hopkinsville, Kentucky, October 1, 1962, edition, (Chapter 3); October 2, 1962, edition, (Chapter 3); October 8, 1962, edition, (Chapter 3); October 11, 1962, edition, (Chapter 3); October 15, 1962, edition, (Chapter 3); October 20, 1962, edition, (Chapter 3); November 3, 1962, edition, (Chapter 3); September 11, 1972, edition, (Chapter 6); February 12, 1973, edition, (Chapter 6); September 17, 1974, edition, (Chapter 13); October 8, 1983, edition, (Chapter 4); October 6, 1984, edition (Chapter 4); October 10, 1985, edition, (Chapter 9); May 31, 1989, edition, (Chapter 6); August 10, 1991, edition, (Chapter 6); May 5, 1994, edition, (Chapter 13); June 17, 1995, edition, (Chapter 10); April 20, 2001, edition, (Chapter 13); January 21, 2014, edition, (Chapter 12); November 23, 2015, edition, (Chapter 15), Source in Chapter 3, Chapter 4, Chapter 6, Chapter 9, Chapter 10, Chapter 12, Chapter 13, Chapter 15

KHSAA.TV, Lexington, Kentucky, Webcast, "2016 Dawahares/KHSAA Induction Class Press Conference," http://khsaa.tv/2016-dawahareskhsaa-hall-of-fame-induction-class-press-conference/, Retrieved November 22, 2015, Source in Chapter 15

Married...with Children, Fox television sitcom, (1987-1997), Chapter 4

Marshel's Wright-Donaldson Home for Funerals Inc., Beaufort, South Carolina, Web Site (February 19, 2012, Entry in Guest Book for Anita Jones Obituary), http://www.marshelswrightdonaldson.com/fh/obituaries/tributes.cfm?o_id=1396625&fh_id=13339, Retrieved October 12, 2015, Source in Chapter 4

Military Brats, Inc., Web Site, http://www.militarybratsinc.org/mbday.cfm, Retrieved July 30, 2015, Source in Chapter 8

Military Brat Life, "Military Brat," (Debbie Adams), Web Site, http://www.militarybratlife.com/articles/military-brat.html, Retrieved August 4, 2015, Source in Chapter 8

Mississippi Burning, Orion Pictures, Los Angeles, California, (December 1988), Chapter 10

Pink Floyd, *The Dark Side of the Moon* (album), Capitol Music Group/Harvest Records, Los Angeles, California, (1973), Chapter 1

Rocky, United Artists, Beverly Hills, California, (November 1976), Chapter 6

Rowan & Martin's Laugh-In, NBC television variety/comedy show, (1968-1973), Chapter 1

Rudy, TriStar Pictures, Culver City, California, (October 1993), Chapter 6

Sands of Iwo Jima, Republic Pictures, Los Angeles, California, (December 1949), Chapter 1

Sports Illustrated, "At Ft. Campbell, football is escape for players with parents deployed," (Andy Staples), September 22, 2010, Web Site, http://www.si.com/more-sports/2010/09/22/fort-campbellmilitarychildren, Retrieved November 1, 2015, Source in Chapter 14

Anna Staatz, Public Affairs Office, Fort Riley, Kansas, "Big Red One Officer Frocked With First Star," December 2, 2009, 1st Infantry Division Facebook Page, https://www.facebook.com/notes/1st-infantry-division/big-red-one-officer-frocked-with-first-star/190518394315 , Retrieved July 19, 2015, Source in Chapter 7

Tennessee General Assembly, Nashville, Tennessee, House Joint Resolution 585 (Memorial, Marshall H. Patterson), February 10, 2014, Web Site, http://wapp.capitol.tn.gov/apps/Billinfo/default.aspx?BillNumber=HJR05 85&ga=108, Retrieved October 15, 2015, Source in Chapter 13

Tennessee Secondary School Athletic Association (TSSAA), Nashville, Tennessee, "Eight To Join The TSSAA Hall of Fame At Annual Induction Ceremonies April 18," Web Site, http://tssaa.org/2015-tssaa-hall-of-fame-inductees/, Retrieved November 24, 2015, Source in Chapter 15

The Eagle Post newspaper, Oak Grove, Kentucky, March 4, 2009, edition, (Chapter 4); December 28, 2011, edition, (Chapter 14); January 22, 2014, edition (Chapter 14), Source in Chapter 4, Chapter 14

The History Channel, "This Day in History (July 29, 1965)," Web Site, http://www.history.com/this-day-in-history/101st-airborne-division-arrives-in-vietnam , Retrieved August 27, 2015, Source in Chapter 9

The Leaf-Chronicle newspaper, Clarksville, Tennessee, "Fort Campbell history much more than the 101st," (Phillip Grey), January 11, 2015, edition; Web Site, http://www.theleafchronicle.com/story/news/local/fort-campbell/2015/01/11/fort-campbell-history-much-st/21602371/, Retrieved January 2, 2016, Source in Chapter 2

The Lone Ranger, ABC television series, (1949-1957), Chapter 1

The Star, (American Media Inc.), New York, New York, January 2, 1979, edition, Chapter 11

The Tonight Show Starring Johnny Carson, NBC television variety/talk show, (1962-1992), Chapter 1

Valley of the Dolls, 20th Century Fox, Los Angeles, California, (December 1967), Chapter 10

Variety magazine, "'Sons of Soldiers' In The Works With Richard Donner," (Dave McNary), February 20, 2015, Web Site, http://variety.com/2015/film/news/sons-of-soldiers-football-movie-in-the-works-with-richard-donner-exclusive-1201437529/, Retrieved October 25, 2015, Source in Chapter 14

We Are The Mighty, "20 important facts about military brats (backed up by research and stuff)," Blake Stillwell, April 28, 2015, Web Site, http://www.wearethemighty.com/20-important-facts-about-military-bratsbacked-up-by-research-and-stuff-2015-04, Retrieved July 22, 2015, Source in Chapter 8

CPSIA information can be obtained
at www.ICGtesting.com
Printed in the USA
LVOW04*0609180816

500658LV00005B/11/P